Lock, Stock & Barrel

Lock, Stock & Barrel

Shirley Ginger

CanalBookShop

Lock, Stock & Barrel

Shirley Ginger

First edition 1985
J M Pearson & Son (Publishers) Limited

Second edition 2021
CanalBookShop
Audlem Mill Limited The Wharf Audlem Cheshire CW3 0DX
www.canalbookshop.co.uk

ISBN 978-1-9160125-8-5

Shirley Ginger has asserted her rights under the Copyright, Designs and Patents Act 1988 to be identified as the copyright owner of the text and images in this work.

Subject to very limited exceptions, the Act prohibits the making of copies of any copyright work or of a substantial part of such a work, including the making of hard or digital copies by photocopying, scanning or similar process. Written permission to make a copy or copies must be obtained from the publisher. It is advisable to consult the publisher if in any doubt as to the legality of any copying which is to be undertaken.

For Maurice, Stephanie and Bruce

Contents

1	Birmingham to Buckby	9
2	Trade & Tribulation	22
3	Stepping Stones	35
4	Café and Camping	49
5	Autumn Reflections	65
6	Oxford Interlude	78
7	Winter Bitterness	96
8	Boats and Pieces	110
9	Spring Greens	126
10	Summer Scene	142
11	The Wheel Spins	160
12	Roll in the Barrel	176
	Postscript	187
	Recipes	191
	Glossary	209

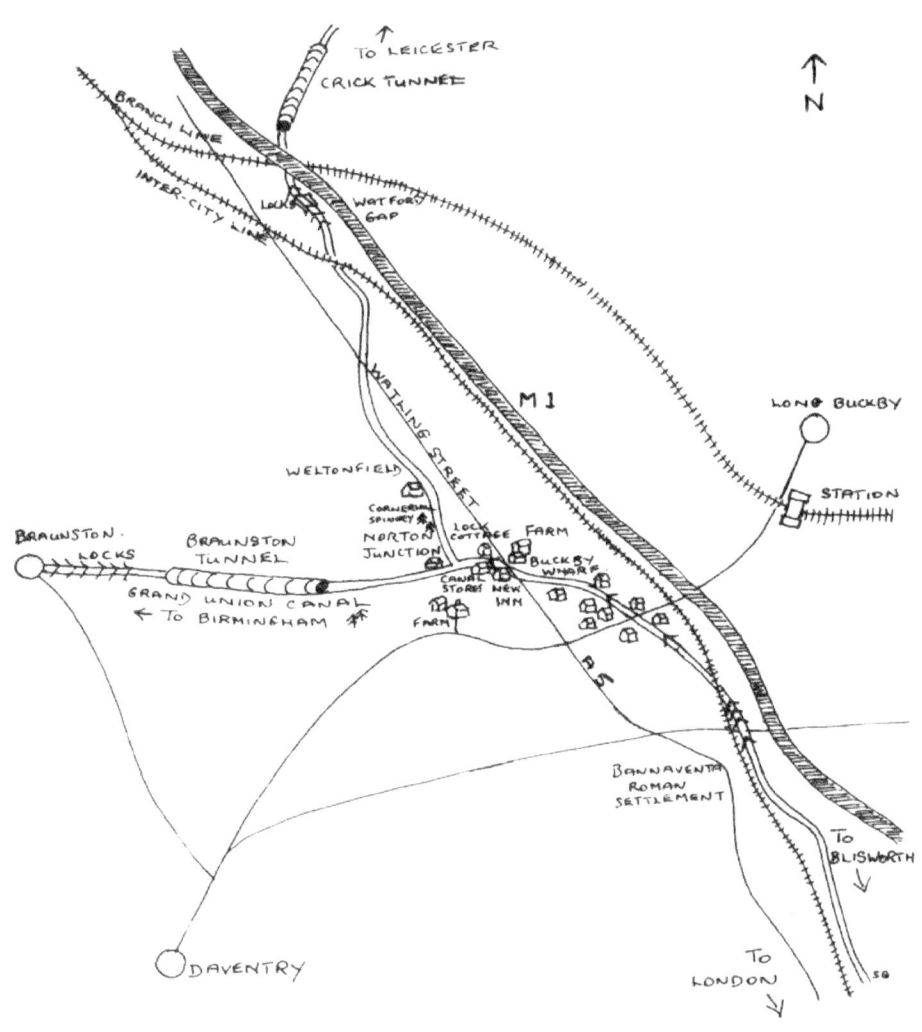

Map of Buckby Wharf and surroundings

-1-
Birmingham to Buckby

I sprawled on the deep pile of the drawing room carpet, the Sunday newspapers spread untidily around me, steadily reading my way through every inch of print. I was not usually so thorough but the weather had put paid to all our plans and I was at a loss to think of anything more constructive to do. The cold February rain was sleeting down the windows, obscuring Birmingham's Post Office Tower. On fine days, one could see it clearly, less than three miles away.

"'The Slow Boat Company'," I read aloud. "'Hire a traditional narrow boat and cruise Britain's delightful waterways at Easter. Begin near Rugby, the ideal starting point for many holiday routes.' How about that for an idea?"

Maurice looked up and I could tell that he was adjusting his brain away from the chess problem in the colour supplement. It takes him a second or two.

"A canal holiday, you mean? Mm. A good idea. The kids would enjoy it and we could take Brynne with us for a change, if they allow dogs on boats."

The terrier that was stretched out at his feet, flickered her short tail without opening her eyes, as he went on.

"Rugby's not far - it might be worth finding out more."

He resumed his former occupation, and as I had learnt after sixteen years, what he really meant was "you find out more." I scrambled to my feet to fetch some writing paper and a pen. It is not in my nature to shelve things that I want to do, especially when a newspaper is involved - they have a habit of disappearing to light a bonfire, or wrapping themselves round a muddy pair of football boots.

I had no idea then that one of those apparently trivial incidents had taken place which can change the direction of one's life. Both of us would have dismissed the suggestion as a flight of fancy.

"Shellover", our hired narrow boat was called, and to our uninitiated eyes, it was beautiful. The name of the boat was painted in large bright letters on the stern and a pair of jolly gothic castles, festooned with painted roses, decorated either side of the cabin. Without wishing to be unkind to the "Slow Boat Company", for we have cause to be grateful to them now, there were a number of hidden snags which made themselves felt in due course.

There was so much play on the heavy wooden tiller that steering a straight course was nearly impossible. When the headlight packed up as we entered Crick tunnel we bounced helplessly from wall to dripping wall lit only by a wavering torch. The refrigerator did not work. This did not matter too much as the Easter weather that year was typically British. "Variable", was how the weather forecast on the radio described it but Maurice had another word for it! It was warmer in the cabin than outside so I put the remaining half of a roast chicken that I had brought with us under the seat in the front cockpit. I was sure that I heard the fox bark gleefully as he made off with it and I think that Brynne heard too, for she lifted her head from her basketful of puppies and growled.

The water pump came on at intervals all night, not only disturbing our sleep with its staccato rattle, but flattening the battery so that the engine failed to start the next morning. A morning to which we awoke in soaking bedclothes caused by condensation trickling from the steel cabin top and sides.

Could it have been an omen, that the telephone box to which the friendly crew of a passing boat towed us that first morning, was the same one that I can see from the window now as I write? In spite of all these mishaps, we succumbed to that phenomenon known as the "canal bug".

"Why?" you might well ask.

It is a difficult question to answer. Even if I listed all the aspects of a canal holiday which appealed to us - fresh air, peaceful countryside, meeting like-minded folk, the feeling of "being busy doing nothing" - I doubt that you would be convinced. Some close friends of ours who shared our tastes in holidays - camping, fell-walking and so on - hired a canal boat on our recommendation and considered that holiday to be a minor disaster. We never really understood why. For some reason, opinions about canals are polarised; love or loathe.

At the end of our week on "Shellover", we cancelled our package tour to Spain which had already been booked for the summer, even though it meant forfeiting our deposit! (That sort of decision was anathema to Maurice who boasted several pints of Scottish blood in his veins.) Instead, we booked a fortnight on a different boat, based further north at Middlewich, in Cheshire.

Just before we left, we saw advertised in the Birmingham Post a butty boat (an old horse drawn boat) called "Iona", for sale at five hundred pounds.

She had a wooden hull, a traditional boatman's cabin and no engine. We went to look at her one evening at her home mooring on the Grand Union Canal south of Birmingham. Peering through the heavy dusk, we could just make out the graceful shape of the seventy foot long hull. There was a huge, decorated wooden rudder with some intricate rope-work on the top of it and a cabin with painted castles on the sides with the words "Preston Brook" in fine Ionic script.

We could not see (even if it had occurred to us to look), the rotting timbers of the fore end, the tell tale patches beneath the tar of the hull, and the leaking cabin roof. Such was the onset of canal mania within us that we arranged to meet the young owners on an aqueduct on the Trent and Mersey Canal during our holiday and there clinched the deal. We were the delighted owners of a genuine narrow boat!

"Iona" alas, did nothing more for us than teach us a thing or two about boats. Our aim had been to repair and repaint and install an engine - if possible without spoiling the original boatman's cabin. The image of a horse was romantic but hardly practical - towpaths being what they are today (which is sometimes not there, because they have fallen into the canal). The more we did to "Iona", the more depressed we became. Every floorboard that we lifted in the cabin exposed yet another portion of rotten hull. The deck planks of both fore end and stern were crumbling. I put my foot straight through the step down into the cabin.

It became clear that she needed a major rebuild of large portions of the hull before we could contemplate the mechanics of installing an engine. Now, "do-it-yourself" was all very well when it came to building a bookcase or redecorating a bedroom but Maurice was not a true carpenter or engineer - even at heart - and he said that getting "Iona" canal worthy was beyond him. We asked a couple of boatyards what it would cost to do the work but no-one was very keen to get involved with a boat of her age and condition.

So it was with reluctance that we sold the old girl to a carpenter. He has made a grand job of rebuilding the hull although it took him several years. But he has ripped out the boatman's cabin and the majestic rudder so that she does not look like "Iona" any more. We suffer terrible pangs of guilt whenever we pass by on our present boat, "Warwickshire Lad".

After "Iona's" departure, we still held the mooring on the Grand Union where we had first seen her. This was important because if we were to get another boat, an approved mooring was a prerequisite of obtaining a British Waterways Board licence. Maurice went quietly to work exploring the possibilities. He found a man, Chris Barney, now a friend, who built boats under the old established name of Braunston Boats Ltd. Chris only built sixty boats in

"He has ripped out the boatman's cabin …"

all, sturdy, well made craft with pleasing traditional lines - and reasonably priced. Ours was number twenty-five.

We liked to think that we made decisions democratically in our family and choosing the name for the boat was no exception. So, between us all - Maurice, myself, eleven year old Bruce, his teenage sister Stephanie - we compiled a list of names and voted on it on the proportional ballot system, like the Eurovision Song Contest. "Warwickshire Lad" won our contest and everyone was happy. The name carried a certain tradition in our family for Maurice had served for twenty years in the Royal Warwickshire Regiment of which "Warwickshire Lads" was the regimental march. That decision made, choosing the livery was easy - the boat would be painted in the regimental colours of dark blue and orange.

For the next seven years, we cruised the waterways of England extensively at every opportunity - rivers and canals, summer and winter, fair weather and foul, annual holidays, weekends long and short, day trips and half-hour jaunts - until it became clear that canal mania was chronic.

By that time, Stephanie was living in her own flat in Shepherds Bush and working for BBC Television and Bruce was striving for those qualifications which ultimately led him to read Geography at Oxford Polytechnic. Much as we loved our Edwardian home within earshot of Edgbaston County Cricket Ground, the large rooms seemed to echo a bit with only the two of us there and the staircases to the two upper floors were silent without the sound of youthful feet and voices.

The time had come to move. From a large house with a smallish garden to a cottage with a lot of land was the general idea and if that cottage were alongside a canal then it would not merely be a home but a way of life.

I had spent two carefree years at Birmingham Art College after leaving school and I had kept up my painting as a hobby. It seemed natural, therefore, to try my hand at the traditional craft of narrow boat painting. My first efforts were terrible. But I persevered and by the time I had completed the decoration on a two gallon water can known as a Buckby Can (after the place of its origin), destined to sit on the cabin roof of "Warwickshire Lad", I thought that my work was tolerable. It was certainly no worse, and in the partial view of my nearest and dearest a great deal better than some of the painted ware that one saw for sale up and down the waterways.

Thus, there came to be added to our pipe dream a shop in which to sell canal crafts. It could either be an existing one or the potential for one - promising outbuildings or even a garden shed! We glossed over the stumbling block of planning permission. We would worry about that when the time came!

Those who are one jump ahead of this narrative, will have realised, quite rightly, that it was not going to be easy to find a property which filled all our criteria. It was not. Eventually, after a long, unproductive, sometimes tedious, occasionally exciting search, we put our town house up for sale and made preparations to live aboard "Warwickshire Lad" for as long as it took to find what we wanted. I think it was a pity that we never did sample the nomadic life - it might have opened up new horizons for us - who knows?

The same week - we saw it! There it was, our castle in the air, advertised in black and white in "Waterways World". We went to see it, twice, the second time with Stephanie and Bruce - and still it floated on rosy clouds!

But it was six months and several heart-breaking, house-selling hiccups later before contracts were exchanged on both properties and the removal men were booked.

We spent the weekend prior to the move taking "Warwickshire Lad" from "Iona"'s old mooring to one at the side of our newly acquired orchard. It was separated from the cottage by nothing more than a few yards of towpath and a hawthorn hedge. There, Maurice, Bruce and I spent the night after vacating our home in Birmingham. I did not leave without a moment of sadness for twelve, happy years spent under its roof. I was to feel many more such pangs - not for the house but for the garden which had been lovingly tended for all those years and was a mass of spring colour as we drove away.

The morning of April 7th was bright and clear - perfect for moving into a new home. Spring-cleaning an empty house is easy and we had everything that we needed on the boat. It was spotless in no time at all. We had resisted the impulse to "put a quart into a pint pot", by drawing plans to scale of all the rooms and designating the best and most essential pieces of furniture accordingly. Stephanie had taken her pick of the rest and hired a van to take it off to Shepherds Bush. Another load went to an auction room.

We did, however, insist on an invaluable item being included in the purchase price of the property. Now known as "The Object", because I could not think what else to call it at first, it was to be the home of anything that we could not accommodate within the house. It was the top of a removal van. Bright green, large, perfectly dry inside, but definitely not beautiful, it sat against the fence between our drive, and the New Inn (our neighbour), ready to swallow up all the awkward morsels with which we might choose to feed it. It still does!

It was midday before we spied the removal vans at the top of the hill taking, to our consternation, the turn towards Long Buckby. It was a common enough mistake although we did not know it at the time. The hamlet of Buckby Wharf, some fifty dwellings, straggles along the canal between two road bridges, separated from the village of Long Buckby by nearly three miles. Originally, it was a canal centred community and with the exception of a few new houses, most of the buildings had origins which were connected with the waterway. Our cottage and shop had been built by the owner of the New Inn in 1922 for the purpose of selling none other than the original Buckby Can to boatmen plying the Grand Junction Canal between London and Birmingham.

No problem with planning permission! Our premises had been designed for the very purpose for which we had bought them - that of selling traditionally decorated canal ware to people on boats!

In about five minutes the vans reappeared having failed to negotiate the low bridge carrying the main railway line. They crept uncertainly down the hill until Bruce's impatient soul could bear the suspense no longer. He ran along the drive and out of the gate, both arms working like a tick-tack man and was half way up the hill before the drivers saw him. Directing them the right way, he followed them in as they drew to a halt alongside their immobile brother - "The Object". It was many laborious hours before all our possessions, in spite of the drastic pruning the other end, were unloaded and stowed in an approximation of their rightful places. Of course, as anyone who has moved house will know, it was weeks before we could lay our hands easily on everything that we had brought with us. There are a couple of things that are still missing!

Our access drive from Watling Street (the A5), was behind the New Inn and really only for service vehicles and ourselves. The front of the cottage and the shop faced the lock and the towpath. This meant that all the substantial pieces of furniture had to be carried right round the building to the front door. As we worked, one or other of us would pause to watch a boat being worked through the lock and listen to the musical sound of pawls being raised and lowered. One thing was plain; the holiday season had begun.

"Come hell or high water", said Maurice as he passed me with his arms full of blankets, "we've got to be open for business by Easter!"

Good Friday fell on the 17th of April that year, and so, although we had ten days in which to get ourselves organised, "the sooner - the better" seemed a good maxim to adopt. We needed some experience as shop keepers before the bank holiday hit us. So we decided to go all out for an opening (unobtrusive rather than grand), on the Friday before Easter weekend. We had three days! Looking back, I think that we must have been soft in the head to give ourselves so little time. But we were very green about the retail trade and went blithely ahead.

We knew enough to take stock first of all. This was done the first evening and well into the small hours of Tuesday morning. There was an extraordinary assortment of goods. Some of it we had expected to find, as a result of our brief inspection on viewing the property. But there was quite a lot of stuff that either puzzled or amazed us. Take the Christmas crackers, for instance - and I wish that someone would - we could not visualise a big demand for them as only a few hardy souls cruise the canals between November and February. Or mouse traps. Half a dozen, perhaps, but a gross? As for toilet fresheners! There were blocks that hung in the loo; blocks that hung on the wall; blocks that were refills for containers that were out of stock (if they were ever in); and discs that were an alternative to all three of those above. And as if that were not enough - all these came in a variety of colours and fragrances to suit every taste! Like the Christmas crackers, they remain unsold to this day.

We had intended to uphold the tradition begun by the original owner of the shop, of selling hand painted canal ware which we would complement by those gifts that would be attractive to the twentieth-century boater but could not produce ourselves. Horse brasses for instance, with the names of different canals round the rims and tea-towels printed with canal scenes, would be popular. However, that first night as we counted the tins of Golden Syrup and the packets of Rice Krispies we modified our intentions. Maybe it would be a good idea to sell food as well?

The first proprietor had died childless and left the business to his niece and her husband - a purveyor of groceries and household goods in the fine, old-fashioned sense. It was on his death that the property was sold to our predecessor barely two years before we bought it. She had not radically changed the nature of the shop, it seemed, and perhaps neither would we.

Our decision had two commercial advantages. One; that it was as a general stores that the shop was described in the current waterways cruising guides. Two; that customers would be drawn in by their need for bread and milk, then - on impulse - buy a souvenir of their holiday.

There was another, non-commercial reason. We felt that we were in debt to the canal system. We had taken a lot from it over the years in terms of the quality of life and here was a chance to put a little back. Few canal-side shops sell provisions to any great extent. There was not another general stores for quite a long way so we would be filling a need. One forgets, in these days of motorised transport, the time that it takes to walk or cycle several miles to buy perishables, top up supplies, or obtain that forgotten tin-opener. We would aim to become known, not just for our Buckby Cans and painted roses and castles, but also as the shop that stocked almost everything. There may not be a choice. One brand of coffee - instant - and one size of jar. But the un-fussy boater would not have to do without.

I think that the most exasperating of our business acquisitions was the till. The shop had been burgled some months before and the ancient till had been smashed. We therefore found ourselves in possession of an electronic machine which not only sounded like an aircraft taking off when it was adding up but screamed at you if you made a mistake, which I did - often. Not content with that, if you stood too close when you pressed the "Cash" button, the drawer added injury to insult by leaping out and thumping you in the solar plexus! I think that I have mastered it now, but many would-be willing helpers have been irrevocably put off by the irascibility of the till.

"We would aim to become known for our Buckby Cans ..."

Somehow, amongst all this decision-making about the future of the shop, we needed to attend to other, more immediate matters. Our lovely garden in Birmingham had not been abandoned with merely a backward glance. We had brought with us a car load of plants.

For close on six months, I had been rooting cuttings, layering shoots, potting seedlings and dividing clumps. In short - propagating by every method that I knew, in order to bring a spot of colour and a memory of the old garden to the wilderness that we had gained. All these precious plants had been reposing in pots and tubs near the wall where Maurice had put them over a week before. They had been deprived of water and dried out by the chill north-east wind. It was imperative that they should be given a drink, and heeled in somewhere. Where? I gazed round despondently. Nowhere leapt to the eye as if to say "here".

Everywhere that I looked, seemed so unforgiving. Couch grass as far as the eye could see, for a start. Docks, with quite the largest leaves that I have ever seen (and no doubt with roots to match), growing on strange humps that looked like coffins that had been chucked about haphazardly. Nettles. Well, I did not mind nettles; butterflies liked them and they made a delicious wine, although there did seem to be rather too many of them.

What I did not appreciate until I started digging, was rubbish. I do not know when refuse disposal came to Buckby Wharf, but I now know what happened to rubbish before it did, and I am thankful at least, that it was in the days before plastic and polythene. Glass and china, bricks and plaster, wood and iron, in the quantities that we found was quite enough!

Finally, I came to the conclusion that the effort of clearing a space in which to heel in the plants temporarily would be as great as preparing their ultimate planting positions. So that is what I did. Of course, the upshot was that many of the larger shrubs could have been better placed if there had been time to give the project more thought. Thus, I am propagating once more (which is what gardening is all about, after all).

With one urgent job done, I thought maybe I had better give a little thought to our living accommodation. The question in my mind constantly was one of priorities and home, shop, garden were all jostling for first place. Order would gradually evolve from chaos without too much effort. Of that I was certain. We had all slept well although my creaky knee-joints informed me that the cottage was damp. But I had been aware, though nothing was said, of wistful glances cast in the direction of bacon and eggs and a still-unconnected electric stove at breakfast-time.

I had the name of an electrician - Dave - and gave him a ring. Incredible! Within an hour, the cooker was fixed up and he had done several other jobs that we had thought of in the meantime. In Birmingham, we would have waited days . . . weeks even. Dave was asked whether he could recommend a plumber. He could. The plumber did better. He arrived in half an hour, plumbed in the washing machine and provided us with an outside tap for rinsing wellingtons and vegetables. The plumber gave us the names of a coal merchant and a television engineer. They arrived the same afternoon, too. It was like "The House that Jack built". The coal merchant recommended an accountant - "a dab hand at screwing anything out of the Inland Revenue".

The crowning touch came a week or two later, when I asked tentatively at the farm across the road, whether they could let us have a load of manure for the garden. I had no sooner returned to tell Maurice that the answer was "yes", than we caught a glimpse in the fading evening light through the window, of a tractor crossing our grass. The fork lift was piled high with succulent cow muck. It had taken a full ten minutes from order to delivery!

The farm, too, was adjacent to the canal, but unlike us, the farmhouse faced the road. Once, it had been on the same level as Watling Street. Then the humped-backed canal bridge was demolished, and the A5 was widened and raised to the level of the new, straight bridge. This had the effect of lifting the road almost to the top of their ground floor windows and very close to them. The increase in noise and dust within must have been considerable.

The pastures, grazed by their prizewinning herd of Friesian cattle, sloped gently south-east and were bounded by a small tributary of the River Nene. The fields stopped abruptly, almost at the foot of the embankment which carried the main railway line. The M1 ran alongside it; I could hear the incessant rumble of traffic as I stood on the canal bridge on that Wednesday morning.

So many transport routes cutting their way through the one valley, taking advantage of the geographical contours - aiming for the Watford Gap, I supposed. First, the Roman road, then the canal closely followed by the railway, and finally the motorway. Not forgetting the aircraft, I thought, as the deafening noise hit me a minute after the American jets disappeared between the radio masts of Daventry and Rugby.

Abruptly, an Inter-City train hurtled along the edge of the lower field, causing the gentle, black and white cows to raise their heads for a moment before resuming their grazing. It was gone in seconds, and all was silent again except for the murmur of the motorway. I thought that it was a pity that all those drivers were not sitting in the one train, for it had looked nearly empty. And I wondered how many lorry loads it would take to fill one goods train - there were certainly plenty of them on the M1 - I could see the tops of them moving very slowly because of the road works.

In the centre of the first field, I had noticed two large coops housing that comparative rarity, the free range hen. Not so long ago, I heard a definition of a free range hen given by a court of law. This means that it is possible to sue a person who claims to sell free range eggs if the hens which laid them do not conform to that definition. As I remember, it went thus: a free range hen is one which spends most of its day with free access to land from which it gets the majority of its food.

There was no doubt about those hens. They were widely spread out over the field, some of them scratching about in the yard, preening themselves in the barn, a few adventurous ones strolling along the towpath. This is where we will get our eggs, I decided forthwith - until we have set ourselves up with our own chickens, anyway. There was no way that we would willingly subscribe to the barbaric battery system.

I pushed open the heavy iron gate and descended some steep concrete steps to the door of the farmhouse. Putting my finger on the button in the centre of the door, I heard the bell announce my presence in an extremely shrill voice. It had to be so. The din of the lorry thundering past above my head would have drowned any other. A tanned face beneath a flowered headscarf smiled at me as the door swung back.

"You must be the new people at the stores? How do you do? Settled in alright? I expect you'll be wanting eggs?"

She disappeared down a flight of stairs to the cellar, leaving me looking at the gleaming brasses which hung on the wall of the tiny hall. A busy lady, I decided. Friendly and pleasant, but not much time to waste in idle chat. Dairy farming is a dedicated business, I know, and hard work. She reappeared a few minutes later, carrying a tray of large, biscuit coloured eggs, faintly speckled, also a winter cauliflower.

"Do have this", she said, "it'll be a while before you'll have anything in that garden."

Thanking her, I carefully carried the eggs up the steps, gingerly balancing the tray as I negotiated the gate and fastened it securely behind me. Crossing the road, I paused a moment, resting the egg tray on the iron parapet of the bridge and looked down at a pair of boats below in the lock. They seemed a long way down, for it is a deep lock and the water was at the lower level (empty, a boater would say, though of course, it is not). A girl, standing by the tiller, glanced up and waved good morning. She was very brown and had long, blonde hair bleached nearly white by the sun. A plump baby of similar colouring, aged about sixteen months, sat on the cabin roof, its harness securely anchored to a brass ring. A lean, lurcher dog stood next to it, with its tail swinging gently.

I smiled, and watched them for a bit as the lock slowly filled and then raised my eyes to look past the top gates to the curve of the canal pound as it swung round the hill towards Norton Junction. The morning sun gleamed on the quiet water as it moved sluggishly towards the opened sluices. A ripple started near one bank, and moved swiftly across to the other, drawing a vee shape, as a water vole went in search of breakfast.

Several boats were moored on both sides of the canal - it seemed to be a popular overnight stop, but no-one was stirring. I glanced at the nearest one, our own "Warwickshire Lad", reflecting glints of sunlight from the polished brass ventilators on its roof and I felt a surge of happiness and hope for the future.

-2-
Trade & Tribulation

I could see the excitement in Maurice's eyes on Friday morning, as he I turned the little wooden sign on the door to "Open" and then vaulted the counter to save himself the trouble of walking around and lifting up the hinged portion. It was an old fashioned shop and we did not want to change it. Both of us had too many disturbing memories of fine Victorian buildings laid flat by Birmingham bulldozers in the name of progress, to feel the need to modernise merely for the sake of it.

Not everybody felt the same as we did. The night before, over a beer at the New Inn, a Daventry builder had scoffed at our intentions.

"Give me twenty thousand and I'll make you a grand little mini-market. You'll never do any good as it is!"

"No thanks," I smiled politely through gritted teeth.

"No shopping trollies and check-outs for us," explained Maurice, "time to chat - get to know people. That's what we're after."

The fellow stared, then shrugged in mock despair and left us, saying over his shoulder,

"I give you three months!"

Among the deeds and papers which had been sent to us by our solicitor, I had discovered the original architect's drawings and the builder's specifications. The shop premises had scarcely been altered since they were built in 1922. The only difference, as far as I could see, was that a glass screen which had enclosed a miniscule office in one corner, was absent. Everything else seemed unchanged. Two dozen iron hooks protruded from a ceiling that was faced with chestnut coloured tongued and grooved boards. At first glance, one might think that they had been the hooks on which hams and sides of bacon were hung. But no, they were too close to the ceiling for that. They would have held the heavy, galvanised Buckby Cans for which the shop was famous, in various stages of their decoration. I devoutly hoped that one day my painting would come somewhere near the standard set by old Mr Lovelock, the originator of the Buckby Can.

We had done our best, in three short days, to fill the shelves. As well as the motley collection of stock which we had bought at valuation, we now had most of the staple grocery items that we thought would be necessary on a boat. Our predecessor had kindly given us the names of some of her suppliers, including that of a large cash and carry wholesaler in Northampton where we had spent a frantic afternoon. The painted ware, which had seemed a goodly array when it was spread out on the dining room table back in Birmingham, looked rather small and lost in the large bay of the shop window.

That first week in trade, our turnover was very low. We learnt a great deal, though about customer requirements and continued bravely to increase the stock, dipping into our fast emptying pockets to do so and pretending that we had never heard of under-capitalisation. Our biggest headache was in getting the first delivery from any new supplier. They were full of promises which were rarely fulfilled. My fingers have never done as much walking as they did that week and I tried not to think of the ensuing telephone bill.

The electricity account had been a shock in itself! Admittedly, I had turned on all the night storage heaters throughout the cottage and shop in an effort to get rid of the damp. But we had only been there a week by the time the meter was read at the end of that quarter. The bill was such, that if we had continued at the same rate, our annual outlay on the one fuel would have been well over a thousand pounds! I think that Maurice nearly achieved the four minute mile as he tore around the premises switching them off!

We awoke on Good Friday morning to a sky of pale, washed blue into which small, cumulus clouds were dissolving. A sure sign, Bruce advised us, of fine weather.

This was cheerful news, for we knew from experience that Buckby Wharf at sunny bank holiday weekends was a popular place for that happy breed of people known as "Gongoozlers". For those familiar with canal terminology, this word needs no explanation; others may be surprised to learn that there have been times when it could have been applied to them.

A Gongoozler is one who stands about near canals, usually at locks, sometimes with hands in pockets, watching boaters at work. They do not mean to get in the way, but as they rarely have more than a smattering of knowledge about canal boating they usually do; tripping over ropes, sitting in a row on lock beams, generally getting between the boater and the work that has to be done. Gongoozlers who stand well back out of the way, are no problem. Those who offer to close the lock gates after the boat has left are a positive asset.

The worst experience that we ever had with gongoozlers took place at the wide lock that links the southern Stratford Canal with the River Avon. Try to imagine the lock, situated in Shakespeare Gardens and right by the river and the Memorial Theatre. It was August bank holiday (we should have known better) and as "Warwickshire Lad" entered the lock to drop down onto the river, it was immediately surrounded by every nationality under the sun. Ciné cameras whirred; Instamatics clicked; everyone jostled to get a better view.

A group of young American girls, enraptured by our "cute little dawg" who was trotting up and down the cabin roof, temptingly held out handfuls of peanuts (to which she was addicted). With one mighty leap, she sailed off the roof, gulped the peanuts and was lost in the crowd. It was a long, worrying time before we found her, having had to refill the lock and reverse back into the canal basin.

Gongoozlers, however, when viewed from the other side of the counter, take on an entirely different complexion. Pure profit! They sit about on the grass, getting in everybody's way except ours, popping into the shop every few minutes; first an ice cream; then a packet of crisps, a bar of chocolate, a can of lemonade; there was no end to it. At last, after they had watched a number of boats worked through the lock and thus grasped the significance of roses and castles, they would feel inclined to have a memento of their pleasant afternoon

"Situated in Shakespeare Gardens …"

and buy one of my painted mugs or a teapot smothered in roses.

We began to have pangs of guilt about the amount of junk food which passed over our counter and entertained thoughts about educating the great British public. I made vast numbers of beef and vegetable pies in individual sized foil dishes, using butcher's mince, fresh carrots and onions, lined and topped with shortcrust pastry. As fast as I emerged from the kitchen, red-faced, carrying the latest batch, they were gone. It seemed marvellous until we sat down and worked out our costs. We could not be sure how much to set off against fuel, but there was no doubt that my time was more cost effective if I painted, than if I made meat pies. People still call in and ask wistfully if I have considered making them again and maybe one day I will.

The sun shone all day, true to Bruce's prediction, and trade was brisk. Some relatives came to see how we were getting on, and sat outside in the sun eating Cornettos, watching the boats from deck-chairs. I carried my enamel paints and brushes out to the garden table, and painted tiny roses on brass miniatures of coffee pots and watering cans and wheelbarrows while we chatted. Bruce and Maurice took it in turns to leap up the back steps to the shop every time the bell on the door heralded a customer. I could not help feeling that I was on holiday, too.

At teatime, Bruce drove our aged Volkswagen Beetle up the hill to Long Buckby station to meet the London train, for Stephanie was coming home for Easter. Festooned with the medley of plastic carrier bags that she always seemed to prefer to one sensible suitcase, she breezed in - radiating energy and enthusiasm for our new venture and delighted with the "truly amazing" station at which she had just arrived. Stephanie worked for the BBC Television programme, "Newsnight", and her conversation as a result, was heavily sprinkled with superlatives.

Admittedly, by comparison with the metropolis, Long Buckby station might be considered quaint. Stephanie, though, was accustomed to arriving at all sorts of stations in all manner of places, in order to meet us at some point during a canal cruise. This was usually fairly easy to accomplish, for in general, railway engineers had followed the line of the canal routes which had preceded them. This was partly because the land contours which were suitable for one, best suited the other, and partly as a deliberate policy on the part of the railways, in order to poach the carrying trade of the canals. In some cases, the railway companies actually bought out the canal companies whose decline they had caused.

One of the most memorable stations at which she arrived, was Chirk, on the Welsh border. We tied up the boat in a wooded cutting, putting it firmly aground on some rocks which had fallen from the towpath, as we did so, and scrambled up the steep path from the canal to the bridge. The railway station was adjacent - small, unmanned, and boarded up. It was a relief to see the train appear round the bend and slow to a halt.

When Stephanie arrived, she told us the story that she had been given by a fellow traveller. Apparently, the land on which the line had been built, had originally been part of the estate of Chirk Castle. It had only been sold to the railway company on condition that the trains always stopped at the station for the benefit of those at the castle. We were surprised that such a condition had survived Dr. Beeching, but grateful that it had.

We were no less pleased to discover that Long Buckby station had been spared, complete with booking clerk. It consists of a booking office at road level and two platforms set high on an embankment overlooking fields of barley and oil-seed rape. One is not aware, arriving from London as Stephanie had done, of the village of Long Buckby at all, situated over the ridge. It seems as if the train is stopping in the middle of nowhere - nothing but sheep and crops, and a few farm buildings in sight. It is not until one has got off the train and walked through the cobbled tunnel beneath the lines, that one sees a small factory tucked almost under the embankment and the row of old shoe-makers dwellings along the ridge; dwellings which once housed those who worked in a factory that now makes pot-noodles instead of shoes.

It begins to make sense that Long Buckby still has a station, where trains top on the branch line between Rugby and Wolverton, and continue, albeit slowly, to Birmingham or London and many places in between. Even so, I was curious as to why Long Buckby too, had not been axed, and I asked a local man who proved to be a fund of information.

Frank told me that it had been scheduled for closure, true enough, but largely through the efforts of the local post-master, it was saved. It was at the time that Daventry, which had already lost its station, was destined for expansion as an over-spill town for Birmingham - a plan since abandoned. This gave some weight to arguments for keeping the station, but more muscle was needed.

The sub-postmaster at Long Buckby, being something of a railway enthusiast, organised the local residents in support, and booked an excursion train to take them all to the coast. The venture was such a success, that British Rail became interested, and he now organises regular excursion trips throughout the year, to places like Bournemouth, Brighton, Hastings and Edinburgh, and every one fully booked, so I am told.

The good weather did not hold throughout the Easter weekend, and as the barometer fell, Stephanie decided to extend the "take-away" menu to include hot, homemade soup and baked potatoes. Unfortunately, the number of Gongoozlers fell too, and we ended up eating the food ourselves. Not that we minded - it was wholesome fare.

Since then, we have had to reconcile ourselves to eating up many foodstuffs which, in the old days would never have passed the threshold of my kitchen. Our cashflow was such, that anything which was dented, broken, or out of date, found its way into our pantry. Fortunately, Bruce, who was living on a shoestring in Oxford, was happy to relieve us of most of the items which were written off from time to time.

Easter week drew to its close with appalling ferocity. The glass plummeted, and as the wind gathered strength from the north-east, it transformed the low, muggy cloud that had been hanging over the Fens all week into huge, soft snowflakes. We were fairly philosophical about it; Maurice joked with the customers, and told them that we had been cruising at Eastertime for twelve consecutive years and had always managed to find snow.

We had woken up on one Good Friday morning, moored by the Wharf Inn at Hockley Heath, to find that an unexpected white world had descended silently overnight. On another occasion, we had spent Easter Monday battling our way through the exhausting guillotine locks on the River Nene against driving sleet and snow. Only last year, we had slipped and slithered across lock beams that were dangerously covered with slush, on the River Soar Navigation at Leicester, during our Easter cruise.

He was very good at cheering up doleful customers and managed to do a grand trade in waterproofs and woolly hats and gloves.

"You're bound to need them next Easter too," he said, somehow managing to keep up the jocularity with everybody, "for I don't suppose the weather will be any better then!"

The large delivery of ice cream which we had ordered to replace that consumed at the weekend, naturally remained unsold. This, we were to regret.

Maurice and I went to bed early on Saturday night. I left the landing light on for Bruce who was celebrating the last night of his vacation with a pint or two of Marston's Pedigree next door. We were so tired that we fell asleep quickly in spite of the wind whining through every cranny in the old cottage, spattering the bedroom window with staccato bursts of noisy wet snowflakes. The cypress tree outside Stephanie's bedroom window roared and rushed like waves breaking on a rocky beach. I could hear it even through two closed doors. The water in the canal broke in real waves over the top gate of the lock as if it were the North Sea instead of an inland waterway.

It must have been about ten past one when Bruce opened our bedroom door, his throaty whisper scarcely audible above the din, "Dad! Mum! The landing light's gone off and I've tried my tape recorder and that won't work either. There must be a power cut!"

"Blast!" Maurice had stubbed his toe as he fumbled his way round a still unfamiliar bedroom. It always impressed me that he could be deeply asleep one second and instantaneously awake and alert the next. It must be his military training. And provided that he was not kept awake for more than a quarter of an hour, he could fall asleep equally quickly. I envied him that. He used to reckon, when he was a young officer, that he could get out of bed, pull his uniform on over his pyjamas, turn out the guard, get out of his uniform, back into bed and fall straight asleep. But if he was delayed by so much as a minute, the magic did not work and he would toss and turn like we lesser mortals for ages.

He went downstairs, trying various switches and ultimately those in the shop, which were on a separate circuit. Not a glimmer. The freezers were silent, too. I listened. There was a hollow-sounding "ding" followed by a curse. I thought that he must have hit his head on a Buckby can as he stood on a stool to look inside the fuse box. I felt a bit guilty about lying in bed, but one of us stumbling about in the dark seemed to be more than enough.

After some more crashing about and swearing, I heard him pick up the telephone, dial, and then report the break in supply. I relaxed. It is all too easy to go back to bed, and either hope that someone else will do so, or that the Electricity Board knows about it anyway. That is very likely what we would have done in similar circumstances back in Birmingham. Now, things were different.

Isolated as we were except for a handful of houses, we could not be sure that anyone else was on the same power line as ourselves, or if they were, that they knew that the power was off - or cared. We did. There were several hundred pounds worth of ice cream in the cabinet, a freezer-chest full of frozen food for resale, and our own domestic freezer in an outhouse was not exactly empty.

"No, they didn't know," he answered in reply to my question, as he snuggled back under the duvet, "but if it's any consolation, half of Northamptonshire is off as well." Then, as his quarter of an hour had not quite elapsed, he turned over and went straight back to sleep, leaving me listening to the storm, and worrying about the ice cream and the frozen food, and whether we were sufficiently insured.

The power was still off at eight o'clock the next morning, when Maurice telephoned again to see if there had been any progress. None. I think that they took their telephone off the hook then, for we could not reach them again. I cannot say that I blamed them, for we heard on the radio that electricity poles had been brought down like ninepins all over the Eastern counties. We would just have to await our turn for reconnection.

I went outside to see what other damage had been done. It was a mild, clear morning, the early sunlight slanting onto the snow. Strange, I thought, how abruptly last night's turmoil had abated. But it was obvious that I had not dreamt it. There were great, glistening snowdrifts reaching halfway up the front doors of the north-facing cottage and shop. Yet the fierce wind had swept the south-facing tracts of grass at the back almost bare, and piled the snow in high ridges up against the thorn hedge, burying it.

The snow was not only uneven, it was not "deep and crisp" either. It was glutinous and soggy, and already melting with a steady drip-drip off the eaves. The dogs played in it, up to their ears in the drifts; their customary black, grizzle and tan fur was coated white and their beards and trousers became hung with shiny balls of slush like the bells of a court jester. These clung fast until the dogs came indoors and shook themselves vigorously, scattering wet snow in all directions. I gave up worrying about the mess.

I walked round the house, examining the ground for fallen roof slates, for our previous home had been wont to scatter those like confetti after a storm, but there were none, to my relief. The orchard looked worse than it was. Apart from a large, old plum tree that had crashed down, most of the confusion had been caused by a deluge of dead branches and twigs. We had got off lightly.

As it was going to be some hours at least, (such was our faith then in the East Midlands Electricity Board) before our power was restored, we set about the task of insulating the freezers. I could just see a few ice lollies, still frozen happily, beneath the glass lid of the ice cream cabinet. We took this to be an indicator that nothing else had thawed - yet, and resisted the temptation to open any of the freezers and have a look.

I eventually located our four sleeping bags, and with these plus an old eiderdown and all the spare blankets, we wrapped up the freezers so that they looked like cocoons. Solemnly, we vowed to each other that we would not raise those lids until electricity was once more surging through the motors, be the customers ever so insistent. Only two people gave us any trouble; an elderly gentleman who was waiting on the doorstep (from which the snowdrift had hastily been shovelled), tried hard but in vain for a choc-ice before he shuffled away, muttering angrily; a determined lady pestered us to let her have a packet of bacon until it became embarrassing, but we did not give in and eventually she capitulated with a laugh. Most people were sympathetic towards us in our predicament, confessing that in spite of the rough night, they were better off on their boats.

The electric till did not work, of course. This was something of a relief to me even though I had to brush up on my mental arithmetic. We kept the small change in a series of cardboard boxes, and the notes in Maurice's trousers pocket - which caused raised eyebrows whenever I found it necessary to run after him and change a ten pound note!

After the first flush of early customers had subsided, I snatched a few minutes to go upstairs and sort out a few more of our clothes. Cupboard space was at a premium, and I looked helplessly at all my inappropriate city clothes - too good to throw out. I compromised. Dragging out a large, teak chest from its place beneath the window, I flung back the intricately carved lid. The delicate scent of the camphor wood lining rose to my nostrils as I packed away silk evening dresses, long skirts and neat suits. Even if I never wear them again, I thought, they might come in useful as dressing-up clothes for my grand-children. Not that Stephanie showed the slightest sign of ever settling down! Closing the lid and fastening the brass clasp, I pushed the heavy chest back into place and rose to my feet. Then I stood for a moment to flex my aching back, gazing idly out of the small window that looked across the pitched roof of the shop towards the New Inn.

That's funny? I don't remember noticing that wire before? There was a thick, PVC covered cable sagging across the slates of the roof and sliding back and forth as the breeze freshened. One end of the cable was attached to a pole alongside the fence which separated our garden from the pub. I tried to open the window, but it was stuck fast. I could not see where the other end went without going outside, for it disappeared towards the gable. Running downstairs, I told Maurice about it as I pulled on my boots and went out to have a look. He followed me.

"A thick, PVC covered cable sagging across the slates …"

We agreed that it was obviously our main electric cable, but as it was not broken, probably not the source of the trouble. "Why's it loose, then?" I asked Maurice, "it's still fixed to the chimney alright."

"I haven't the slightest idea," he said helpfully, going inside to serve a customer who had just arrived. Exasperated, I walked over towards the lock and stared back at the situation from a slight distance.

Suddenly the light dawned on my befuddled brain! The pole was leaning over towards the shop! It was obvious when viewed from the lock-side, but foreshortened when seen from the bedroom window. I went over to have a closer look. The steel wire rope which normally ran from the top of the pole to a stay in the ground, had snapped. The pole was at an angle of about twenty degrees, and pressing against the bulging fence. I measured the distance with my eye. If it fell, it would crash across the front of the shop, and probably hit the bedroom beyond. My stomach contracted.

Maurice tried, unsuccessfully, to get through on the telephone to the Electricity Board, all afternoon. We rang the police, in desperation, who advised us that the Electricity Board were not taking any more calls, in view of the magnitude of work in the aftermath of the blizzard. There were poles, they said, down like dominoes everywhere. This pole had not even fallen. I said yes, that was the point. It might fall on a customer entering or leaving the shop - or me. Surely it was quicker, and safer, (and cheaper), to fix the stay before the pole fell, and not wait until afterwards? They agreed with that, and said that as the Electricity Board telephoned them every few hours for news, they would certainly pass on the message.

Dusk fell; the wind grew stronger and the pole began to see-saw a bit on the edge of the fence. We got out the silver candelabra that we used to have on the table when we had dinner parties, lit all the candles, poured ourselves a large whisky each, sat down and stared at each other. We did not need to speak; the words hung in the air between us. What could we do?

Bruce had returned to Oxford as planned, for the roads were clear and he had hitched a lift quite quickly.

"We could move into Bruce's room tonight," I said, "just in case . . ."

"Good idea," Maurice nodded, "and what about moving the stock out of the shop window - it would be a shame if all your hard work was smashed?"

He started to clear the window, carrying all the painted ware to the back of the shop, and stacking it on the deep freeze.

"It would be safe enough here, and we won't be opening this tomorrow, that's certain."

"Will the insurance cover all of it?" I asked, nodding towards the freezers and in the direction of the electricity pole.

"I bloody well hope so!" he exploded, "I told the broker when we were moving in. We should be fully covered."

"Is it an act of God?" I asked, with a tremor in my voice, "and isn't that excluded?"

He looked up at the dark ceiling, as if he thought, like Don Camillo, that God was there and ready to chat.

"No, of course it isn't an act of God - it's the usual incompetence of a Nationalised Industry!"

I nearly smiled.

Another early night, even though neither of us felt very sleepy, but Maurice had to be in Birmingham by nine o'clock the following morning. Although he had resigned from his job, it would be the end of June before he was free to devote all his time to our new enterprise. Now that his fortnight's holiday was over, he would be commuting daily until then, leaving the Wharf at twenty minutes to eight and returning after seven in the evening. We lay in the dark, torches handy, talking and worrying for a long time, listening to the wind moaning and half waiting for that dreaded crash.

I woke early, and dashed to the window of the bedroom in which we had not slept, and looked out at the offending pole.

"It's still there!" I called to Maurice, who was in the bathroom, shaving. Then, after pulling on jeans and a sweater, I rushed downstairs to put the kettle on the camping stove before going outside. The pole was definitely leaning at a more acute angle, I reported, and there was something else which I had noticed.

"There is a telephone wire attached to that pole; it was hidden by snow yesterday. I'll ring the GPO - maybe they will do something!"

"So, after Maurice had driven off after a hasty breakfast, I managed to get though to the Post Office without any delay, and reported the dangerous condition of one of their telegraph poles.

It was barely a couple of hours later, that a bright yellow British Telecom van drew up on the bridge and three men wearing hard hats of an equally sulphuric colour, came along the towpath. I heaved a sigh of relief and went out to talk to them.

"Yes, lady," said one, "that pole is in a very dangerous condition - it could come down at any time."

"Can you fix it?" I said anxiously, certain that it was leaning over more acutely than at breakfast time.

"Sorry," he shook his head, "it's not our pole."

"Not your pole!" I squeaked, "But there's your telephone wire fixed to it!"

"That's right, but the pole belongs to the Electric - they just allow us to put our line on it. We can't touch their pole."

They had started to walk away while he was speaking. I ran after them.

"Will you tell them it's dangerous?" I called. They nodded assent and drove away. I did not believe them, anyway.

I rang Maurice at work, and told him what had happened.

"Pretty typical," he said acidly, "and there's more bad news. I've spoken to the insurance broker - and he's made a nonsense - said he hadn't realised that we'd moved, let alone that we were trading!"

Another miserable night passed, and another morning inspection of the electricity pole. By that time, it had achieved an angle of forty-five degrees. It was the fence that seemed to be holding it up and that was beginning to split. Another high wind, and undoubtedly it would give way.

I pulled a chair up to the telephone and decided that I would not budge until I had spoken to someone at the Electricity Board. Amazing - I got through immediately. It was Tuesday morning. The voice on the other end made all the right noises and as we were speaking, the freezers rumbled into life. Restraining myself, I did not check the contents until the red warning lights had gone out to tell me that the temperature was at the correct level. Everything was fine except the kippers - it must have been the salt. I reckoned that the insurance broker could sweat a bit before we gave him the glad tidings.

Wednesday morning - Thursday morning. The pole was still, miraculously, at the same angle and swaying gently in the wind. Then I had a brain-wave. With hind-sight (if there is such a thing, except in rabbits), we were stupid not to have had the idea before. Put it in writing! Nobody, least of all those in Nationalised Industries, likes to have their mistakes down in black and white - in duplicate.

I sat down and wrote a polite, but succinct letter to the East Midlands Electricity Board, put a first class stamp on it and just caught the afternoon post from the Wharf box.

By eleven o'clock the following morning, the pole had been made safe!

-3-
Stepping Stones

Trade slackened gradually towards the end of the Easter holidays, with the intermittent start of the summer terms; the state schools were the first, then the private schools and the polytechnics with the universities lagging behind. After that, parents of young families below school age and retired people took advantage of the less expensive rate of boat hire.

As the type of customer altered - so did their needs. The demand for uncut wholemeal bread which had fallen off as the school holidays ended (undergraduates invariably asking for thick, white sliced), resurged with vigour. We were faced with urgent and unexpected pleas for disposable nappies.

It was very difficult to develop a rational buying policy. Even if our capital had been unlimited, our shop was so small and our storage space so meagre, that we could not have carried nearly enough stock to satisfy everyone.

We learnt quickly, unfortunately, the sad fact that people were so accustomed to shopping in large supermarkets that they were impatient to find that we did not have the same wide choice available. Neither could we hope to match the prices of the multiple stores who were able to sell their goods often more cheaply than we could buy ours. Another quirk which we observed with some amusement, was that many customers have forgotten how to look a shop assistant in the eye and ask for what they want. I think that about three-quarters of the people who walked through the shop door, immediately turned their back on me without a word and stared at the opposite wall of shelves. It did not make any difference how we re-arranged the goods, varying the display from boring household disinfectants to exciting trinkets - that is the direction in which they would initially stare fixedly! Now, Maurice stands behind the counter and I sit painting on the other side. That stumps them! They usually watch me - silently.

A principle which we found hard to swallow, was that our tastes were not necessarily shared by our customers. Still, we were there to please, so we tried to hold in stock any item for which we had been asked at least twice.

On weekdays, while Maurice was working in Birmingham, I had to manage single handed. This meant staying within earshot of the shop bell, which could be a bit annoying if there was nobody about and there was other work to be done. I began to notice that the quiet times and the periods of intense activity on the canal fell into a pattern. At the beginning of the week there was a lull, especially on Tuesdays; Wednesday brisked up a bit; Thursday and Friday were hectic and so was Saturday (except for a hiatus around midday). Sunday largely depended on the weather.

This pattern was primarily the result of one factor. A factor which might have influenced a less obsessive purchaser against buying our shop. A factor which is constantly uppermost in our minds even now. It is Blisworth Tunnel which takes the Grand Union Canal from the village of Stoke Bruerne to that of Blisworth in Northamptonshire, on its long journey from London to Birmingham. Blisworth - a tunnel which has been closed now for four long years, severing the main artery of the canal system in England; withering trade on the southern side and cutting it to the bone on the north. A tunnel which is, at last, being repaired at the cost of four and a quarter million pounds.

The effect which the closure of Blisworth Tunnel has had on our trade is hard to quantify even now. We knew when we offered for the shop, that the tunnel was temporarily closed for repair. We did not worry too much, though, for through traffic was being maintained at that time, by the British Waterways Board. They arranged for each boat to be steered through the tunnel by their own helmsmen while the occupants were ferried over the top in a mini-bus.

Work on the tunnel continued at the same time, coupled with a detailed inspection. What we did not foresee, was the radical rebuilding which was found to be necessary at an estimated cost (then) of one and a half million pounds that the Board insisted they could not afford. Even so, in the spring of the first year at Buckby Wharf, we were blithely optimistic that the money would materialise and that Blisworth would be re-opened for navigation by the following season. We were content to use our first summer building up our stock and getting to grips with the retail business.

One obvious effect which a truncated canal and the consequential loss of a through route had on canal traffic, was to make it predictable. The pattern which I had observed was no accident. Let me explain.

A narrow boat hire company, for example, based close to the northern portal of Blisworth Tunnel, might have eight boats ranging from four to ten berths each - a total of about fifty potential customers. Their "turn around" day might be Saturday, which meant that boats were required to be back at the base between nine and ten on a Saturday morning, to leave with their new hirers on board at three o'clock in the afternoon. The tunnel being closed, their only option was to go north. Most of them considered the idea of turning right down the seventeen locks to Northampton, an unattractive proposition, so continued straight on towards Norton Junction and our shop.

Now, cruising time by canal is calculated in "lock-miles". The maximum speed permitted by British Waterways is four miles per hour (fifteen minutes per mile). The average time that it takes to work through a lock is also fifteen minutes. The experienced boater would probably be quicker in the locks than the novice, but cruise the pounds in between more slowly in order to preserve the banks from wash damage. Thus, the twenty-two lock-miles between Blisworth and Buckby Wharf could be calculated as taking about five and a half hours. Therefore, the early boats from this base could be expected at about half-past eight on Saturday evening, and the remainder throughout Sunday morning. Simple!

Once I had worked all this out with reference to the ten or so nearest hire bases (and you would be surprised at how long that took), I was able to make life very much easier for myself. Instead of attempting several times to do something relatively trivial, like making the bed, scampering downstairs each time that I heard the shop bell ring (and incidentally losing pounds in weight as the days went by), I was in a position to organise my chores. Of course, there were deviations (privately owned boats and gongoozlers, for instance) from the pattern.

Customers from the road, though, did fall into a different, but discernible pattern of their own. Lorry drivers, for example, called first thing in the morning and late afternoon, and the local school children arrived when the school bus disgorged them at a quarter past four. And I could always tell when there was a hold-up on the motorway - the A5 would suddenly become chock-a-block and drivers would sprint into the shop for cigarettes to soothe their shredded nerves.

With the warmer spring weather, I itched to lick the garden into shape. There was so much to be done. A lot of it had to wait until the weekends when we were both at home and could take it in turns to mind the shop or work outside. I tested the soil with a proprietary soil-testing kit, and decided that where there was virgin soil, it was slightly acid, but the deposits of builder's rubble and plaster had made parts of the garden alkaline.

One such place lay opposite the back door which opened onto a small, paved terrace. It was the ideal place for a herb garden. Most herbs prefer an alkaline soil, and just there, they would not only be handy for picking but we could enjoy their fragrance when we sat outside on warm , summer evenings. I do not believe that a garden should be merely a place of work - one must make time to sit and appreciate it. The evening is ideal for that.

As many herbs originate in Mediterranean countries they are somewhat tender, but the spot that I had chosen would be sheltered from the cold north-easterlies by the house. We sorted the rubble into bricks, cement and stone. Putting the bricks on one side for future use (one can never have too many bricks), we built a long, curved wall to protect the herbs from the prevailing west wind, using large chunks of cement as a core, and disguising them with lumps of local sandstone and flint, so that the wall had a pleasing appearance.

For my birthday, Maurice gave me a replica in stone, of a mediaeval monk's head carved in relief. It was one of a set of eight which illustrated afflictions that could be cured by herbal remedies. My monk was suffering from baldness, and for some reason (perhaps Toadflax was the cure), he had a rather engaging toad sitting on his forehead, which was why I chose him in preference to toothache. We sat "Baldness" in the wall, to guard the herb patch.

Digging out the couch grass and other perennial weeds from the bed took a long time but as it was close by, I was able to do it in between customers. I would pull off my gardening gloves, kick off my galoshes and saunter into the shop, smiling nonchalantly as if there had been no frenzied activity occupying me outside at all! I do not think that I can have been very thorough with the weeding though, because the bind-weed has reappeared with a vengeance this year, curling over the rocks and stones to blow its pale pink trumpets at me in triumph.

The nucleus of my herb garden was going to be the half dozen essential plants which I had brought with me. By that, I mean herbs that I cannot do without in the kitchen - thyme, parsley, rosemary, sweet bay, lemon balm and chives. Mint is vital too but I do not let that loose in the garden.

In Elizabethan England, when most large homes had a garden of sorts, herbal plants were usually separated by type into small, geometrical shaped beds which were arranged within rectangles. These "knots" were divided from each other by low, clipped hedges and narrow paths of camomile or coloured gravel. Delightful though knot gardens are, they are too formal for my way of gardening - not having a fleet of gardeners to clip the hedges and rake the paths.

As long as the plants were labelled, and I could find what I wanted when I needed it, I preferred my herb garden to have the appearance of a large, informal flower bed. So I decided to expand the collection with a combination of shrubs and herbaceous perennials, not bothering too much in the planting, as to whether

"We sat 'Baldness' in the wall ..."

they were culinary, medicinal or aromatic herbs, but taking account of the height, spread and flowering time of each one.

I had read about a nursery garden which specialised in herbs, so off I went to Thornby one rainy Sunday afternoon and returned with boxes full of exciting plants. They had such engaging English names. I have never been a great one for the botanical names of plants because I have an appalling memory. I find, for instance, that "Hamamelis virginiana" is instantly forgettable, whereas its popular name "Witch Hazel" lingers quite unbidden.

I confess that I did not necessarily buy herbs because they would be useful in any way, but sometimes because they conjured up pictures of my granny's cottage garden or were steeped in folk-lore and history. I bought Rue, the herb of grace, because it reminded me of Ophelia; Lad's Love, Sweet Cicely and Jacob's Ladder I chose for no other reason except the music of their names.

In no time at all, I filled my herb garden with plants and there are still more that I would like to have - Feverfew is one. Several customers have told me that it is an infallible cure for migraine so it must be worth growing. Once the plants were established, I intended to offer "Fresh Garden Herbs picked on request" as a speciality in the shop.

We had brought roots of several different varieties of mint with us, too. There was common mint, orange and apple mints, peppermint, and of course, ginger mint. These, we decided to confine in an old bath which we found lying fortuitously amongst the nettles. We chose an inconspicuous place not too far from the back door, and Maurice set about digging a trench in which he could sink it up to its rim. It turned out to be the place which had been used as a dumping ground for bottles, for years. He dug up hundreds, of all shapes and sizes. Some were quite old. There were ancient ink bottles, medicine bottles with ground glass stoppers, lemonade bottles with glass marbles in their mouths. Bruce collects old bottles so he was pleased. I was not - I have to dust his collection.

I planted the mint, carefully labelling each variety, in a mixture of good soil and cow-muck and it romped away. Unfortunately, all the mints ran into each other and mixed themselves up so that I cannot tell the difference between them. They have kept their individual flavours, though, so sometimes the new potatoes taste of peppermint or ginger, or even plain mint, which makes life interesting.

The vegetable patch was a very pathetic place. I stood looking at it sadly, wondering where to begin. It was a Saturday morning in early May, and I should have been revelling in the opportunity to wander about outside at will, with the warm sun on my back and no need to cock one ear for the bell, for Maurice was on duty. He had found time in odd moments, to turn over a good sized oblong of land at the side of the cottage, parallel with the towpath hedge. Judging by the great heap nearby, he had removed a considerable quantity of couch grass, dock, nettles and other weeds, although there were plenty more where they had come from - I could see that. I had raked the patch more or less level, thrown in its general direction the contents of several packets of vegetable seeds and hoped for the best. There had been plenty of rain lately which was just as well as the soil was light and sandy and there had been no time to incorporate any humus before the season for sowing the early crops would be gone.

The seeds were all through; in fact the percentage of germination looked pretty good when I thought of the cavalier treatment that they had received. The problem was predators. Slugs mainly. Huge, black garden slugs, each with a yellow foot. Some of them were five inches long, and Maurice's heap of weeds was black with them. Then there were field slugs. A delicate pinky-brown in colour, and very, very slimy. Ugh! I once ate a lettuce leaf harbouring one of those - I was responsible for washing the salad so I could blame no-one else - and the gorge rises within me now at the memory of it. No amount of salt mouth-washes could clear that milky slime away.

Squatting down on my heels, I stirred a patch of soil with a stick to see what else had woken up on a warm morning after a shower to decimate my precious seedlings. The first fellow I saw was a fat, grey cut-worm that had already eaten halfway through the stem of a broccoli seedling. I stirred some more. Two cheeky orange wire worms having a dance - no doubt to celebrate the meal that they had just made of the next door broccoli. A chafer grub lay nearly immobile; he was a Whopper and must have been actively eating to get to that size. A leather jacket and a millipede were both hiding under a stone. At that point, I stood up in despair, and that was the moment too, when Maurice galloped out, thrust a mug of coffee into my hand and sprinted back to the inevitable summons.

I walked back to the house slowly, sipping my coffee and meditating. It looked as if our aim to become self-sufficient in vegetables was heading for dismal failure. We had got to do something drastic to get our plants past the vulnerable seedling stage - preferably without the use of pesticides.

"Chickens! " I announced as I walked into the shop. On the far side of the counter, the lady who was trying to decide between two decorated wooden spoons looked rather startled.

"To eat the slugs," I explained kindly. She seemed confused but settled hastily for the red spoon, paid for it and vanished out of the door.

"You really mustn't do it!" Maurice was at his most severe.

"What?"

"Walk in and talk as if there was no-one here. It isn't just that they're strangers, and they don't know how your mind works . . ." he muttered something that I did not catch, then added "they're customers and it puts them off buying."

"Oh! Sorry, I forgot. Business is business." I tapped the side of my nose and went on.

"It's just that we did say that we were going to keep hens eventually. Well, we must put our skates on. Get them now. It's the only way we'll get any veg at all. Let them loose all over the place to eat up everything they can find before we start. And you must cut the grass - it's so long all round the vegetable patch that the slugs simply lurk, ready to pounce when we're not looking."

"I don't think slugs can pounce," said Maurice, "but I agree with you in principle. We'll need a hen-house - and some pullets, of course."

"I'll ask at the farm. They've just bought a hundred point-of-lay pullets from somewhere; they don't keep a cockerel for their hens because a lot of people don't like eating fertilised eggs, apparently."

"Oh! Really? Perhaps we'd better not have one, then - we want to be able to sell our surplus eggs in the shop."

There were several ways in which we could start keeping poultry. The most interesting and natural way would be to buy a broody hen and clutch of fertilised eggs for her to hatch and rear for us. She would teach them how to forage for their own food, and keep them warm at night while they were chicks. The difficulty would be in finding one for sale, for modern hens were hybrids which had had all the broodiness bred out of them in order to increase egg production.

I scanned the local paper, affectionately known as "The Gusher", but came up with nothing. Another method, also interesting, would be to buy day old chicks and rear them in an artificially heated pen - a brooder. The drawback to that was our lack of a suitable outhouse with enough space for it.

The easiest way for us to start, although more expensive, would be to buy half a dozen young hens aged about twenty weeks - pullets at "point of lay". After a week or two to settle into their new quarters, they would begin to lay small eggs, a few a week. The eggs would increase in size, until we were getting one large egg nearly every day from each of them - we hoped.

I went over to the farm and asked about the hens.

"Penny's Pullets," I told Maurice on my return, "in a village called Canon's Ashby."

"Fine," he said, "now the next thing is a hen-house, which I suspect will be more difficult. You've looked in 'The Gusher', of course?"

"Mm. Can't you build one?"

"Of course I can," he said, looking pained, "my carpentry is quite good enough for chickens. But it needs wood, you know, and wood is expensive."

"But there's heaps of it lying about," I gestured airily around the estate.

"I absolutely agree," he said, somewhat icily, "but most of it, as you would have found out if you had examined it (his brilliance at turning the tables always impressed me), is either rotten or totally unsuitable for making a hen-house."

"Humph!" I was sceptical but for once did not argue, merely added, "Well, we can't have hens without a house. I'll ask Chris when he comes tomorrow - he may hear of one on his travels."

Chris was our milkman. He had his own dairy, and although the discount that he gave us on milk to sell in the shop was not as good as the large companies and he did not deliver on Sundays, he was flexible. I think that flexibility is the advantage that small firms have over big ones which are hide-bound by rules and systems. And, of course, the desire to oblige the customer even at the cost of extra time and effort. We knew that we could telephone Chris at home to order extra milk in a hurry and if he was unable to deliver it, we could always drive over to his farm to collect it. One Sunday morning when we had unexpectedly run short, the boats were coming through the lock as if they were on a conveyor belt. Chris and his family were just about to go out when I 'phoned, but we arranged to meet near a pub called The Buckby Lion, halfway between his farm and the Wharf. He rolled up in a large horse box, in the front of which all his family were squashed with my crate of milk, and two superb show jumpers in the back. I realised then why he did not deliver on Sundays!

Chris said that he would keep his eyes and ears open for a hen-house for us and a couple of days later he turned up trumps.

"I've found you a hen-house! " he called, as he humped the crates off the lorry. "An old girl up Ravensthorpe way has died, and her niece is selling off her stuff. There's a hen-house; she used to keep bantams but it's big enough for hens. There's other bits and pieces with it. Forty quid."

Maurice and I looked at each other and nodded (I had already priced a new one).

"Is it in good nick?" Maurice asked him.

"Not bad at all," answered Chris. "I reckon it's worth it. Tell you what - if you want it, I'll fetch it over for you tomorrow afternoon on my lorry after I've finished the milk." '

What more could we ask? In due course the hen-house arrived on the back of Chris's lorry, and with Graham, his eldest son, the four of us lifted it carefully onto the grass. There was also a wire run on a wooden frame which would be useful, for although we wanted the hens to range free, if they were not confined for the first few days they would not know where to come home to roost. In addition, there was a small drinker and several feed troughs. All we needed were the pullets.

I telephoned "Penny's Pullets" to check that they had some point-of-lay available and we arranged to collect them from Canon's Ashby, which was about fifteen miles away, early on Saturday afternoon - the time when we were least busy in the shop.

Canon's Ashby turned out not to be a village at all but a group of buildings, all of which were part of a sixteenth-century manor house and a mediaeval Priory Church. The priory itself was clothed in scaffolding and according to Mr Penny was being renovated by the National Trust. His poultry farm ran alongside a high, brick wall which must have enclosed the monks' kitchen garden, a lot of which now seemed to be Mr Penny's vegetable plot. How we envied him the shelter of the mellow wall and the dark, weed-free soil, no doubt enriched with poultry manure over the years.

He seemed a diffident sort of man with a shy smile on his ruddy face and a gentle voice which was softened further by a Northamptonshire burr.

"Six point-of lay, you said on the 'phone? I've got some beauties: Warrens they are, and laying already. " His eyes lit up as he spoke of his hens. He was clearly in a business that he loved.

We had walked along a brick path as he talked, towards a large, wooden shed. He opened the door. It was a light, airy building with windows set high up near the roof and out of jumping range of foxes. Feed hoppers hung from the rafters and swung clear of the deep, straw litter on the floor, and so did the drinkers. There must have been two hundred pullets in there, contentedly scratching about in the straw. The air was filled with their cooing and clucking.

"I'll pick you out some nice big, brown ones," he said, "if you'll just hold these sacks open, and tie the tops when they're in - leave 'em open a bit for air. Two to a sack."

He opened the door of a sort of shed-within-a-shed in the corner, where the feed bins were stored and found some empty paper sacks and pieces of baling twine which he gave to us. Effortlessly, he caught a couple of birds - they all looked brown to me - and thrust them head downwards into the first sack.

"Will they be alright upside down?" I asked. He smiled.

"They'll right themselves, don't you fret."

I peeped through the opening at the top of the sack. I could not see anything except feathers, but there was a great deal of squawking and fluttering going on, so I supposed that that was what they were doing. I tied the top with string, leaving a gap about the size of a saucer. When all three sacks had their quota of chickens, we carried them to the car and put them on the back seat.

"What do I owe you, Mr Penny?" asked Maurice.

"You'll be wanting a cockerel," he answered in reply, setting off in the direction of another large shed.

"We weren't, actually," I gasped, running to catch up with him. "You see, we want to sell eggs, and people don't like the blood spots."

By that time, he had reached the building and opened the door. I could see past him into the shed. There were another hundred or so birds, but only half of them were hens, the rest were cockerels, some of which boasted the most beautiful colours that I have ever seen on a domestic fowl. I glanced at Maurice, who had come to a halt, puffing slightly, beside me.

"Oh well," he shrugged, "might as well, I suppose. They are rather handsome, aren't they? I like that lemon one, Mr Penny."

"I like that glossy dark brown one with the peacock-blue tail," I said. "He's a proper nursery rhyme cock-a-doodle - can we have him?"

Mr Penny seemed suddenly to have gone deaf. He grabbed a big fellow, unusually marked, but rather drab I thought, with different shades of grey and a spotted black tail. Maurice and I made ineffectual gestures in the direction of the other, prettier birds as Mr Penny shoved the cock into a sack, and briskly tied the top.

After we had settled the bill, and driven off with our heaving, muttering load of sacks, we looked at each other and Maurice burst out laughing.

"How did he do it? We didn't want a damn cockerel - quite the reverse!"

"I know, and having pushed us into having one, he didn't even let us choose one we liked. He foisted that . . . brute on us! I wish I knew how he did it - I've always prided myself on my ability to resist pressure selling!"

"He's such a mild sort of chap," said Maurice thoughtfully. "That's how he did it. It would have been churlish to argue. Ah well, I'm sure the hens will be happy even if the customers aren't. We can expand the flock if we want to, as well."

"I wonder. Warrens are hybrids, you know. We may never get one to go broody."

"We'll just have to wait and see," said Maurice unperturbed as usual.

As soon as we arrived home, we freed the hens and cock from the confinement of the paper sacks (considerably relieved that they emerged unscathed) into their new quarters, and left them to get used to the feel of sunshine and a light breeze to ruffle their feathers as they peeked at the grass. After half an hour, I went to have a look at them. To my surprise, there was not a bird in sight in the wire run. They were all huddled inside the hen-house, one or two on perches and the others in the straw beneath, looking very dejected. The fine cockerel was crouched in the farthest, darkest corner, his handsome tail drooping onto the floor. Far from being pleased with their new freedom, they obviously wished that they were back at Penny's Pullers, tucked up safely in a nice barn.

"Come on girls," I said cheerfully, "you'd rather be here than a battery, I'm sure! Out you go, and look for some nice beetles and things!"

I pushed them, one at a time, out of the pop-hole into the run and shut the door behind them. The cockerel had glared at me with what I imagined was belligerence, but was probably his natural expression. However, I prudently put on a pair of leather gardening gloves before I ejected him to join his harem.

At dusk, I re-opened the door. They were going through the motions of pecking up the corn that I had scattered by then but they were pretty quick to scuttle back inside as soon as they could. It was several days before they would venture out without a prod and at least a week before they looked cheerful about it. I had to teach them how to roost at night, for they had not been used to perches, by picking them up off the straw in the dark, and setting them gently on the wooden bars across the henhouse.

At the end of a week, we removed the wire run, and let them do their worst with the vegetable garden. They scratched up the few remaining seedlings but the advantage of having the invasion of pests halted was worth it in the long run. The slugs have never been as prolific since.

The cockerel became very arrogant. He strutted round his flock, waving his tail feathers and holding his head, on which a fine red comb and Wattles were fast developing, high. We named him Aragorn. He seemed to be a good husband although the pullets clucked in annoyance at his advances. He twittered at them to tell them the whereabouts of the choicest morsels, which he never took for himself, even when I threw a fat worm at his feet. We became accustomed to being surrounded by a flotilla of greedy beaks whenever we did any digging. It was some months before Aragorn learnt to crow properly; to begin with, he sounded like a cross between a boy whose voice is breaking and a late season cuckoo. When he did manage it (loudly and at dawn), the jubilant cry must have rung out across the canal, for a hitherto friendly neighbour became most unpleasant and never spoke to us again! Unfortunately, as Aragorn matured he grew fiercer and after I had received a few vicious jabs with his beak at the back of my legs, I took to carrying a stick when I fed the chickens. I always felt uneasy if he was behind me, even so.

 Grass-cutting was next in our line of action and not just around the vegetable plot. Altogether, it was a mammoth task. Not only was it long and growing on uneven ground but as it had not been cut for years, the old, dead growth was tangled with branches and briars - and rubbish, of course.

"The cockerel became very arrogant ..."

Maurice bought an excellent implement for the job called a brushwood cutter. It had two cutting alternatives. On its long handle, it could either have a revolving blade for cutting woody undergrowth or a length of nylon string which whipped around faster than the eye could follow it, slicing through the grass. It was slow work and tedious. He tried to do an hour or so of grass-cutting on every fine evening and Bruce helped when he came home. Inch by inch it seemed, the grass was cut. Fresh grass grew almost as fast as the old was removed but at least it was the new season's grass - bright and green. Haymaking seemed to be a good idea but there were so many brambles and trails of ivy matted in the old grass that it was useless. We had no alternative but to burn it in huge bonfires.

An awareness of wind direction was quite important before we lit our fires, with so many boats moored close to the garden and the A5 not far away. Also, with a pub next door it seemed politic as well as safer to know which way the smoke would blow. I had long hankered after a weather-cock in any case - at last I had a good excuse! I found quite a cheap one in the Cash and Carry wholesaler's, which Maurice erected on a tall post that he set up on a ridge. We automatically glance at the weather-cock now, before we put a match to a bonfire. It is quite a realistic rooster, not unlike Aragorn in appearance but very much less aggressive!

-4-
Café and Camping

As midsummer's day approached, the number of boats on the canal multiplied. The amount of holiday traffic on the A5 increased too. I had painted two large sandwich-board signs, one saying in big letters "Shop on Left", and the other saying, "Shop on Right". Maurice carried the former a hundred yards along the road towards Daventry and placed it well back on the grass verge so that it faced the oncoming traffic. The other one was positioned similarly to attract customers approaching from the opposite direction.

As we had hoped, the boards had an immediate and favourable effect on trade. Traffic from the south (the London direction) had negotiated a series of bends where Watling Street looped round the Roman settlement of Bannaventa and arrived at the top of the hill where the Daventry to Long Buckby road crosses the A5. At that point drivers could see in front of them a straight, fast road, and that is how they covered it - fast, very fast indeed. I knew that the wording would have to be brief and large in order to be read at such a speed, for before we had the signs there, most drivers had flashed past unaware of the canal and our shop which was half hidden by the New Inn.

Once the signs were in place, we discovered that we were as an oasis in the desert to many of these drivers. They told us that ours was the first shop that they had seen for many miles, and there was the added bonus of easy parking and a pleasant spot in which to stretch their legs and perhaps those of their children and dogs, too. They often lingered, to breathe in the fresh country air and watch the boats on the water. After several requests for tea, we discussed the possibility of opening a tea-room.

"You can't possibly cope with the shop and a tea-room at the same time," said Maurice, "it will have to wait until I've stopped working in Birmingham."

"But it's only been at the weekends that people have asked us for tea," I said, full of enthusiasm for the idea.

"Well, I suppose we could give it a try on Saturdays and Sundays to begin with - it'll give us an indication whether or not there's enough demand to make it worth while."

"Where shall we have the tea-room, then?".

"Hm. Difficult."

The ground floor of the cottage consisted of a tiny, narrow hall with a room on the right as one entered the front door and a room on the left which also had a door to the adjoining shop. It had once been a "two up, two down" but an extension had been built on the back in which the kitchen and the cloakroom were situated. These were approached through a doorway at the far end of the hall and one which had originally been the external back door.

We were loathe to sacrifice one of our precious ground floor rooms entirely. Maybe, with a little ingenuity, we could adapt the one next to the shop into a tea-room at weekends, and then back into our dining room for the rest of the week? Patrons could enter via the shop and have the facilities of the tea-room and cloak-room without stepping along the hall to the foot of the stairs and the parlour door which was alongside. This arrangement worked very well when we came to put it into practice. I painted some pretty little signs reading "Toilet" and "Private" and such-like, and we hung them on unobtrusive small hooks so that they could be removed the moment that the tea-room was closed.

We did not expect a tremendous influx of tea customers all at once, so we decided not to buy any special furniture until we saw how things went. In the centre of the room, our own round dining table would seat six people and we added a card table in the window for a cosy twosome or even four, if necessary. I unpacked some linen tablecloths which years before had been hand embroidered with cottage garden flowers by an aunt of mine. I had never used them; swinging city socialising did not include afternoon tea.

I think that it must have been those cloths that told me which sort of tea-room that I wanted. I could see it in my mind's eye: fresh flowers in vases on the embroidered tablecloths; homemade preserves in little pots; hot, home-made scones; mouth-watering cakes - coffee, chocolate, cherry and ginger (and not silly little cup-cakes either but good thick slabs cut from a gateau) filled with cream or butter icing.

I remembered the time when Maurice and I were courting (such an old-fashioned word that seems now, but that is what we were in the 'fifties), he took me to tea at a place called "The Grey Cottage" in Ilmington, in the Cotswolds. There were polished oak tables and wheel-back chairs, with a copper warming-pan hanging on the wall of the room that was obviously the owner's dining room as well as the tea-room. We had strawberry jam on hot buttered scones, followed by wedges of delicious coffee and walnut cake served to us be a softly spoken lady with silver hair. The "Grey Cottage" to me, has always been the epitome of the perfect tea-room, and time and again we have searched in vain for its equivalent. I had my model - all I had to do was copy it as faithfully as possible and wait for the customers to come rolling in!

A few days before the end of the month, Maurice was given a farewell party by the members of his staff in Birmingham and I closed the shop early in order to catch the train from Long Buckby. There were many sad faces at the end of the evening, not least of all that of his secretary Lynn who gave us a handsome brass fender which exactly fitted the parlour hearth. The rest of the staff had clubbed together and presented him with a cheque to buy a large, soft-fruit cage. How well they understood our new life-style! Nearly all of them kept their promise to visit us at Buckby Wharf, too.

It seemed odd, at first, having him home every day. But we soon got into the swing of things, and developed a pattern of work, indoors and out, and shared all the chores. I had long questioned the accepted roles of the sexes, according to which we had both been brought up most strictly. I, for instance, had wanted to study medicine but was given a firm negative by my father (with whom I dared not argue) on the grounds that it was not worth it as I would only get married. So I became a nurse instead, but my heart was never in it to the same extent. I think that was why I grabbed at the "Open University" when it became available for it gave me that missed opportunity for a higher education and I revelled in it.

Maurice, however, proved himself a far better cook than I had ever been - painstakingly achieving the most imaginative dishes. He admitted that I was more meticulous (and legible) when it came to book-keeping and accounts and so they became my province entirely. We shared the odd jobs about the house and garden although I studiously left to him anything involving power tools. I am not mechanically minded really, except with simple things, and when machines make a lot of noise, I get nervous. I dislike electric drills for that reason though I am not bad with a bradawl or a screwdriver.

Even the painting was divided between us. Maurice primed the articles to be decorated and covered them with a base coat of glossy black, dark green or blue. When that was quite dry, I went to work on the roses and castles, building them up in bright enamel colours.

We applied a similar division of labour to the land. Maurice did the heavy digging, the tree felling, the chopping. He used the rotovator, the brushwood cutter, and later, the chain-saw. I did the sowing, the thinning, the planting and pruning, the hoeing and weeding.

It worked remarkably well. My nephew's wife said to me one day, when they dropped in to see us.

"Don't you quarrel? Under each other's feet all day?"

"No," I replied, puzzled. Should we have done? But we never were under each other's feet. We were both too busy doing whatever job that we had allocated to ourselves, usually one of us indoors and one outside; the inside person always having the dual task of minding the shop. We practically had to make an appointment with each other for a discussion!

"I'll make a start digging the bed for the fruit cage this morning," Maurice might say, "if you'll come and tell me where you think it ought to go."

"Give me half-an-hour," I would reply, "to finish painting the yellow lines round this Buckby can - then I'll be free."

We sited the fruit cage alongside the vegetable garden and at right angles to it, leaving a path wide enough for a wheel-barrow between the two. With the shorter side of the bed facing south, maximum sunlight would fall along the rows of bushes to ripen the fruit. I ordered the "soft fruit collection" from Highfield Nursery, because it worked out cheaper than buying individual plants. The raspberries were divided between early and late fruiting varieties, so I did ask for an extra half dozen of the mid-season Golden Everest to make up the row.

The extent of available land must have gone to my head a little, for I actually worked out the spacing of the fruit bushes on a piece of graph paper. My usual method (if one can call it that) is to squash plants into vacant corners and move them when they get too big. It is surprising how much room a young blackcurrant bush, for instance, will need when it matures. And the agony of scratched legs will tell you when gooseberries have been set too close together! I speak from experience.

Maurice groaned when he looked at my plan and saw the size of the area which had to be dug. We had deliberately chosen one of the worst spots in the whole garden, for we were anxious to get rid of an eyesore. Even after the vast pile of old timber and iron had been shifted, it was a daunting task. There were two of the coffin shaped humps, both of which sprouted docks and nettles, to be dug out. A barren ridge which ran the length of the east side of the plot would have to be levelled. All the rest was bumpy and riddled with buttercup and dandelion. We had had a progression of bonfires all over that piece of ground in an effort to sterilise it, but the perennial weeds rose with renewed vigour like a phoenix from the ashes.

"The fruit bushes won't arrive until the autumn, thank goodness," I told Maurice, "so we've heaps of time to get it done. Little and often, I would say, and we'll all do a stint in turns then it won't seem so bad."

"Well, I might as well make a start now, as I said before."

July was a splendid month. The sun shone on most days, and although the weather was hot, it was not sultry, for there was always a fresh breeze off the canal. I longed to stretch out on a sun bed in the garden, but there was no time to spare for that. Instead, I spent my mornings on the terrace, desperately trying to keep abreast of the painting. I should have been gratified that my work was so much in demand. But it seemed to me, that as fast as I painted things - Maurice sold them. Sometimes the enamel was scarcely dry. Once, it certainly was not. I can visualise him now - the schoolmaster who gingerly carried a set of freshly-painted miniatures back to the school trip-boat as a present for his wife. I had arranged the ornaments on a cardboard-box lid for him, and he teetered across the lock beam holding them aloft like a wine waiter with a tray of drinks. He was puce-faced from holding his breath when he reached the other side!

My afternoons were spent indoors, for then the tea-room came into its own. I added the word "Teas" to the shop signs that were on the road-side and we waited, the larder crammed with home-baked goodies, for the scores of folk who had been yearning for "Ye Olde Tea Shoppe" and never found one. People the same as us. Stephanie telephoned, excited, to tell us about a review that she had read, of a new book about running a tea-room. It was exactly like our sort of tea-room, she insisted, so I rang Bruce in Oxford and instructed him to visit Blackwell's, and bring the book home with him at the week-end. We have always believed devoutly in the printed word, which accounts for the ridiculously large reference library that we have amassed over the years. One glance at the ominous lack of book-shelves in our new home sparked off the notion of selling second-hand books. We had a catholic collection of non-fiction for sale, ranging from Maurice's fusty tomes on Roman Law to my glossy Open University set books, with books like "Hamsters as Pets" and "Modern Surgery for Nurses (1954)" in between. They sold, I am ashamed to say, faster than my own hot cakes!

I hope that I have not given the impression that the tea-room was a failure. It was not. But neither was it an unqualified success. One thing it was certainly not - dull. Broadly speaking, the tea customers fell into two main types: there were those who were pleased to find "our" sort of tea-room and there were those who were not. We learnt quite early on that our predecessor had also had the idea of selling teas - to the latter.

A group of motor cyclists, male and female (though I was not sure which was which as they did not lift their visors and they all wore black leather jackets and blue jeans), initiated us. Having banged in vain on the front door of the cottage, they marched into the shop in a phalanx. One of them said, gesturing with his thumb.

"Where's the caff, then?"

"Through here, please," I smiled, lifting the hatch and ushering them through the shop to the tea-room cum dining room.

"Cripes!" He looked at the bowl of sweet peas on the table and picked up the menu.

"You've gotta be joking! C'mon chaps," the thumb worked again and they all walked out - pausing briefly to buy six Mars bars and six cans of Coke. These they consumed in seconds as they sat on the lock beam, before they zoomed off in a haze of blue exhaust fumes.

Of the customers who fell into the other category, several of them were memorable for different reasons. There was a couple from Walton-on-Thames who arrived during one of our quiet periods and sat long over their tea, entertaining us with stories of their bee-keeping activities. They told us about the dances which are performed by the workers in a bee colony when they return to the hive from a food source, in order to share this valuable information with other worker bees. They described how their bees had swarmed and settled on the hanging basket in the porch of a bee-hating neighbour and how they had recaptured the swarm. We picked their brains about bee-keeping, and by the time that they left to continue their journey north, Maurice had decided that bee-keeping was a distinct possibility. I had reservations. I am a coward about bee-stings.

Another couple that I recall, drove up in separate cars. They sat at the window table but ignored the view, touching fingers and talking softly. He looked anxious and she had great, mournful dark eyes which clung to his face. She hardly touched the piece of chocolate cake that he bought for her. I guessed that the wedding ring that she wore, was not his and felt sad for her. Maurice accused my imagination of working overtime.

There was one family which I would prefer to forget. The young woman wheeled a pushchair containing a wriggling, grizzling toddler through the shop and across the tea-room floor, leaving dark tramlines on the carpet. Her husband had insisted on bringing in their spaniel (fresh from swimming in the canal) which wiped its muddy feathered paws, its flapping ears and furiously wagging tail on everything else! Our own two dogs growled in annoyance on the other side of the kitchen door, fighting each other to get at the intruder each time we went through it. Meanwhile, the baby dropped bread and butter (jam side down) on the carpet and its mother knocked over the mug of milk onto the tablecloth as she tried to beat the dog in a race for the baby's tea.

When they had gone, leaving a trail of debris behind them, I rushed about clearing up the mess and resetting the table before anyone else arrived.

"Thank heaven for carpet tiles," I called to Maurice from the stock-room, as I rinsed off the mud and jam under the cold tap, "but I think we could do with some paper cloths to put on top of the linen ones."

"Nothing would stand up to that sort of onslaught," he replied, "but I think that we say 'no dogs' in future. It isn't as if we don't provide somewhere for their owners to leave them."

There was a much photographed post outside the shop door. It had a hefty iron ring at the top underneath a notice which said "Dog Mooring". Scores of people would whip out their cameras and persuade their pets (or spouses) to pose beneath the sign. I was driven nearly potty on one occasion though, when two dogs were tied to the ring by a person unknown and left there for three hours. They barked without a break. By the time blissful silence reigned once more, I had spent my fury with the paintbrush. The sign now says, "Dog Mooring - While Owners in Shop".

The weekend arrived and so did Bruce - with the book I had asked him to buy for me. I read it avidly. Surely it would solve all our problems? Alas no. I was disappointed. It was true that the author had run several tearooms successfully in various country towns so she knew her subject. But the circumstances were fundamentally different. Firstly, her establishments were larger than ours, they were really restaurants. Secondly (a vital difference), her trade was constant both during the week and throughout the year. She did not have to cope with the extremes that we faced; total inactivity in the tearoom one day and pandemonium the next! I had wanted to be told how to keep a ready supply of fresh food available in case it was needed without wasting an excessive amount if it was not. She did not say.

Maurice thought of an answer.

"What we need is a microwave oven." It was a statement that was not altogether unexpected, but I sighed. I had spent most of my married life trying to curb his appetite for kitchen gadgets. My cupboards were overcrowded with machines that chopped, sliced, liquidised, extracted, crushed, ground, deep-fried, toasted, kneaded . . . Some of the equipment was better at its job than others, and most of the things that had turned out to be utterly useless (a pancake-maker springs to mind), I had managed to spirit away to jumble sales. Until that moment, I had successfully resisted a microwave and he could hardly slide one of those into a kitchen drawer, unobserved.

"What good will that do? Except break the bank!"

"It will allow you to do a lot of baking all at once, freeze the stuff, then thaw it as it is needed. You won't need to waste so much as one scone that way."

I had to admit that it sounded a good idea, so I capitulated and he bought one. It has been very useful in other ways but it did not solve that particular problem. It is surprising how long it takes to thaw and reheat a few scones, even in a microwave, while the customers sit drumming impatiently with their fingers. One moment of inattention with back turned while the teapot is filled, means one million electromagnetic waves too many and a perfectly delicious scone is turned into old boot leather!

Our other major problem, which was also not dealt with by the author of the book, was how to discourage people who did not want a full tea with scones and cakes. With seating for ten persons only, and our style of accommodation, customers had to make it worth our while. We could not afford those who just wanted a brief cup of tea and a long sit down, or the ones who really wanted to use the lavatory and were prepared to buy a cup of tea and no more, to pay for the privilege. The latter were the worst, for they tended to be in large family groups - while Mum and Dad had a "cuppa", the children would troupe into the cloakroom, one after another until it was reduced to a shambles. After one lad managed to wrench the porcelain toilet-roll holder off the wall and sneaked off leaving it in shards on the floor, I reckoned that the time had come for action. I printed a neat card headed "Set Teas Only" - laying out the menu and prices, and stuck it in the shop window. Matters did not improve noticeably. I tried umpteen different ways of wording the card but people continued to misread the intended information and the aggravation went on . . . and on.

There were several economical cake recipes in the book, however, so I added it to "The Backyard Poultry Book", "Self-Sufficiency", and "The Real World of the Small Business Owner" in the bookcase, and thought ruefully - here we go again with our reference books!

One evening quite late, there came a knock on the door. Two young men stood there. They wore shorts and training shoes, and their bicycles, heavy with loaded panniers, leant against the fence. They were cycling, they said, from Southampton to Llangollen and camping every night. They had ridden many miles that evening, searching for a camp site before they stopped to quench their thirst at the New Inn. Pauline, listening to their plight as she drew two pints of Pedigree for them, had suggested that if they asked us nicely, we might oblige with a patch of our orchard.

"Sure, come round the back and I'll show you a decent spot," said Maurice cheerfully, "we're on a bit of a slope, but if you pitch your tent pointing downhill you won't roll into each other."

The next morning, the two campers came into the shop and bought themselves eggs, bacon, bread and milk for breakfast. They seemed very cheerful and offered to pay for what they thought was a "jolly good site". Later, after they had packed up and loaded their bicycles, they came in again and bought chocolate and fruit juice to take with them on the journey.

"Well! Well!" exclaimed Maurice, after the young men had ridden away, "Are you thinking what I am thinking?"

"Absolutely! Why didn't we think of it before? Good old Pauline! It's so easy. We've got an outside tap for drinking water. There's a loo outside, too. Is that in working order, by the way?"

"Yes. It just needs a good clean-out." I grimaced.

"I can imagine. Bruce has a list of camp sites from last year - it'll give us an idea of what's required, and what to charge."

I found an old free-standing ice-cream sign behind the "Object" (anything that came into the category of "might be useful" found its way there) and without more ado began to paint on it the silhouette of a tent.

As Maurice lugged the sign (heavy, because of its concrete base) up the hill, it crossed my mind that perhaps planning permission should be sought for a camp site.

When we applied for a licence to sell milk and ice-cream, we had also asked for permission to serve hot drinks and snacks (which I reckoned included teas as well). We were wrapped around with rules, it seemed to me. Some of them were archaic. The ice-cream licence, in fact, permitted us to make it and not just to sell it. It dated back to the time when all sorts of people were stirring up frozen messes in their back kitchens and selling ice-cream that was stiff with dreadful microbes. The fact that I only wanted to sell ice-cream which was manufactured under aseptic conditions by a gigantic company with world-wide outlets, was neither here nor there. I still had to have a licence to make it, in order to sell it!

Oh, well! I inwardly shrugged off the question of planning permission for a camp site. We might as well wait and see. It might not be necessary. I am afraid that "wait and see" was fast becoming a maxim of ours. With all our little enterprises, so many ingredients were put into the pot to melt or to boil. It seemed sensible to wait and see which ones cooked and which ones went sour, before we took any drastic action. In my view, applying for planning permission (which might be refused) could definitely be construed as drastic action.

With campers in mind, it became a matter of some urgency that we should finish clearing the orchard of lumber and litter. And if we did not reduce the length of the grass by at least eighteen inches, a new game might be invented, called "Hunt the Tent Peg". A garden contractor quoted us a couple of hundred pounds to clear the grass and undergrowth.

"Ridiculous," said Maurice, when he saw the estimate, "we'll do it ourselves - all I need to do, is hire a motorised scythe."

It was certainly cheaper and it had to be quicker as we only had the motorised scythe for twenty-four hours, but it was back-breaking. We gained a few hours as the van turned up late to collect the scythe, but even so, we worked against the clock and long after it was too dark to see properly.

Maurice scythed, gripping the handles of the machine with all his might as it leapt like a bucking bronco across the tussocks. I raked the cut grass and brambles into heaps, and then he went over it again with the scythe. Again I collected great piles of cut grass, using the wide, wooden rake that finally split in protest before the task was completed. We just about made it, more or less. I would not have described the orchard as being a smooth, green sward exactly, but by the time that we had finished, a camper with good eyesight could have located most of his tent pegs. Both of us were so stiff afterwards that every joint and muscle screeched for a week!

The day after we cut the orchard grass, the weather broke. We stood together at the window, smugly watching the angry blue-black clouds rolling over the hill, split every so often by sizzling streaks of lightning. Great plopping drops of rain hit the terrace and bounced up, breaking, to land again in a shower of droplets.

"We just made it," said Maurice, and sneezed. I looked with sympathy at his streaming eyes. He was suffering terribly from hay-fever.

"Well, at least the rain will settle the dust and pollen," I replied, "while we wait for the campers to discover this lovely new site."

The camp-site project turned out to be much less hassle than the tea-room. We were not overwhelmed with tents and caravans, but there was a steady trickle of campers seeking an overnight stop; enough to make us feel that the effort had been worthwhile. There were never more than two or three tents at a time, or more than one caravan or Dormobile. This suited us fine, for we did not want our camp site to be too obtrusive. Just one complaint from an irritated neighbour might bring the planning question to a head prematurely.

Like the tea-room, the camp-site was never a boring enterprise. The caravanners who stopped with us were much of a muchness - generally middle-aged couples who were on their way to or from the south coast. The "real" campers (the ones who chose to sleep under canvas) though, were diverse characters who provided us with a deal of entertainment.

There was an elderly vicar, for instance. He and another, younger man (brought along for his pedal power), were cycling from Sheffield to Rome on a tandem! The trip was in aid of the church fund and sponsored by a local firm. Very sensibly, their benefactor had already presented them with return rail fares for themselves and the tandem. The vicar asked Maurice if he would mind waking them when he let out the chickens first thing in the morning. He had not then sampled Aragorn's raucous cry which was scarcely muffled by the closed hen-house, or he would not have worried about oversleeping.

It may have been the sound of a cock crowing that informed the neighbourhood foxes that we kept chickens. On several different nights we had heard the bark of a fox. It is an eerie screech that makes the blood run cold and penetrates the deepest slumber. Maurice threatened to get a twelve bore shotgun if they attacked our little flock, or maybe a long-bow. I think that he fancied himself as a Robin Hood, for the latter idea really appealed to him.

One weekend, a group of young men pitched their tents in the orchard. On the Saturday night, I heard again the unearthly sound of a vixen calling to her mate. I got out of bed and went to the window. We always left a light on outside when we had campers, so that they could see their way around. On the far side of the drive and just outside the pool of light, I could see the dim shape of a fox. It stood quite still - its eyes glinting in the darkness.

"Maurice! Wake up! Quick! I can see it - the fox. I can see its eyes. Look!"

"Good God!" he had stumbled to the window and was standing beside me. "I wish I had that long-bow - I could get it easily from here - an arrow straight between the eyes!"

"You're looking in the wrong place," I said, for he was staring in the direction of the stump of a sawn-off telegraph pole that stood nearer the house.

Suddenly, there was a movement. From behind the pole, where he had been half hidden in the shadows, emerged one of our campers. He was rubbing his forehead, his eyes gleaming in the light but unfocussed for all that. He was very drunk.

"Jush looking fra wadder dap," he slurred, "and dis damn thing goddin de way," he lurched in the direction of the pole and clung to it. The fox melted into the hedge.

Maurice closed the curtains and looked at me.

"Good job I didn't have a long-bow," he said drily, "or I would have shot him."

After the young man we nicknamed "Fox's Eyes", departed with his friends, we welcomed (with some relief) two smart gentlemen in city suits. They asked us whether we had any objection if they pitched their tent on the short grass directly in line with the kitchen window. We were not too keen but they were so polite about it that we agreed. We wondered why they did not want the greater privacy of the orchard but when we watched them mincing across the soaking grass in their natty foot-gear the next morning, we understood. They told us that they had come from South Wales to attend a course in Daventry. Unlike most of the other students whose employers paid their expenses, they were self-employed and trying to cut their costs. Oh dear! How miserable they were. They had never camped before but had borrowed the tent from a friend. The course lasted for a week - and it never stopped raining. They had a frightful

"Two smart gentlemen in city suits ..."

job to keep themselves smart and they gave up trying to cook breakfast after the first morning. A watery sun peeped through as they were packing up on their last day and I tried to convince them that camping could be fun. They both smiled at me pityingly, and said

"Never again!"

The weather cheered up again towards the end of August, and with the onset of the bank-holiday weekend there were several tents dotted about under the apple trees. They looked colourful and lent a certain gaiety to the holiday atmosphere. There was a cluster of small, two-man tents pitched in a semi-circle at the top of the orchard, in a secluded corner. The occupants had a long way to go to wash and being young they ran laughing and singing.

Aragorn did not like it. In fact, Aragorn strongly disapproved of that group altogether. Moreover, he took grave exception to the long, swishing skirts of the girls and their squeals when they realised that he was after them aggravated him even more. I could understand their fear because he looked quite the opposite of friendly. Positively evil!

He would begin by standing very tall and stretching his neck to lift his head up high, glancing about himself with malevolent eyes and wiggling the bright red comb on the top of his head. Then - suddenly, he would lower his head until it was a few inches off the ground and stretch his neck forwards, beady eyes fixed on the plump calves which were his target. His scaly legs marked time quickly while his toes, armed with long talons, opened and shut like the spokes of an umbrella. He was off! Like an aircraft starting down the runway; beak lowered to attack, wings lifted with flight feathers drooping, tail flowing behind him - the miniature Concorde was after his prey! Who could blame the poor young lady for running as if the devil himself was after her?

Anxious to prevent trouble, we moved the hen-house out of the orchard and warned new arrivals to the camp-site to keep away from the rooster.

All this time, the tea-room had been flourishing. Stephanie had come home for several weekends and with her usual energetic zeal had enlarged the menu. The most popular addition was poached eggs on toast. We poached the eggs in the microwave. They took seconds to cook (when things went according to plan). Occasionally, the eggs exploded into tiny fragments for no apparent reason. We tried all the tips which the experts recommended, but there always seemed to be one rogue egg in a batch that splattered itself all over the inside of the oven. Very unnerving!

At about this time, my mother came to stay for a couple of weeks. She was old and very frail but she had hung on to her impish sense of humour. She would seat herself at the table in the tea-room window, drinking her tea genteelly and smiling out at passers-by with a graciousness not unlike the Queen Mother. As soon as there was an influx of tea customers, she would get to her feet and go outside to finish her tea on the terrace!

"Well done, Rene!" whispered Maurice, as he helped her down the steps and arranged her in a deck-chair, "you've done the trick again."

Occasionally, she pottered round the shop, re-arranging the window to her satisfaction, and chuntering a little to herself at the bad manners of some of our customers. I think that she never completely reconciled herself to having a daughter "in trade".

During the fine spell, our neighbour who farmed nearly all the land on our side of the A5 for many miles, decided to burn the stubble off the field which lay behind us. He called in the shop to warn us that he was going to fire the field.

"May we have some straw first?" asked Maurice.

"Help yourself," he smiled, "take the lot, if you like!"

We filled all the sacks we possessed with first-rate barley straw - it was only for the chickens and lasted us nearly twelve months.

Then he set the field alight. It was a fantastic sight: orange and yellow flames fifteen feet high sped across the field and up the hill before the breeze. The sound was deafening; crackling and popping and hissing along the line of our hedge, but separated from it by the ploughed strip. It was all over in a few minutes. The field, which moments before, had been the colour of sunshine, was black and funereal with a grey pall of smoke drifting across it.

There is a continual debate about the pros and cons of stubble burning. Those in favour - mainly the farming fraternity, argue on the grounds of soil sterilisation and economy. Those against - the ecologists, the housewives, the police and fire services, marshall a variety of reasons. The ecologists are concerned about pollution of the atmosphere, the waste of natural resources, the threat to small mammals and insect life. The police worry about smoke blinding motorists, and the fire service about fires which get out of control. The housewives (and I speak as one) are fed up with the clouds of ash fragments which invade their homes.

Perhaps I am cynical, but there is no doubt in my mind that in our society today, principles have to be paid for. When a method of dealing with stubble more cheaply than burning it is discovered, I am sure that farmers will adopt

"Orange and yellow flames fifteen feet high …"

it, willingly, and not before. Otherwise, those who shout loudest against the practice must put their hands in their own pockets. Do you think that they will?

A summer invasion for which sunshine was responsible, was by thrips - commonly called thunderflies. Tiny, slender insects, less than a tenth of an inch long, they swarmed in their thousands. They settled on anything and everything, inside and out. They stuck to one's skin and tickled your hair, crawling inside socks and beneath collars. Life became one big itch. Customers came into the shop shaking their heads and flapping their arms.

At dusk, the thunderflies disappeared - at least, those that were free to do so, disappeared. Dozens of the minute creatures were trapped inside the frames of pictures, between glass and painting. They crawled through microscopic cracks, never to emerge. They found their way into "sealed" cellophane wrappers of articles that were for sale - crepe bandages, cotton wool, toilet rolls. How could we sell such products?

"The cotton wool is absolutely sterile, Madam, except for twenty or thirty little black bugs crawling about inside!"

Spiders had a field day! Enormous webs were hastily spun across every window and quickly became black with the tiny flies. During the night, a vast web was hung across the shop doorway like a curtain, and the first customer walked straight into it - flies and all!

It was almost a relief when the summer drew to a close. The calm, cool evenings acted on us like a tonic. We were beginning to flag but the school holidays had not yet finished. The thought of a rejuvenating cruise on "Warwickshire Lad" was a tempting prospect. Perhaps later, we promised ourselves - when the season had finally ended.

-5-
Autumn Reflections

The huge pear tree which dominated the orchard began to show pale gold and lemon tints of autumn at the edges of its leaves. I had identified it in the spring as a pear tree by its characteristic shape and mass of creamy blossom. We had looked forward to a heavy crop as one of our favourite chutneys was made of pears, heavily spiced. But we were disappointed, for there was no fruit. It could have been a variety which was sterile and needed a mate for cross-pollination. More likely, the hard frost which we had suffered on the fourth of May had nipped its early blossom. I considered the question of pruning. Then I rejected it! No-one without forestry experience could have dealt with it safely. It was a splendid tree, though, and quite a landmark among the others as one looked down the hill from the Daventry road. Even if it never fruited, we would appreciate its beauty, especially in the spring.

Looking at the other trees which surrounded it on all sides, I was conscious of a task that we had, so far, neglected. We had not touched the poor trees and neither had anyone else done so for years - if ever. I made disapproving noises to myself as I collected a big basketful of grub-eaten windfalls and carried them back to the house.

Improving the quality of the apple crop was a tall order, so Maurice decided to set about it systematically, military fashion. He took a large tin of old emulsion paint and a brush and daubed a number on every single fruit tree. After an hour or so, he came back into the shop and said.

"Guess how many trees there are."

I thought for a minute, dividing the time that he had been gone by the time that I guessed it would take to paint a number on the rough bark.

"Thirty-six."

"You're way out - there are sixty-seven altogether!"

"Good heavens! Who ever needed that many?"

"They're not all apple, and some are in a very bad way. See what you think. I suggest that we start an orchard note-book - take it with you."

It took me the whole afternoon to write notes about every tree, and pretty dismal reading it made. On the bright side - I had discovered a damson, a Victoria plum and a greengage. There were many different sorts of apples, some for cooking and others for eating, and of these there were both early and late season varieties. They were probably all trusty friends, I thought, which was to be expected in an old established orchard.

I recognised the early yellow cooker, Grenadier, which dates back to 1860, and the yellow eating apple, James Grieve. There were Bramley Seedlings - enormous misshapen trees, and probably the best known eating apple of all - Cox's Orange Pippin. Worcester Pearmains were easy to identify and there were some tasty rough-skinned russets and many more.

With little or no fruit on some trees, it was difficult to be certain what they were. Even now, we are not sure. Maurice has a testing munch now and again as he picks the fruit and divides them into cookers and eaters. He has less of a sweet tooth than me and some of his "eaters" make my eyes water. We are always happy to give customers a testing munch too, before they buy, and if they can identify the apple for us - so much the better!

It was the condition of the trees that was so depressing. There were three that had nearly been choked to death by ivy and another which was growing almost underneath a fine oak tree in the corner. Every single tree required extensive pruning and thinning (some needed felling), and all of them were thickly coated with crusty green lichen. On many trunks and branches I could see gaping wounds that looked horribly like canker.

I bought yards and yards of grease bands which are supposed to trap the caterpillars of the Winter Moth and fastened these round the tree trunks with string. It was very messy and expensive so I gave up after I had done about twenty trees. Maurice said that he would give the whole lot a winter wash when the trees were dormant instead and hope to cure a range of ills in one go.

I managed to prune half a dozen of the smaller trees that autumn and removed from the others the low branches which swiped us in the face when they got the chance. Bruce chopped down the largest ivy-strangled tree, unfortunately bringing down half the Victoria plum with it.

I think that we must have paused then, to survey the scene. It looked much as it might have done in the wake of a typhoon! And we had barely started in our pruning and felling programme!

"What on earth are we going to do with all these branches?" I asked Maurice in dismay.

"How about a wood-burning stove," he suggested, "in the shop instead of that great night-storage heater that is so expensive to run?"

"Brilliant! There must be a chimney somewhere - you can see the stack outside."

We found the fireplace eventually, hidden behind a shop fitting, and the only blockage in the chimney seemed to be a sack of straw. Maurice shopped around and came up with a basic, no trimmings wood-burning stove for about fifty pounds. It looked a bit like a road-mender's brazier although it had an exotic Spanish name. Once it was installed and working, it threw out a sweltering heat in which we gratefully basked.

There was one drawback - our stove was fussy. It wanted absolutely dry, seasoned wood in pieces which were about ten inches long and three or four inches across. These, it golloped greedily. If it was neglected - even for a short while - it sulked and went out.

Reluctantly, we stacked the wood that we had cut from the orchard to season for the following winter and bought off-cuts from the timber mill to feed it temporarily. We resolved to limit our pruning and felling so that each year we would have a plentiful supply of wood and kindling but not so much that storing it became an embarrassment. The trees had gone so long without being pruned, I rationalised, that another year or two would hardly matter!

To our pleased surprise, one of the hybrid hens became broody. Each time I went to collect the eggs - there she was, sitting in a nest box on two or three. She clucked angrily when I disturbed her. It was rather late in the year to raise chicks, for the nights were long and chilly although the sun was warm at midday. But the chance of hatching some of our own eggs was too good to miss, so Maurice made her a snug broody box out of a tea-chest and fitted a sliding door to keep her safe and warm at night.

I put a layer of damp earth on the bottom of the box as eggs should not be allowed to dry out, and made her a comfortable nest of hay. To test out her broodiness, I put in the nest a beautiful alabaster egg that Maurice had brought back from Singapore. In she went, fluffed out her feathers and with a chirrup of satisfaction, settled down on the nest. She kept the egg warm and turned it over regularly, so after two days I removed it and entrusted her with five eggs which had just been laid by the other hens.

In three weeks, three of the eggs had hatched; the other two must have rolled into a corner without her noticing; they were just bad eggs by the time that I found them.

We placed the broody box in front of the kitchen window so that we could keep an eye on it. I did - constantly. The chicks were talented time-wasters (my time). Within hours of hatching they were out on the grass with their mother, watching and imitating her as she scratched at the earth and pecked at morsels of food. She took great pains to teach them by example - over-acting in her zeal as she pecked at the dry mash, scattering it in all directions. She did the same with the water. The chicks quickly grew as they learnt the skill of food gathering. There were two pullets and a cock. They were all yellow at first, as if they had hopped off an Easter Card, but after a few days I could see a budding tail with a hint of russet on one. He eventually became quite brown, but the pullets paled into a rich cream colour.

When they were several weeks old, I propped a long twisted branch up against the broody box for them to use as a perch and learn how to roost. They made a great game out of this, chasing each other up the branch to the box roof then fluttering off it to land with a thump on their poor mother's back and cling there. She never complained although as they got bigger I could see her sagging at the knees as they landed.

"As if they had hopped off an Easter card ..."

This seemed the right time for the youngsters to become independent, so I returned the broody to the main hen-house at dusk one evening. I hoped that she would get some peace. It was some time before she did, for the other hens resented her presence and peeked her, especially at feed times. We felt sorry for her. It seemed such a poor reward for her labours.

The exciting world of television entered our lives briefly in late September, and for once not indirectly through Stephanie. We were used to hearing her amusing anecdotes of famous personalities with whom she came into contact on "Newsnight". We had had to stay, too, various friends of hers whose names appeared in the credits on the small screen. This time - it was different!

It all began when a handsome (in my opinion) man cast about up and down the lock-side and towpath before walking in through the shop door and buying a bar of chocolate. This device frequently heralded a request for something quite different (usually a favour) so we waited expectantly.

"I wonder whether you can help me," he began. We said that we would do our best.

"Do you know who all these boats along here (he gestured) belong to?"

"Us, for one," said Maurice, "the others belong to different people. Did you have something particular in mind?"

We had been asked that sort of question before. It usually meant that the enquirer was hoping to buy a boat - possibly one of those that he had just seen, and more than likely a neglected-looking one that he hoped to get cheaply. He would then be subjected to Maurice's lecture on boat buying, for he was always ready to share what he considered to be his hard-won canal wisdom with everyone else. I think that we are overly anxious to prevent people to whom the canals are a novelty, from starting off on the wrong foot by buying unwisely and then regretting that they had ever come into contact with the wretched waterways in the first place! It never ceases to amaze us - the number of hasty decisions there are to spend several thousand pounds on what turns out to be a shell of rotten marine-ply with a dead-beat outboard engine (or similar fiasco). And I thought that we were impetuous over "Iona"!

But it was not to be the day for sermons.

"I work for BBC Television," came the reply, "and I want to film here - an educational, documentary type of thing. What are the chances of getting a boat to come through this lock at a certain time on a certain day?"

"Very good," I answered, "we'll do it for you ourselves if you give us some notice."

"No problem," said Maurice, adding shrewdly, "particularly if there's a fee."

"Oh yes." The man was nonchalant. "How much notice do you need?"

"A couple of days will be enough. We're not as busy as we were, but we ought to warn our regulars that we'll be shut for a few hours."

"Fine! I'll be in touch."

As it turned out, we were not given even a couple of hours notice. For several days after that, the weather was wet and windy. Gradually, the wind calmed and the rain became intermittent with patches of sunshine breaking through the clouds. It was during one of these bright periods that the telephone rang and a female voice announcing herself as the producer's assistant asked whether we could be ready to film in half an hour.

Heavens! No time to worry about hair or clothes. I slapped on some lipstick and looked in the glass. What a fright!

"It's 'Warwickshire Lad' he wants to film - not us," said Maurice, not even bothering to drag a comb through his own unruly mop.

So I quickly smartened the boat instead of myself; I rubbed Brasso on the tiller and polished it with a rag, and put the Buckby Can in its accustomed place, with the stale of the mop (striped like a barber's pole) stuck through its handle in the traditional way. I had wiped a wash-leather over the windows and was just chalking "Closed for Filming" on a large slate when Bryn, the producer, arrived with his assistant.

"How long will it take you to get to the next bridge?" he asked.

"Twenty minutes."

"Twenty minutes" he looked at the clouds which were scudding across the sky.

"Yes. Fifteen minutes to get through this lock and another five minutes to the bridge."

"Oh well. Be as quick as you can. I'm afraid the rain will come before we're through. That's why we couldn't give you more notice - sorry about that. We want to film the canal, the railway and the motorway at the same time."

"Hang on!" exclaimed Maurice, "are you sure you mean the next bridge and not the one after?"

"Yes, of course!" Bryn sounded impatient, "it's a modern, concrete road bridge with an iron railing."

"The next one isn't. It's old red brick, no railing and roses growing up it," I said.

"Let's look at the map," said Maurice, spreading out the Ordnance Survey.

Sure enough, the canal bridge from which the railway and the motorway were visible and the one which Bryn had earmarked for filming, was the new one which carried the Daventry to Long Buckby road. It was situated not one but two locks away from us and a good half mile. It would take forty minutes by boat.

Bryn groaned when we told him. Not being a boating man, he had parked his car at each of the road bridges in turn to examine the filming potential of each but he had not walked the towpath. He had not thought of looking beyond the first bend even, to discover what secrets lay in store on the canal.

Maurice tut-tutted as he wound up the paddles to fill the top lock and muttered to himself.

"Time spent in reconnaissance is seldom wasted."

As I steered the boat gently into the lock, I thought how great it was to be on board once more, and cruising. It was ironic to think that we had moved to Buckby Wharf to be near a canal and yet since living there we had not had the chance to go boating at all. Tansy, the younger of our two dogs, obviously felt the same, because she sneaked on board the moment that she heard the engine start and ran back and forth from bow to stem in great glee.

We reached the bridge five minutes before Bryn and his television crew.

We still had no idea what the film was about or what we would be required to do. There was also a man whom we immediately recognised as Fred Housego, the London cabbie who had won the "Mastermind" quiz a few years before. Fred and another, older man who said that he was an historian, got two bright yellow folding bicycles out of the boot of the car and wheeled them onto the towpath. We became more perplexed.

Fortunately, we had plenty of time to talk to the two of them between "takes" and found out what we were supposed to be doing. Bryn was making a series which was ultimately entitled "History on your Doorstep". It's aim was to encourage the television viewers to look around themselves at the districts where they lived and seek out local history. The programme in which we were involved was centred on transport and the marks which man had made on the landscape in consequence. Hence the bicycles, I supposed. He had noticed as I had done, the way in which several different transport routes were funnelled towards the passage between the hills which was known as the Watford Gap.

Bryn's idea was that we should bring the boat slowly out from beneath the bridge at exactly the same instant that an Intercity express streaked across the embankment behind us. He wanted the camera focussed on the bow of

"Warwickshire Lad" as it emerged from the bridge hole, then panning upwards to focus on the train, and after the train had gone, the lorries on the motorway would come into view. It was a marvellous idea!

There were certain difficulties when we came to put the idea into practice. The trains ran every fifteen minutes but as we were tucked beneath the bridge, engine throbbing, we could not hear them coming. We depended on a signal from Bryn to tell us when to start forward. His impatience at the length of time that it took for the boat to get under way was obvious, in spite of his efforts to control his agitation. He kept making roly-poly movements with his arms, which Stephanie had told us meant "faster - time's running out" in television language.

Bryn would signal; we would come out; he would shout, "No good - go back and do it again!" We did not bother to ask why, for we were fully occupied in bringing the boat to a halt. He was totally unable to come to terms with the fact that boats do not have brakes! Worried lest we should miss the next train, he would hop up and down in anguish while we gradually slowed to a stop and then went astern towards the bridge hole.

Not many narrow-boats steer well in reverse and "Warwickshire Lad" is worse than most. At about the sixth attempt, he insisted on taking the stern rope and hauled us back into position. Then he threw me the rope in a great jumbly heap which fell in the water and straight away wrapped itself round the propeller in a tight noose. Maurice was furious. Not only because, in fifteen years boating we had never committed the cardinal sin of catching our own rope round the prop, but also because he had to strip off his shirt and pullover and plunge his arm up to the shoulder in dirty, cold water to disentangle the two.

"This will take some time." Maurice called pompously to Bryn, to punish him. In fact, he freed the rope quite quickly and we began the manoeuvre all over again. Bryn was slightly more subdued after that and actually told us generously at the next "retake" that we had been perfect but the cameraman was at fault!

Eventually, Bryn pronounced himself satisfied and allowed us to proceed (with some relief) towards the lock. We had put Tansy up on the cabin roof out of the way during the episode of the bridge hole, and the cameraman (perhaps he was getting his own back) surreptitiously filmed several sequences of her trotting from one end of the roof to the other. She was quite the star of the finished film!

The lock was full and we could see another boat up above, approaching it. We explained to Bryn that not only canal etiquette but British Waterways Board by-laws required us to wait for the other boat to make use of the full lock, lower the water and come out, before we entered the empty lock. I am not sure that he fully understood the reasons but he decided to make the best of it and snapped his fingers at the camera-man to film the boat, "Buttonweed", as it emerged from the lock. The camera went on rolling as the two boats passed each other and the steerer of "Buttonweed" and myself exchanged greetings before we were lost to view in the gloom of the lock chamber. The great gates swung shut behind us.

I heaved a thankful sigh that that was one episode that could not be repeated. For in late September it might be some while before another boat came along to fill the part of "Buttonweed". An actor's working life must be more tedious than folk like me had ever supposed.

As we-entered the lock, the lock-keeper appeared as if by magic, in the most beautifully laundered set of overalls that I had ever seen him wear. He gave me a wink as the water level rose, so I think that a little bird must have told him that he might be on TV. He made an eye-catching figure, in bright Waterways blue with his startling white hair in contrast with his weather-beaten, brown face and I heard the camera whirring as it pointed first at him then at Maurice as he pushed the heavy balance beam to open the top gate and finally at "Warwickshire Lad" as we chugged slowly out into the pound and pulled into the bank to await further instructions.

We paused, holding the mooring ropes while Fred and the historian were filmed as they sat on the lock beam and talked history to each other. But our brief glory was over. The producer's assistant paid us off and thanked us for our co-operation (was that what it was?) and promised to let us know when the series went out on the air. When it did, we enjoyed it enormously. We were amazed at the professionalism of all the programmes, not least of all the one that we thought of as "ours". It had seemed such a shambles at the time!

"Don't worry, Mum," said Stephanie airily, when I told her about it but before we saw it, "all filming's like that in the BBC - utterly shambolic but they turn out great. It's all done in the editing, you know!"

Except for a flurry of families at half-term, there were only a few boats passing us daily in October. Their crews were similar sorts of people to the ones that we remembered during the off-peak spring season and so we were ready to meet their demands.

There were quite a lot of fishermen about though, who had not been around in the spring which was the close season. They were taking advantage of the quieter waters with fewer hired boats to disturb the fish. There is tremendous animosity between fishermen and boaters. Boaters argue that without boats the canals would silt up and become nothing more than stagnant ditches in which no self-respecting fish would breed. Fishermen sometimes agree with this in principle but in practice they wish that the boats were anywhere but the stretch which they happen to be fishing at any given moment!

I do not fish. Therefore I must be biased. I do, however, throttle down when our boat approaches a fisherman and steer as far away from him as the depth of the canal will allow. Occasionally, they are so well camouflaged that one does not see them until it is too late which I do not consider to be my fault. They could wave a hat or a hand when they hear the boat engine if they felt inclined.

I am sure that there are boaters who (probably through ignorance rather than intention) fail to slow down for fishermen. But I am fairly certain that if more fishermen smiled and passed the time of day instead of glowering surlily, they would stand a greater chance of getting those boaters on their side in the future.

Having become accustomed to the scowls, my only gripe is the amount of litter that they leave behind them. It is no good fishermen pretending that they are not the culprits either! Take circumstantial evidence for a start.

Imagine a circle of flattened grass about the circumference of a large green umbrella with the perimeter just touching the edge of the canal. As you walk past you glance within this ring; your eyes momentarily rest on a putrid gathering of swollen maggots and hastily move away. Close by, you notice some coils of nylon line, maybe a hook or two, several lead weights, the wrapper from a sliced loaf , empty crisp packets, a couple of cans which had once contained beer or cola and spread freely all around, numerous sweet and chocolate wrappers.

That, I would say, is about the average detritus which is left after a day's fishing. One sees these blemishes, too often to count, all along the waterways - but never far from road bridges because fishermen are not renowned for walking even moderate distances.

Do I sound more than at touch tetchy? In my own defence, I would say that I have spent an hour unravelling fishing line from one of our dogs, whose hind legs were securely bound together with the hook buried deep in her flank; I watched, helpless, from the boat in the middle of the Trent while a fisherman gathered together all his rubbish and put it in a plastic carrier bag - and slung it into the river. We have all collected scores of lead weights, floats and hooks before they could be swallowed, fatally, by some poor creature. Miles of nylon line must have gone into our dustbin over the years too, and this tirade does not even take account of the general unsightliness of it all. When one thinks that more people reputedly take part in coarse fishing than any other sport - the mind boggles. To me, it is aptly named!

However, fishermen - and fishing children - are customers too. I made a resolution that whenever I strolled along the towpath with the dogs, I would bring back any litter which I recognised as having come from our shop. It is surprising how much there is!

I was patiently waiting in the queue at Long Buckby Post Office one morning, having inadvertently picked the day when pensions are paid out, to post a parcel. I occupied myself as I usually did in such a situation - by reading everything in sight and there is generally plenty to read in a post office. It took a moment to register in my mind; on the glass above the post-master's head was stuck a poster which said "Part-time Post-person required (Male or Female), for twenty-eight and a half hours per week, six-thirty a.m. to eleven-fifteen a.m."

I read the notice several times before it was my turn to be served - my eye kept being drawn back to it. The post-master took my parcel and as he was weighing it, he said.

"I saw you reading. the job advertisement - are you interested?"

His saying that crystallised an idea that had been forming in my mind. With the shop being seasonal and with Blisworth Tunnel closed, a part-time job would not come amiss. I explained all this to the post-master who was most encouraging and gave me the application forms. I filled them in there and then. Feeling very pleased with myself, I drove home to tell Maurice what I had done.

"Are you sure that you can cope?" he said anxiously. "You know you hate getting up early in the morning, and with winter coming and icy roads . . ."

"Of course I can cope - I'm as fit as a flea - it'll be nice to ride a bike again and I'll get to know my way around, and meet people. The worst part will be getting up early, I agree, but I expect I'll get used to it. The best thing about the job is that I'll be finished by a quarter past eleven - with the rest of the day to do things here."

Things did not work out precisely as I had anticipated, but it was in a happy state of ignorance that we gratefully accepted Stephanie's offer to look after the shop and chickens for a week while we went away on holiday.

It was hectic trying to get away. Boats require a good deal of maintenance and "Warwickshire Lad" had been shamefully neglected since our arrival at the Wharf. Maurice rushed about changing engine oil, checking pumps and electric circuits, filling up with diesel and so on. I gave the cabins a cursory lick and promise, took down the fly-blown, cobwebby curtains and put up fresh ones at the windows. I checked the contents of the galley, added a box full of groceries, another one of fresh vegetables from the garden, plenty of our own eggs, homemade wine and beer, and we were away!

Stephanie had brought a friend with her for the week-end and we were relieved that we were not leaving her quite alone. We left her and Vicky happily playing records and swapping news. Although they both worked for BBC Current Affairs, we were informed that "Nationwide" and "Newsnight" were two different worlds and they had a lot of catching up to do! It certainly seemed like a different world from ours - particularly in view of our own recent television experience!

We also left Tansy behind. It was a pity, really, as she would have enjoyed the trip but Stephanie said that she would feel uneasy without a dog after Vicky had gone back to London. Instead, we took with us Brynne, now an old lady and rather a liability about the house. She still liked going out on the boat though and curled up on a rug on the cabin roof to watch the world go by, with an occasional gentle forage along the bank when we stopped.

In her younger days, Brynne had been an excellent ratter. Looking rather like a small Airedale, originally the Welsh Terrier had been bred for tackling vermin. Quite early in her life she had demonstrated this inherited characteristic. When she was scarcely more than a pup she had put paid to a rat which was almost as large as herself with a single bite - presumably on the back of the neck, although there was not a mark on him to show how she had done it.

Her greatest delight when we were canal cruising, had been to trot along the towpath just ahead of the boat; a small machine moving at a steady three miles an hour, short tail vertical like a companion rudder. She would walk for tens of miles, sometimes totting up thirty or more in a day, pausing only to flush out the many water voles in her path. I never saw her catch one, for their escape routes were too numerous but the challenge was ever present.

Even when we tied up the boat for the night, she did not relax. She would find the tunnel of a rat or vole and burrow deep into it, the earth flying up behind her. At the same time her tail would wag in eager anticipation and her face wore what I can only describe as a demoniac grin!

Strangely, her daughter Tansy had inherited nothing of the ratting instinct nor learnt it by example. She was aware that Brynne had an absorbing interest and would sniff vaguely at all the spots that her mother had found irresistible,

"Brynne wore a demoniac grin …"

but it was clear that she had not the least idea why. Once, quite by chance, she disturbed a young rabbit and she jumped backwards with a yelp of surprise. What a lucky rabbit - to come face to face with Tansy and not Brynne!

Now, however, Brynne was old, deaf in one ear and nearly blind. Although she was still alert to the scent of a rodent, they were able to skip past her to safety. My heart grieved to remember the dog that she had been once, and I think I sensed that this was to be her last boat trip.

-6-
Oxford Interlude

It was not until early afternoon on the first of November that we were ready, after several false starts, to let go from our home mooring. There was a faint mist already rising from the fields and the air was dank and chill. We chugged slowly along the line of moored boats and as we passed the end of our orchard the smell of decay and rotting branches drifted over the hedge. The surface of the water was thickly coated with fallen oak leaves and looked solid, like a road. I heard Aragorn crow loudly to his wives when he heard the boat engine and we looked at each other and smiled. We could still hear him, less distinctly and gradually becoming more distant even after we had turned left at Norton Junction. Maurice said it was impossible, but I fancied that I could detect a faint crowing until Braunston Tunnel cut off the sound entirely.

I still think that canal tunnels are eerie places, even in the summer when there is more boat traffic and one is unlikely to be alone inside. Then, there might be the headlight in view of a boat which is travelling at some distance behind. There may easily be a pin-prick of light in front which grows larger and reveals itself as a boat coming the other way, to bump and scrape past you with an apology (or a curse) from one steerer to another. But in November, there are almost no boats to be seen. True, there are a good many hardy boaters who cruise all the year round but sprinkle them over the waterways and they do not meet each other very often.

Canal tunnels in November, to those with an over-developed imagination, abound with spooks and Braunston is no exception. All tunnels have their regular ghosts, with similar names that are mostly derived from the original apparition which was supposed to have been seen first in Crick Tunnel - Kit Crewbucket. Even my fertile fancy has never conjured up a phantom yet in any tunnel but bats there are - in plenty!

In most tunnels, it is possible to see both ends at once and it is reassuring to see one circle of light get bigger as the other one gets smaller. But Braunston has a kink in it which can be claustrophobic to those who are that way inclined. It was a difficult tunnel to build, for it is not based on rock but on quicksand, and a miscalculation on the part of the contractors caused it to have its characteristic "S" bend. Even so, it was a remarkable engineering feat when one considers that it was opened in 1796 and is nearly a mile and a quarter long. One wonders how many of our modern underpasses will still be standing in two hundred years.

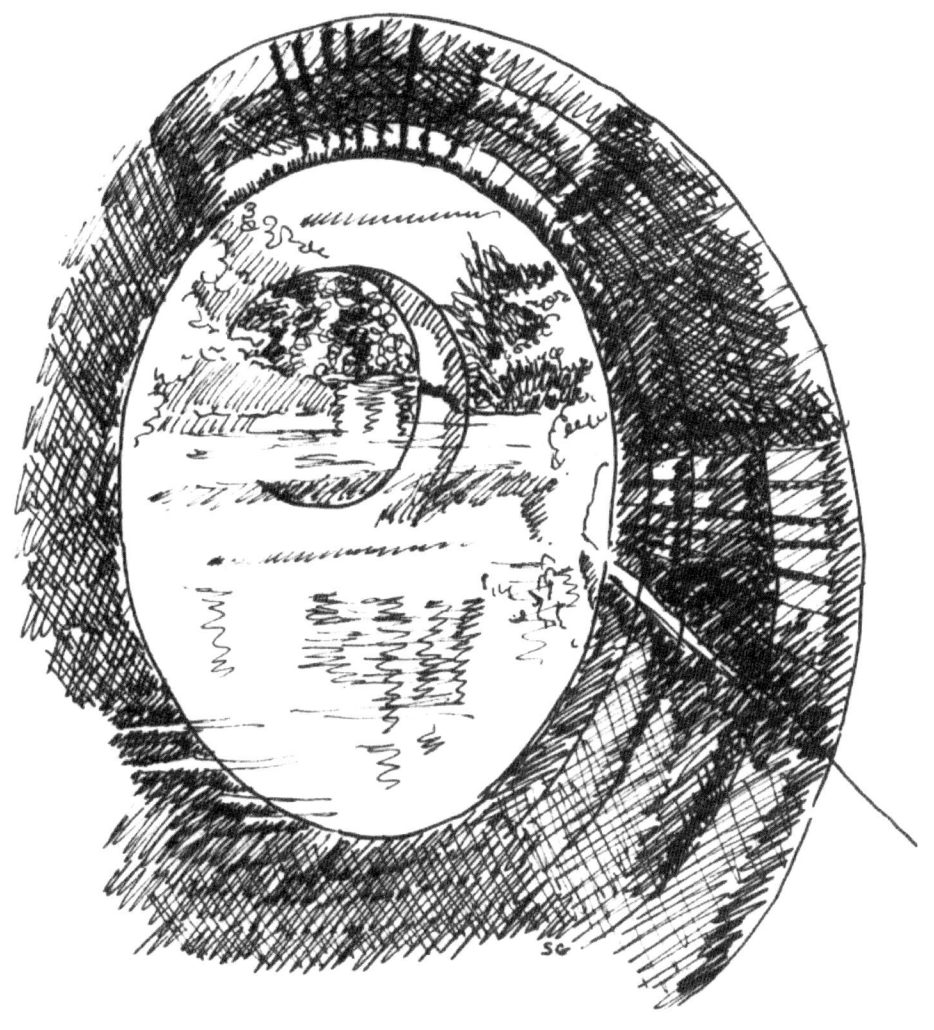

"As we came out of the darkness of the tunnel ..."

As we came out of the darkness of the tunnel into the daylight, I popped up from the brightly lit cabin where I had been skulking to relieve Maurice of his dripping waterproofs. Braunston Tunnel is also wet. The water seeps off the hill through the sandstone and trickles between the rows of old brick-work which line the arch. The lime in the mortar forms multicoloured stalactites of a strange beauty that sparkle in the beam which is thrown by the headlamp. Then the water drips onto the unsuspecting boatman below, either in a cascade of small droplets or great single plops.

We came upon Braunston Top Lock with its adjacent cottage almost as soon as we left the tunnel. The lock-keeper's wife bred German Shepherd dogs and she was returning home with three of them just as we approached.

They are handsome, intelligent dogs and these were well-trained and obedient. To my surprise, she unfastened the window of an outhouse and opened it. Why not the door? A word from her and they jumped through, one at a time, as lightly as a cat. Some people say that you cannot trust Alsatians, which is rubbish! There is a deal of truth in the saying that a dog is as good as its owner. But in my view, like Border Collies, they are working dogs and not household pets.

There are six locks in the Braunston flight and like all the other locks on the main line of the Grand Union, they are broad locks. This means that two narrow boats will fit in the lock, side by side. In the hey-day of the canals, most working boats travelled in pairs. The motor boat, steered by the boatman, would tow behind it a boat without a motor, called a butty, which would be steered by his wife or one of his children. When they arrived at a broad lock, the boats would be "breasted up", which meant that the butty would be allowed to swim alongside the motor and they would be tied closely together, fore and aft. Thus, the two boats could enter and leave the lock simultaneously on the one motor. This saved a lot of time, especially in flights of locks.

Today, one still sees this method used by the camping boats. These are ex-working boats whose cargo holds have been sheeted over with canvas and converted for use as rough and ready accommodation for parties of school children, scouts and the like. They often travel in pairs, a motor and a butty. When we see them arriving at Buckby Top Lock we know that we are in for a hectic time in the shop. After one frantic afternoon on my own when three pairs of campers arrived in convoy, I put on the door a notice which says, "Camping Boats and School Parties - Five Children Only in the Shop at any one time Please."

We like to use broad locks in the company of another boat if we can. Not breasted up which would look rather incongruous, merely sharing the lock. There is often a shortage of water on the canal system today, mainly because the system itself is old and leaky and many of the pumping stations have disappeared. Sharing a lock not only means sharing the work but also means halving the amount of water which is going to waste. The other advantage is that two boats of roughly the same length placed beside each other in a wide lock get bumped about much less by the water churning through the sluices than one boat on its own.

It dawned on us as we started down the flight, that this was the first time that we had cruised without Bruce. We missed his muscles and his jokes! With a crew of three - there is one to steer, one to open paddles and gates and then to walk or bicycle to the next lock, and one to shut paddles and gates behind the boat. With four, there is the added bonus of one to keep all the other inner men sustained. We took turns at each task - no unions on "Warwickshire Lad"!

As there were now only two of us, one had to steer and the other one was lumbered with all the effort. There was no doubt that if we were not to return from holiday more tired than when we left, we would have to change our hitherto slick system of locking. In other words - take it slowly.

We did not see another soul as we worked down the flight. Dusk was falling by the time we came out of the bottom lock and moved slowly past the dozens of beautifully painted boats which are always to be found tied up in Braunston. From their tall, black chimneys, plumes of acrid smoke wafted in ethereal fantasies over the still water. We caught the occasional appetising whiff of suppers cooking and my stomach gave a sympathetic rumble.

It was black as pitch when we reached the canal junction known as Braunston Turn, where the Grand Union meets the Oxford Canal and we turned sharp left under a cast iron footbridge. The stretch between Braunston Turn and Napton Junction had been built by the Oxford Canal Company, who later charged the Grand Junction Canal Company (as it was then) an exorbitant toll to use it. Today it is one of the most picturesque stretches in our part of the country; the canal meanders through quiet farmland and the towpaths are too overgrown for any but the most intrepid hiker.

The boat headlight lit the mist eddying across from the puddle banks as we sought one of our favourite places to tie up for the night. At last we saw it; just past a bridge that was festooned with swags of trailing ivy, there was a place where we knew that the water was deep enough for the boat to come in close to the side. I could hear the munching of cows beyond the towpath hedge and on the opposite side of the canal a rolling hill which showed traces of ridge and furrow cultivation was grazed by sheep. I could just see them in the cool light of the rising moon.

Maurice made the boat fast while I walked with Brynne a little way along the towpath. I stopped as she rummaged about in the reeds at the edge of the bank and looked at the stars reflected in the quiet water. Then I took a deep and satisfying breath. Mm. This was what canalling was all about!

I awoke the next morning soon after day-break, which in November is not very early. One of the drawbacks to cruising in the winter is that the days are short. But there is the blessing of plenty of water beneath the hull to make up for it; often in summer "the bottom is too near the top" on the Oxford Canal.

Contentedly gazing at the cabin ceiling on which a dancing kaleidoscope informed me that sunshine was playing on water riffled by a breeze, I considered whether or not I should get out of bed. My nose told me that it was cold and so did the condensation of my breath in the air. I am usually careful to remain asleep long enough for Maurice to light the stove and make the tea but this time I was too impatient to see what the day would bring. Anyway, it was his holiday too.

We had not made any definite plans. British Waterways Board maintenance work is mostly carried out during the winter months and although I had checked their published list of "stoppages" where sections of canal are closed to navigation, I had not made use of the system which informs canal users of emergency repairs. One dials a number known as "Canalphone" and is treated to a recorded message; like machine-gun fire, a list of restrictions and closures rattles over the telephone - too fast to make a note even if one can write short-hand. I dare say "Canalphone" is helpful if one is quick on the uptake. I have to let the tape run through at least twice and even then I sometimes end up none the wiser!

We could not complain therefore (although I am sure we did), when, after following the canal as it lazily wandered around Napton Hill we arrived at Napton Bottom Lock to read, in familiar Waterways blue letters, "Claydon Locks will be closed for repair from November 2nd."

I cannot remember exactly, but I know that although we might have scraped through before they closed, we would not have been able to return for nearly two months! Oh well! We cogitated for a minute or two before deciding to go as far as Claydon Top and then turn back. The South Oxford in winter is too good a treat to miss entirely.

In the middle of our discussion, a boat appeared round the bend and pulled in alongside the water point behind us. While the tank was filling, the steerer strolled up the slope to the lock-side for a chat. His was the first boat we had seen on the move that morning and Maurice told him so, adding:

"I didn't know there was a stoppage at Claydon from today, did you?"

"Oh no!" the man wailed, "That's all I need! I've just bought the boat - been having engine trouble off and on since I left Braunston. I'm supposed to be taking it to London to live on the damn thing. What on earth can I do?"

"If you look sharpish you might just make it," said Maurice, "they're not putting the padlocks on till four o'clock according to the notice - if you can get past us in the next pound you're welcome to go in front - we're in no hurry."

"Thanks!" The man sprinted back down the path to turn off the tap and make preparations to follow us through the first of the narrow locks.

The substantial house which is set back from the canal alongside the water point used to be a public house called The Bull and Butcher. By contorting myself I could decipher the name still engraved on the fan-light above the door although the glass had been recut and reset. L.T.C. Rolt bemoans the passing of the pub in the Preface to the Second Edition of his book "Narrow Boat". It is a sad loss because now the nearest hostelry is a fair trek up Napton Hill. Scarcely worth the effort, we thought, on the one occasion we tried it and found nought but fizzy beer.

Incidentally, in the book itself, Tom Rolt anticipated the early departure from the waterways scene of our Canal Stores. I would dearly love to be able to show him the Buckby cans hanging from the ceiling today - more than forty years after he bought his own from the same shop!

We made slow work of the nine locks which lift the Oxford Canal to its summit level, for having let the other boat go in front, every single lock was against us and had to be emptied. Still, the view got better with each one until I could see straight across the valley to the windmill on top of Napton Hill. It began to get chilly before we had left Napton Lock a couple of miles behind us and as the sun disappeared a raw wind started to eat into my bones.

"Let's stop now," I said to Maurice, "I know it's early but I'm perished. It's pleasant here, too."

So once again we tied up in the middle of nowhere. It was uncanny - the silence. Usually, the Oxford Canal is buzzing with boats. Every bridge has to be approached with caution for nearly all of them are situated on blind bends and you can almost guarantee meeting another boat head-on if you are not extremely careful. But we had not seen a single vessel other than those tucked away safely in the Old Engine Arm since our friend had disappeared ahead of us.

It was an excellent spot. The water was good and deep with no obvious rogue rocks underneath to scrape and reverberate through the hull and keep us awake. (Not that there was much fear of anything doing that!) The bank was firm and level and clothed in short grass. In fact, as a mooring it was a rarity on that particular canal. In our parlance, it was a "Stephanie Type Mooring". She is very fussy about our overnight stops and has been known to bully us into trundling along for ages after the rest of us wanted to tie up because she would not tolerate being so much as six inches out from the side.

Maurice made a mental note of its whereabouts so that he could find it again. His brain is packed full of such jottings and he gets very put out if he has earmarked a place for us to tie up and finds that someone else has had the audacity to put their boat there before him!

On one extraordinary occasion in Leicestershire, we were just hammering in the mooring spikes when a local man advised us that there was a much better spot around the next bend where the water was deeper and we would be out of the wind. Thanking him, we shifted the boat. There was not a living soul in sight in any direction and not a sound either. After supper, Bruce opened the stern cabin doors and went outside. He was back in seconds.

"You'll never believe this - but there's a boat moored right next to us, actually touching!"

Maurice and I scrambled up the cabin steps to have a look. It was true.

And yet the canal disappeared in silence and tranquillity as far as the eye could see. So we moved. Then they moved - as soon as we had gone below.

"Perhaps they're lonely," I suggested.

"Invite them on board for a coffee, why don't you?" said Bruce, grinning.

"This is too much," said Maurice grimly, "they've got the whole Welford Arm to choose from - why up our back end?"

He and Bruce waited until it was quite dark and then, very gently they eased out our mooring spikes and towed "Warwickshire Lad" silently out of earshot of the other boat. Wrapping a rag around the hammer, they made us fast once more.

"That should fix 'em," said Maurice with satisfaction.

But when Bruce flung open the doors next morning - there they were! Their bow fender and our stern fender nestling close together like peas in a pod.

I think there must be those who dislike spending the night in deserted stretches of countryside as we prefer to do. They like the security of knowing that there are other people and boats at hand. Near a pub is the best place for that. If we moor for the night close to a road bridge or a public house as we do occasionally, then we should not complain if there is noise and bustle going on half the night. But if we seek out peace and solitude, others should respect that choice too. There is room for us all.

It was still barely dusk so Maurice tramped off to gather some fallen elm branches to take home for the stove in the shop. I was quite happy to snuggle up in the cosy cabin with a book. We used to have a portable television set on board but we gave it away some years ago. It was vital when I was reading for my Open University degree; we used to have to stop abruptly in the most inconvenient places so that I could watch the broadcasts associated with my course. The engine interfered horribly if we kept going and in those days there was no video. Now, we have twice the bookshelves instead, suitably loaded, and a set of chess-men and a board. I enjoy having a week without television although I do miss "Gardener's World".

Later that evening as we were getting ready for bed, we felt a slight movement of the boat and heard the scrape and slide of gravelly mud along the hull and a protesting creak from the mooring ropes.

"Hello!" said Maurice, "don't tell me someone's coming up the locks at this hour."

Sure enough, after a bit, the faint sound of a diesel engine penetrated the thick silence and steadily increased in volume. I opened the curtains a crack and peered out into the darkness. A headlight pierced the black, dazzling me.

"I can't see very well," I said, "but I think it's called 'Cropredy Man' and it's not going slowly."

"Lechlade or bust," said Maurice, quoting a Thames lock-keeper with whom he had once struck a rapport, "if he's hoping to get to Cropredy he's in for a disappointment - the padlocks will be firmly on by now."

But when the next day we reached the last point at which we could turn round to come back and walked along the towpath to Claydon Top Lock, there was no sign of the boat that had passed us in the night.

"He must have talked B.W.B. into letting him through," said Maurice generously.

Once, we were travelling down the North Stratford towards Kingswood Junction when a fisherman called out to us.

"The lock-keeper's after your blood!"

"Why?" we replied, injured expressions to the fore.

"For taking a crowbar to the padlock on the top lock last night!"

We had done nothing of the sort. True, a boat had passed us while we were tied up and having tea. And true, when we arrived at the top lock we were surprised to find the gate was not locked as we had expected and the padlock and chain were lying broken on the grass. We had worked down the flight then - well - wouldn't you have done? But use a crowbar - never!

Maurice nudged "Warwickshire Lad"'s bow as far as he could underneath the bridge which carries the towpath across the feeder from Boddington Reservoir. With some help from me shoving on the long shaft and a breath or two of fresh breeze blowing from the opposite side, we eased the boat round so that it faced the way we had come. "Winding" it is called when it is done properly, because I suppose, one utilises that element of nature. To see a seventy foot long boat nosing deep into a slit in the canal bank known as a "winding hole" and being expertly manoeuvred with the minimum of effort is an experience to behold and a tribute to the steerer. Personally, I try never to "wind" "Warwickshire Lad" beneath the eye of a beholder because I generally make what is known as a "dog's breakfast" of it!

Leaving Brynne burrowing into the bank after a water vole under the pretext that she was guarding the boat, we strolled along to Claydon Top Lock to see what was happening. Very little. A padlock on the lock-gate stared rustily. Obviously work on the repairs had not yet begun. With a stoppage of two months I suppose there was no hurry.

The group of old red brick buildings were basking in the wintry sunshine. The largest had once been a blacksmith's forge and had great double doors opening onto the canal so that the heavy iron work could have been easily loaded into boats for transportation to where it was needed. But no metallic ring of hammer on anvil could be heard, and the only smoke came not from the stack on the forge roof but the stove chimney of a narrow boat tucked close into the bank alongside.

"Vixen", I read aloud as I glanced at the boat, "I wonder who that belongs to - didn't I read somewhere that these old workshops were being developed into a craft centre?"

"Mm," said Maurice, "that was a year or two back. Not a lot seems to have happened. The one in the middle is obviously a gift ship now although it's closed for the winter. It looks as if someone's patched the roof and put up a bit of new guttering."

"What a shame - there's so much potential - the forge would make a great art gallery for local artists."

"Including you, I suppose," he replied with a smile, "while I grow runner beans in that little walled garden. The trouble is that there is no road access - who would come and admire your paintings? You'd never have boaters pausing long enough to walk round an art gallery. You know what it's like at home - everyone expects to get their shopping done before the lock has finished emptying or filling, and narrow locks are pretty quick."

"You're right, of course", I said, reluctantly turning away from the sun-warmed cluster of brick and the patch of faded, forlorn African Marigolds in front of the gift shop.

We cruised gently back the way we had come; the engine ticking over so quietly that it failed to disturb a dog fox scuffling about in the undergrowth on the sharply sloping sides of Fenny Compton "Tunnel". The lid was taken off the tunnel over a hundred years ago and it is open to the sky. There is still the feel of one, though, in parts where the cutting is deepest and the trees hang densely overhead. It is very narrow and in places submerged stones from the old tunnel wall clutter the channel and make it difficult for boats to pass each other. We could see one far away at the northern end but it did not seem to be moving. When we eventually reached it, we found that it was loosely tied to some scaffolding that was standing in the water. No-one seemed to be about although smoke was curling out of its chimney. As it was completely blocking our way, Maurice called out.

"Anybody aboard?"

A young man appeared at the top of the cabin steps with a mug of tea in his hand. He looked surprised to see us but amiably pulled his boat out of the way so that we could get past. It did not have an engine, apparently, and so he was bow-hauling it to Claydon on his own. I could not imagine how he could possibly manage to keep his feet on the steep overgrown sides of the "tunnel" and pull along a fifty foot narrow boat single handed but he just shrugged and said.

"I'll manage O.K. I expect."

We called briefly at Fenny Marine to use their pay-phone and find out if Stephanie was alright. She was a bit lonely but expecting another friend to arrive that evening and was in the process of preparing an exotic meal (at our expense, no doubt). Not that we minded in the least, I was glad that Irene was going to keep her company until we got back. She said the shop was "as dead as a door nail" and hoped we wouldn't think that the awful turnover was her fault. It comes as a shock even now, that as far as trade is concerned, the season ends with a bang on the last day of October. Maybe one day we will be able to afford to close the shop during the winter months. It is a difficult decision whether to forgo the little custom there is out of season or tie up capital in goods that nobody is going to buy for three months.

Fenny Marine were obviously in a similar dilemma, for their normally well stocked shelves of maps and books had a depressing half-empty appearance and the food counter was almost bare. But they have a good chandlery store which is probably patronised all the year round by the large number of owners who keep their boats permanently in the marina.

The thin pale sunshine scarcely took the chill off the crisp air as we followed the tortuously winding course of the eleven mile summit pound. The canal almost seemed to double back on its tracks round Wormleighton Hill. We savoured the emptiness; the feeling that the waterway belonged to us and entered all the bridge holes with confident abandon.

It was still a little too early (even for us) when we drew alongside our mooring of the night before, although it looked tempting, so we pressed on to Marston Doles at the top of the Napton Flight and tied up opposite a derelict warehouse.

Another "Stephanie Type Mooring" although Brynne was not too pleased as the bank had been piled which meant that ratting was out as an evening occupation. I like Marston Doles; it is a friendly sort of place. The warehouse is a handsome building in spite of its dilapidated state. Made of dark red local brick, the date 1865 is written high on the wall in Staffordshire Blues that had also been used to surround the loading doors.

"Yet another place with bags of potential," I said to Maurice, "and look at the very acute angle the wall on the canal side makes with the other one. How strange - it has the exaggerated perspective of a stage set."

"A trapezium," he said, knowledgeable as always. "I expect the canal company didn't own enough land to build it square on. They had to have one wall next to the canal for loading so they compromised on the other."

The yard was flanked by a row of stables that used to house the towing horses and on the other side were some red brick cottages with well kept gardens, one of which boasted a splendid ancient box hedge that would have done justice to a stately home.

Maurice went for a walk to sniff out any dead elm that might be lying around while I took out my sketch-book and tried to capture the evening light on the mellow Victorian walls. He came back just as I was putting away my paints and blowing on my finger-tips.

"Finished?"

"Not really. My hands were too cold - I need mittens; the sort with no fingers. If your palms are warm so are your fingers. The sun's going in, anyway." I nodded at the inky-coloured anvil cloud edged with silver-gilt creeping across the sun as it dropped towards the vale of the Itchen.

The next day dawned bright and clear in spite of the ominous sky the previous evening. We sped down Napton because all the locks were with us, give or take a few leakages; "a good road" in the language of the working boatmen.

"This is heaven", I said to Maurice as he peeled off yet another outer garment. "Out of season! Whose season! Not God's - that's for sure!"

"Don't speak too soon", he was pessimistic as usual but opened a bottle of beer to indicate that at least it was warm enough for some evaporation to have taken place.

Napton Junction is the best place for crab-apples I know, so we stopped there for lunch and picked two large carrier-bags full in about twenty minutes. Then, we had no sooner started off again than I spied sloes galore glimmering mistily from the overgrown towpath hedge. By no means every year is a good one for sloes. In fact many years can pass without seeing more than a scanty crop. These were the size of Californian grapes and there were hundreds. The towpath had disintegrated so we pushed the boat as far in as we could and Maurice held it there on the long shaft while I picked the sloes. Blackthorn is well named and after a dozen vicious jabs I decided that the kindest thing for the tree and myself would be to prune and pick afterwards as I do with blackcurrants. So I fetched the secateurs from the galley drawer (I keep them there so that Maurice does not confuse them with his tools) and soon the roof was covered with long sprays of fruit. I am sure it was largely due to my ministrations that there was an excellent crop on the same bushes the following year too - plus the unusually mild March when the blackthorn flowered.

We motored beneath the left-hand span of the elegant iron bridge at Braunston Turn to spend the latter part of our holiday cruising as far as time would allow up the northern section of the Oxford Canal. The bridge under which we passed almost straight away is one of two notorious bridges which carry the A45 over the canal in Braunston; the parapets are demolished with monotonous regularity. Years ago I saw a film in which Robert Powell crashed a sports car into one of them, to disappear in a spectacular sheet of flame into the canal. I think he must have started the habit.

Within minutes we were out of Braunston and away into the pastoral scene once more with the canal playing hop-scotch between Northamptonshire and Warwickshire. The hawthorn hedges were glowing with garnet red haws, the occasional vermilion splash of colour giving away the presence of wild rose hips. We stopped after half an hour so that Maurice could cycle into Willoughby to buy some fresh bread from the bakery there. My success rate of home-baked bread on board is pitifully low. The oven always seems to blow out at the crucial moment. Sometimes even the ducks turn up their beaks at my efforts.

The Ordnance Survey Pathfinder map still shows an inn at Navigation Bridge, Willoughby Wharf although, alas, it has followed The Bull and Butcher into oblivion and been converted into a "gentleman's residence". So I put the kettle on for a cup of tea while Maurice lifted the folding bicycle out from under the seat and assembled it for action. I think he is very brave to ride it at all because it has a nasty trick of folding itself up when you are in the saddle and once precipitated him painfully into a timber yard. I find it nerve-racking enough to discover after a mile or so that the handle-bars are no longer at right-angles to the wheels but when the pedals start dropping off, I wish I had walked! It behaved better before its ducking in a lock on the Macclesfield, I remember. Still, it is an essential part of the boat's equipment when it comes to buying necessities like bread and milk and is handy when one wants to finish a cruise at a different place from where one began.

You leave the car at strategic points where the road is near the canal and every now and then somebody cycles off, puts the folding bicycle in the boot of the car which is driven to another spot a little ahead of the boat. Then the bicycle and the driver board the boat, cruise for a few miles and repeat the exercise. It sounds more laborious than it is, especially if people take it in turns. It is a device often used by guests who join us for a day or two's cruising while we are on holiday.

This time Maurice returned without mishap, an appetising wholemeal loaf, still warm from the oven, tucked into the saddlebag.

"I don't know where the day seems to have gone," he said, "just look at the time!" We'd best not go further than Barby Hill tonight, though, there's the motorway and the railway after that so it could be noisy."

A brilliant moon, phosphorescent in the navy-blue of the eastern sky, was rising to outshine the saffron glow on the western horizon. Against the pale range light a line of leafless trees on a distant hill was silhouetted, a filigree of dense black.

"There'll be a frost tonight, I think, with that clear sky," Maurice said, "I think I'll put the canopy on the front to keep us warmer."

"Let's pick some rose-hips before we go tomorrow then, they're better when they've been frosted. We've done so well with fruit this trip - there'll be enough for wine and jelly too. Keep your eye out for some late blackberries and elderberries as well, I'd like to make some hedgerow jelly this year."

Maurice was right about the frost. The canvas canopy was hard and unforgiving when we rolled it back in the morning and a film of ice, thin as rice paper, had formed on the water near the bank. As the sun rose, a spectrum of light shimmered on rime along the twigs of the high hedge in whose lea we had been snugly moored.

There were rose-hips close at hand. I followed the curve of the towpath round a slight bend and found my way barred by an impenetrable wall; the great hedge lay massacred on the path; slashed to a height of two or three feet, torn tree stumps gaped open with sap still oozing from the ragged bark, hips and haws lying like drops of blood among the wreckage.

A Waterways flat floated nearby, one end tied to a spike in the ground.

"Typical", I murmured bitterly to myself, remembering the man who had had a go at our own hedge before we managed to stop him.

After that we did not feel like lingering so let go without delay and ate our breakfast from the cabin top as the boat carved its way along the bright morning mirror of the waterway. A man digging his allotment garden caught the scent of coffee and bacon wafting across the ripples from our stern, raised his head and smiling enviously, called "Can anyone join in?"

The three Hillmorton locks are among my favourites; they have so many good features - pleasantly situated for a start but that is not all. The locks are in pairs, both chambers in working order, unlike some of the twin locks on the Trent and Mersey Canal. This cuts down delays in the summer and in wintertime means there is a good chance of finding one side in your favour whether you are going up or down. But I think the best thing about them is the ease with which even my rheumaticky wrists can swing the massive cog-wheels to draw the paddles.

Newbold-on-Avon is a compulsive stopping place during "opening time", I am afraid. The only problem was which of the two pubs should we choose.

Davenports or M&B? They are both good brews so we decided to be scrupulously fair and dispense our largess equally. It was lucky that both "The Boat" and "The Barley Mow" were right on the wharf and next door to each other because it was in a very benevolent frame of mind that we boarded "Warwickshire Lad" and headed north once more.

We had come to the point in our holiday when we needed to do a spot of calculation in order to decide when we ought to turn around to come back, for Stephanie had a deadline to resume work at the BBC. Maurice is the mathematical genius in our family so I left it to him.

"Certainly Hawkesbury Junction," he announced, "we can't go further than that and be sure of getting back on time. But if you want to do any more sketching we ought to make allowances for that and turn round at Stretton Stop."

"Hawkesbury would be the natural place, I suppose, as it's at one end of the Oxford Canal but I really would like to do a painting of the B.W.B. Yard at Hillmorton."

"Stretton Stop it shall be then, but tomorrow, not tonight. I want to catch "Rose Narrowboats" when they're open and buy a new front fender. It's falling to bits in spite of your efforts."

"Have a heart! The poor old thing doesn't owe us anything."

"I really would like to do a painting of the yard at Hillmorton ..."

Actually, the round rope "button" on the bow was the same one that Chris Barney had put there when the boat was new. Rope fenders are expensive, so when it became worn and ragged I knitted a rope covering for it using a crochet stitch and a strong metal hook Maurice codged up for me. A professional fender-maker laughed at me when I told him my method, but I made side fenders too, on the same principle with a roll of old carpet in the middle and they were perfectly successful. It is tough work, though; you need strong fingers. I was relieved that Maurice was prepared to buy a new one without first trying to persuade me to make one from scratch!

The toll-house has gone, and Stretton Stop is now only an easily swivelled footbridge which enables people to cross from the towpath to the boats moored along the old Stretton Arm. We turned into the arm to "wind" which Maurice achieved neatly and after a brief pause just short of the bridge carrying the Fosse Way overhead we returned the way we had come.

By midday we were back at Hillmorton and made ourselves comfortable within sight of the bottom pair of locks and opposite a patch of arrow-head growing in the water at the edge of the channel. A family of moorhens were weaving in and out of the emergent spikes like dinghies in a boat-handling competition.

The British Waterways buildings, which are situated along a short arm of the canal above the bottom locks, were originally built by the Oxford Canal Company as workshops. Now they house the Board's Section Office, the Maintenance Yard and, until recently, provided a base for part of the British Waterways hire fleet. The composition of functional buildings and landscape has been thoughtfully conserved (the fact that the occupant of one of the offices there is Peter White, architect to British Waterways, may have something to do with it) and altogether makes an attractive picture.

Because most of my sketching is done in the winter months, I am conscious of the skeletons of trees. A beautiful tree, like a human being, has good bones. I was drawn by the strong vertical thrust of the tall trees on either side of the bridge in contrast to the horizontal slate roofs of the workshops.

The sun was warm on my back when I started painting but in no time at all it slid away over my left shoulder and the rosy brick-work melted into purple shadow. That is the trouble with painting from the life - it changes by the minute. As the sun sank lower my feet, buried in fallen leaves up to the ankles, grew numb. So did my fingers. But I persevered, determined to complete at least one picture before we went home. The light was almost gone by the time I had finished but I was not displeased with the end result; secretly I thought it was one of the best I had ever done.

Maurice could tell that I was happy. He poured a generous slug of rum into my tea to get the circulation going again and said that we might spend the night where we were.

"We've bags of time to get home tomorrow, it's only four and a half hours from here - barring accidents." He always says that, not meaning accidents exactly, but delays. They are frequent occurrences on the canal; drained pounds, for instance, or broken paddles. Once, because a bridge on the Birmingham Canal had collapsed, we had to make a detour along the Wyrley and Essington and the Walsall Canals to Pudding Green junction. It added about five hours to our journey but was not too worrying as we were on home ground with time in hand.

There was an occasion though, on the Shropshire Union Canal, when we had an anxious moment or two. We had tied up the previous evening in swirling fog at the only place we could find that was deep enough for us to get anywhere near the bank - by a public house at Bates Mill. We were still snoring in bed the next morning when a bang on the roof heralded a visitor. Maurice stumbled out to be greeted by the information that there was to be an emergency stoppage at Wharton Lock, scarcely more than a quarter of a mile ahead of us.

"If you've got any sense, mate," advised the friendly fellow boater, "you'll go through the lock now, before Waterways arrive at 8 o'clock."

"Thanks! Come on chaps (to Bruce and me) - we're moving!"

I cannot pretend that I did not grumble incessantly as I took the tiller and (still wearing pyjamas) steered the boat towards the lock. I ducked below modestly as the Waterways men appeared and Maurice went to talk to them.

"They'll let us through the lock now," he said when he returned, "although by rights the stoppage is on already. It's a brickwork job, they say, and could take anything from half an hour to four days - they won't know till they drain it and see the extent of the damage."

"Gosh! Four days! We'd never be home before you had to go back to work!"

"Exactly. We've been remarkably lucky - we'd have had to leave the boat here and try to get home by train somehow."

Some friends who were travelling behind us in a locally hired boat told us later that the stoppage was lifted after half a day which would not have been too disastrous. But it is a factor worth taking into account when planning a holiday.

Another day of Indian summer dawned and we set off home in brilliant sunshine.

"We have been spoilt for weather this holiday," I said, "I really feel I can face the winter now." (They call that sort of remark "tempting Providence".)

Close by Barby Wood we went under a road bridge. On the grass verge nearby I noticed a battered black car parked not far from the mooring of an old seventy-foot working narrow boat in need of a coat of paint. I mentally bracketed the two together and thought no more about them.

A little later as we rounded Barby Hill, there came into view a welcome sight. Only a good stone's throw from our overnight stop a few days before and even less from the sorry hedge, was a young couple skilfully layering with care and precision a field's length of old thorn. We could not resist drawing close to exchange a word or two. They lived on the boat, they said, finding work where they could. It had been the Waterways intention to slash this piece of hedge too, they told us, but the farmer who owned the field had sent the men packing.

"You'll have it done properly or not at all," he had said. And so they did.

We were glad of company up Braunston flight. Peaceful waterways are all very well but man is a gregarious animal and we are no exception. It was pleasant to have some conversation and we were content that "Warwickshire Lad" might share the locks with "Vixen", last seen outside the old forge at Claydon.

The Lloyds ran the gift shop at Claydon Top Lock together with another couple. I got the impression that the men were the entrepreneurs and the women were the artistic ones. Napton flight too, was due to be closed soon for routine maintenance, Sue Lloyd told me, and they did not fancy being stuck between Claydon and Napton for a chunk of the winter. So they were moving south on the Grand Union as far as Weedon which was more easily accessible by road.

We saw the Lloyds again the next day when Sue brought some of her work into the shop to offer me on a wholesale basis. We bought quite a selection; it was delicately executed and unlike anything I produced myself.

By then, of course, our holiday was over.

-7-
Winter Bitterness

I had never in my life as a routine, arisen in the morning earlier than at half past six - even when I was a student nurse. If one is not a "morning person" - and I am certainly not - half-past five in the winter seems like the middle of the night. Of course, I can get up when I have to on occasion. I never failed to see Maurice off on a military exercise at whatever uncivilised hour that the army chose. But there is a grave difference between getting up at some God forsaken hour now and again or even for a week or two at a time and doing it for six days a week for forty-nine weeks of the year.

At first, I worried that I might oversleep in the mornings but I never did. I woke without any trouble and although I always had two alarm clocks which were set ten minutes apart, I rarely needed the second. I was in bed and asleep by half-past nine in the evening, though, which did not make me very good company.

I was trained as a postwoman for three days by a jolly little person called Doll. Although she said that she was nearly sixty, she was bubbling with energy. She also never stopped talking.

A regular annual event is a television news item about the Christmas mail. The viewer gets a glimpse inside a great city sorting office to see the mighty Post Office at work. Inside the centrally heated hall, young men in shirt sleeves swiftly conjure the Christmas cards from the moving conveyor belt into pigeon holes. Probably there will be a shot of the postman with whom the public are familiar - the one who drives up in a bright red van and delivers the parcels to the door.

It is a pity about the Official Secrets Act because all I can say is that it was not a bit like that in Long Buckby! By the time that Doll had finished explaining everything to me, I was more than a little apprehensive.

There were four of us altogether, not counting Doll, who, when she was not training me, acted as relief.

Walter was the head postman by virtue of serving for the longest time - thirty-five years and coming up for retirement. He was short and stocky with a round, ruddy face and a gentle way of telling me that I had done something very wrong - like leaving someone's garden gate ajar so that their dog got out.

Then there was Jim, who became my favourite. He had worked there for nineteen years and was also nearly due for retirement. He was not very tall either, and a bit arthritic. He had an earthy sense of humour, and quietly helped me to lift the heavy sacks up onto the bench and unobtrusively gave me a hand to sort when he saw that I was getting flustered. Walter and Jim were both keen vegetable gardeners and constantly compared notes. I learnt a lot from them. It was like being in the audience for a daily edition of "Gardener's Question Time" and as I got on top of the sorting I asked plenty of questions myself.

Maria was the fourth member of the team and a part-timer like myself. She was Italian by birth and married to an Englishman who worked for the motor industry. So frequently was the poor man on short time, that they could not have managed without the extra money that she earned. Maria was nearly sixty too. I began to feel quite young! She was very prickly at first. I heard that my predecessor and Maria had been at daggers drawn and I think that she was anticipating a battle with me too. After a week or two, though, she began to soften and we eventually became friends.

Our working day began at six twenty-five with the arrival in the market square of the mail van. We unloaded it between us for nowadays we have "equal pay for equal work" and I could not be expected to leave all the heavy lifting to the men. It would be after seven before I wrapped myself up even more warmly and went outside into the chill morning air to load my formidable steed - the post-office bicycle. It was a sturdily built machine, much heavier than an ordinary bicycle and it had no gears. There was a hefty tray in front which I found rather unnerving when I set off, for when I turned a sharp corner the handle-bars and front wheel turned at right angles together but the tray still faced straight ahead. Jim advised me to put a folded mail bag on the tray to conceal the wheel and that helped my equilibrium.

What with the weight of the machine and that of the parcels, sometimes it was so heavy that I could not hoist it up the kerb. The loads got heavier as Christmas approached. On one occasion, I could scarcely see over the top of the parcels which I had piled on the tray and the leather straps would barely fasten. It was icy and as I turned a corner, the wheels slid. I ended up in someone's rock garden with bundles of Christmas cards slithering down the pavement and parcels flattening the alpines. One box clearly said "Fragile - With Care" in big red letters! I gave it a furtive shake as I picked it up but there were no sounds of tinkling glass or china so I delivered it without a comment and waited in trepidation for the recipient to pounce on me the following day. Nothing was said, so I think that I was lucky - except for my multicoloured bruises.

I travelled to work first thing in the morning by car, as the thought of cycling along three and a half miles of lonely, unlit lanes at that hour made me nervous. This meant that the Beetle had to be brought home again, so I left the post-office bicycle at the office and picked up my own to deliver the mail to the inhabitants of Buckby Wharf. These houses are widely scattered, some with no road access at all and one or two where I would not choose even to ride a bicycle for fear of ending up in the canal! This made it difficult to deliver large, heavy parcels.

It was invariably long after the designated time of eleven-fifteen that I threw the letters addressed to ourselves onto the dining room table and collapsed into a chair. Eleven fifteen! How could I have been so naive as to think that my morning's work would end on the dot? If one thinks about it rationally - how could I go home at a quarter past eleven and put my feet up, just like that? Not if I had a bag half full of letters and two or three parcels left. What would I do with them? Take them back to the office and deliver them the next day? Of course not. One worked until the work was done. Quite simple - even if I was only supposed to be working part-time! My plans for spending the greater part of my day painting or gardening flew away with this realisation - even if I had had any energy left. With legs that felt like planks and tired in body and spirit, I was usually so sleepy that my eyes were closed before Maurice had time to hand me the mug of hot chocolate that he always made for me.

The weather turned bitterly cold in the second week of December. We were hard pressed to keep the wood-burning stove in fuel without using un-seasoned wood. So Maurice bought an ingenious log-making gadget that converted newspaper into combustible bricks. It was remarkably efficient. He soaked our old copies of The Guardian, The "Gusher" and The Sunday Times in water in a plastic dustbin. Every time that he walked past, he gave the printed stew a casual stir until it had the appearance (but not the smell) of grey soup. It smelt vile - particularly when it started to foment! Then, he dolloped it into the machine which was rather like an oblong colander or a lemon press and squeezed out the water. The wet bricks were then lined up beneath the "Object" where it was dry and draughty. Eventually, they dried out sufficiently to burn on the stove or in the fireplace. They lasted longer if they were slightly damp. A really dry newspaper "log" perked up a dismal fire in no time and they were handy when there was any slack coal which would not burn by itself.

Every night there was a hard frost and the biting north wind that blew all day kept the air temperature down in spite of the sun shining in a clear blue sky. The ground was as hard as iron. Wild creatures were desperate to find food and so we loaded the bird table with kitchen scraps and hung a split coconut from the cypress tree for those supreme trapeze artists - blue-tits. All the neighbourhood birds made free with the hens' corn, to Aragorn's annoyance. He tolerated the smaller birds such as sparrows and starlings but he disliked the magpies and darted at them, twittering angrily. He hated the crows even more but must have been a little frightened of them for he kept his distance in spite of making a fearsome display with his wattles and wings.

There were several huge rats that regularly helped themselves to poultry-feed too. Maurice managed to catch the largest fellow in a trap which he carried to the canal by hooking the end of the garden hoe beneath the trap handle. The rat was so heavy and active that he set the trap in motion like a fairground swing - the trap-door flew open and the rat plummeted into the icy water and swam vigorously in the direction of the bank. Maurice thought that he eventually got the better of the rat with the working end of the hoe. I devoutly hoped so! I am not especially squeamish but I cannot control an involuntary revulsion of rats and snakes: an irrational fear that manifests itself by nausea and a prickling of the scalp.

Neither did rodents confine themselves to the garden. I discovered mouse droppings in the kitchen one morning - on the draining board and the top of the refrigerator. Then in the airing cupboard I found the clean towels and bedlinen bespattered with telltale traces of mouse. As the days went by, the mess became less of a shower and more of an avalanche!

I began to get the familiar prickling sensation at the back of my neck and in the roots of my hair. It was only mice - wasn't it? I understood why we had inherited a gross of mousetraps! I caught one culprit in the airing cupboard with a great "splat" and drops of blood everywhere. Thank goodness - it was a mouse after all even if it was plump and well fed. I kept a trap permanently set in the same place but I never caught another. I knew they were still there, though. I could smell them.

It could easily have been witchcraft that charmed into our lives a handsome black cat called Lucifer, for he arrived at the most opportune time. Three years before, Stephanie and her flat-mate had chosen to provide a home for two abandoned kittens - a brother and sister. Stephanie adopted Polly, who was a tiny tortoiseshell and timid. Nicky plumped for Lucifer who was big and black, and (so she thought) brave. Maurice and I called them "flat cats" because they never went outside the spacious, second floor flat in Shepherds Bush. They were happy though, playing with each other and rampaging through all the rooms, chasing each other under the beds and up the curtains.

This contented state of affairs continued until the cats were full grown and even Nicky's departure for the other side of the world did not unduly ruffle the smoothness of their lives. Stephanie undertook to look after Lucifer as well as Polly for the year that Nicky would be away.

It was when Lucifer slipped out one evening and did not return until the following morning that the situation became decidedly unsettled. Stephanie did not think that it was other women he was after, for he would have been a sad disappointment to them, but Polly clearly assumed the worst! From then on she persecuted him. Big though he was, his little sister bullied him to such an extent that he would not come out from under the bed either to eat his meals or to use his earth box. The position from Lucifer's point of view was miserable; from Stephanie's - intolerable.

After several expensive trans-Atlantic telephone calls, it was agreed that Lucifer should come to Buckby Wharf on condition that he came to stay for good.

"Maurice and I called them 'flat cats' ..."

It would have been unfair to him (and us) to expect him to revert to flat dwelling after an outdoor life. As a country cat he would have to take his chance with the A5 and the canal as well as the hazards of farm and field.

Stephanie and Lucifer arrived by coach in Daventry late one evening when hoar frost was sparkling on the pavements and competing with the Christmas decorations in the shop windows. He was packed in a wicker bicycle basket that was covered with chicken wire. Stephanie insisted that this Heath Robinson contraption was better than a proper cat basket (for which he was too large anyway) as he could see her all the time. Even so, he looked very scared. His normally sleek black coat was sprinkled with dandruff - a sure sign in a cat of violent emotional upset.

My intention (although it may have been going from one extreme to another) was that Lucifer should be an "outside cat". I thought that he would be less likely to suffer from the attentions of the two dogs whose incivility towards our previous feline had been marked. So we made him as comfortable as we could in the storeroom outside, buttered his paws and shut the door. Stephanie visited him frequently and he eventually calmed down but he would not come out even when the door was left open. Maybe he thought that Polly was out there - waiting to pounce!

Stephanie had to return to London after the weekend, so it was left to me to coax and cajole and generally try and persuade him that his days of persecution were over. It needed patience but it was not too difficult as beneath the dense dark fur was hidden an affectionate spirit.

Within three days of his arrival, it started to snow. The first flakes were small and gritty and took an age to clothe the ground. When they did so, the soil which had already been deeply frozen for several weeks, was insulated against any minor thaw. Thus it remained for nearly two months.

So Lucifer moved indoors. Only Stephanie was not at all surprised. She nodded when I told her (sheepishly) and said.

"I knew he'd get round you - he's good at that - and you're so soft!"

Brynne took no notice of him whatever. Her age was telling and she was too concerned with her own problems. Tansy was jealous. She growled whenever she saw him approaching but he had the sense to give her a wide berth and clearly regarded her as less of a menace than Polly. He did not go out very much for he disliked the snow and when the wind ruffled his fur he thought that it was attacking him - and shot indoors! With no soil visible in the garden, I could not really expect to train him away from his earth box at first but it did annoy me to see him come in to the house specially to use it!

It went on snowing, off and on, for a week. After each fall the sun thawed the surface and then at night it froze again so that everywhere was as slippery as glass. The A5 was cleared and gritted, but on the minor road to Long Buckby I never saw a snow plough. A Volkswagen is built for these conditions and coped quite well at first. But in Germany the winter temperature is consistently low - once it freezes at the start of winter, it does not thaw until the spring. Each fall of snow on the road is packed down by heavy wheels and a layer of grit is thrown on top. So it goes on, getting thicker and thicker but with few patches of ice.

Neither the conditions nor the remedies are as tolerable in England in my opinion. After one hairy journey at six o'clock in the morning when I was first of all forced off the road by the coach which fetched the workers for the pot-noodle factory, and later skidded on a double bend, I asked Maurice to fit chains on the rear wheels of my car. Then I negotiated the winding road with confidence, and was the envy of many a motorist as I whizzed up Station Hill past their stranded vehicles.

The pavements became more and more treacherous. The lanes in the village were pitted with deep ruts in the snow and were filmed with ice where the sun slanted. It was impossible to ride the bicycle but I needed it to carry the weight of the Christmas parcels. Laboriously, I pushed it through the soft drifts and across the crusty ridges, leant it against garden walls which were so deeply covered in snow that the handlebars disappeared from view entirely.

Some people thought it was funny when the Post Office issued us with chains for our boots, but few of them swept their paths clear of snow. Being new to the district as well as the job, I often stumbled into flower beds and rockeries as I searched for the way to the door.

The lack of consideration which many members of the community have for public employees came as a most unwelcome surprise. The extreme thoughtlessness of a few came as a bitter blow.

On one estate, almost every family owned two cars. The second one was invariably parked outside the garage and completely blocked the way to the front door. In order to get to the letter box, I either had to sidle alongside the vehicle, soaking my clothes with snow from it and from whatever grew alongside the drive or tramp across the garden. The second method attracted complaints from the irate occupants of the house, the first made me wet and miserable for the rest of the morning. One man parked his car so close to his

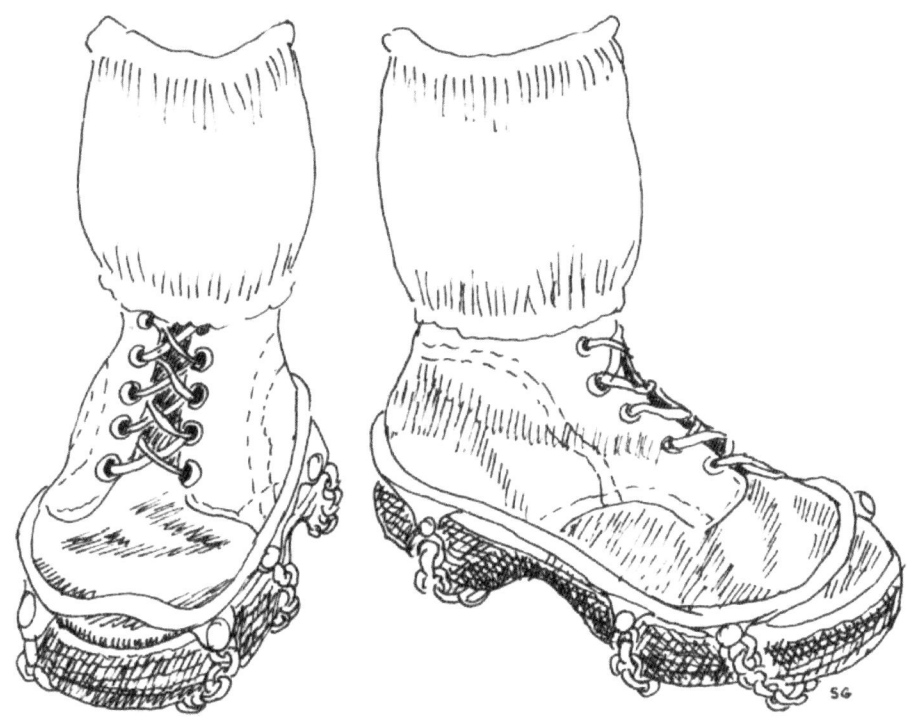

"The Post Office issued us with chains for our boots …"

rose border that although I held my breath as I squeezed past, I tore my trousers on the thorns. I smiled in spiteful malice a few mornings later when I saw that he had misjudged his parking the previous evening and squashed the offending rose bush quite flat!

It seemed obvious to me that the combined effect of the seasonal mail and the weather conditions would have made the late deliveries understandable to most reasonable people. Either I was wrong or there were a lot of unreasonable people on my "walk". It was bad enough when they grumbled to my face which happened quite often, but behind my back made me really annoyed. It was silly of them actually, because I always knew who they were (even when they smiled sweetly) and there are heaps of ways that a post-man can get his own back without breaking any rules!

The Sunday before Christmas was a day of compulsory overtime and that morning there was a terrible blizzard. The mail van was nearly an hour late and none of us were pleased to see it. If the driver had not brought the mail we should not have had to deliver it! I read later in the "Gusher" that all the Daventry postmen were told they need not go out at all. Perhaps it was just as well that I did not hear it at the time or Long Buckby might have had a mutineer on their hands!

It was hopeless attempting to push the bicycle, so I left it behind and fought my way down Station Road in the teeth of the wind with stinging snowflakes driving horizontally into my face. Halfway through the morning I met Walter crossing the market square. He asked me how I was doing.

"Terrible," I said through stiff chapped lips. "I can't open half the garden gates for drifts and it's up to my waist in front of the Court."

"You'd best call it a day, then. If you don't get in that car of yours now - you'll not get home at all."

I did get home (thanks to the chains), went to bed and slept like an exhausted child. When I awoke it was quite dark. The snow was still falling.

I think that Long Buckby must have been one of the few rural districts which did not lose a single day's delivery of mail in the winter of 1981. Left to me, it might have been different I have to admit. I am not of the same generation as Walter and Jim. They are of the old school - tough, hard-working and diligent. I did not hear them question the orders of those whom they considered to be their superiors. Me - I am argumentative. I missed them when they retired, though. The atmosphere in the sorting office changed, and not, I thought, for the better.

My sister, who lived in Nottinghamshire, was having a family gathering at Christmas and I was rather relieved not to have to make the effort to cook the meals which are traditionally expected of one during the festive season. I've always thought it silly that one compares prices and counts the pennies all year only to spend more money on an unhealthy blow-out during a couple of days than one would normally spend in a month. Perhaps one day I will have the guts to stand by my convictions!

I cannot say I remembered very much of that particular Christmas. When I was not dozing in an armchair, I was manfully trying to participate in the jollifications like a zombie on holiday! Alcohol made me more sleepy. The nicest Christmas present I could have had but no-one believed me, would have been forty-eight hours uninterrupted slumber!

We returned home on Boxing Day evening, worried about the hens and

Lucifer who were fending for themselves. We did not feel that we knew our neighbours well enough to ask them to spend some of their holiday looking after our livestock. We left two days rations for all and hoped for the best. Lucifer was fine - he had had the run of the house, unmolested, and looked positively-pleased to see us. The hens were alright, though probably a bit hungry as a fresh fall of snow had obliterated their feed trough and they had not had the wit to scratch it away. Hens are not clever. We had left the hen-house door open and were uncommonly lucky that we had not lost them all to the fox for the next day I saw his tracks encircling the house and criss-crossing the orchard. We made a nightly ritual of locking up the hens at dusk after that.

My sister had pressed on us the gift of a bantam cock and three hens. She had been persuaded to buy them from a friend of hers who bred rare and decorative fowl. Her garden, though large, was purely ornamental and chickens - even Silver Spangled Hamburgs - did not fit into her scheme of things. She would not let them range in case they scratched up her plants, and the small house and run had to be moved daily for the sake of the grass.

I found them to be a mixed blessing. It was the wrong time of year to take on more stock which would have to be fed, and these did not lay eggs in winter as a return. They did not lay much in summer either, as it turned out. Still, bantams had a good reputation for broodiness and when she offered us their little house and run too, we accepted. I asked her to get rid of the cock though, as he and Aragorn would fight. But no, when she arrived without warning early in the New Year with the whole lot in the back of her station wagon, there he was, glaring wickedly through the bars of the bantam house. Her friend who was an expert in these matters and knew better than me, had told her that two cocks were most unlikely to fight when they were ranging free in an area as large as ours.

He was wrong. At first there were mere skirmishes. Then Aragorn decided that he preferred the bantam hens to his big brown ones. Gimli, as we had named the fierce little bantam cock, grew angry. They fought to the death, which for Gimli was a bloody one.

1982 brought no noticeable improvement in the weather. Tempers were beginning to fray. Even children had seen enough of the snow. There had been six inches of ice on the canal for so long that they were careless of the dangers in their fragile playground. Beneath the bridges and wherever there was a slight stirring of the water, the ice was as thin as Edinburgh Crystal. In other places a blow with a sledge-hammer would not have shattered it. The lock neither filled nor froze because of the water constantly trickling through its leaking gates.

Owen and Iris Bryce lived on their boat called "Bix" (after the jazz-man) which had been ice-bound since the beginning of the freeze. I delivered their letters to the cabin door and they expressed their gratitude tangibly by inviting me on board one bitterly cold morning for a steaming mug of coffee and homemade biscuits. With my fingers and toes coming back to life beside their stove, I listened to their tale.

They had moored their boat alongside the cottage of some friends, not intending to stay for more than a few days. The night before they meant to leave there was a hard frost, not severe enough to freeze the whole canal but just the short exposed stretch between the boat and the sheltered bend below the lock. Owen tried to break the ice with a long boat-shaft but only managed to make a small hole or two. They attempted to use "Bix" as an ice-breaker boat, ramming the frozen surface with the bow and moved a couple of yards but no more. The next night was milder so they tried to be patient until the ice thawed. After two days it had melted considerably but it was still hard going, so Owen decided to wait for one more day. It was a mistake. During the night a sudden drop in temperature caused an even fiercer frost that confined "Bix" as if in clamps of iron. That had been three weeks before and there was no sign of a change in the situation.

Iris told me that they did not really mind being frozen in as it happened nearly every winter and they were used to it. Usually they had the foresight to be stuck near a bus stop or a railway station. This time they had been taken unawares. I think it was a launderette she hankered after most of all! The previous day, apparently, a British Waterways Board official had marched up to "Bix" and banged loudly on the cabin roof to attract their attention.

"It's time you moved this bloody boat out," he barked, "you've been here too long already!"

I did not get the impression that Iris and Owen actually fell about laughing but I thought it was quite funny really.

A converted ice-breaker could have obvious advantages for the full-time boat dweller. The craft were sharply pointed fore and aft and were originally horse drawn. Several men would rock the boat vigorously from side to side as the horse inched forward, dragging the vessel through the cracking ice. Thus a passage was cleared for the loaded boats - until the channel froze again.

We were tempted to buy an old ice-breaker (appropriately named "Scott") before we bought "Iona". "Scott" had a wooden hull too, but it was strengthened with strips of iron at each of its pointed ends. An engine had already been installed and living accommodation (of a sort) erected.

There was one beautifully panelled cabin in which the owner (a mature bachelor) had built a massive king-size double bed surrounded by fitted stereo cabinets. Nothing else! No galley and no space left for one. The mod-cons were restricted to a wash basin with no water and a "bucket and chuck it" reposing in the engine room! The asking price was high although dismantling the owner's handiwork would have been nearly as expensive as starting from scratch with an unconverted boat. The manager of the boat-yard where it was berthed was unable to track down the owner's whereabouts that we might negotiate a deal. It was a shame because "Scott" lay there for months becoming more and more derelict. Presumably it was sold eventually, because we have seen it recently on the waterways, looking trim and freshly painted. I would love to know what the interior is like now. Has it been altered or is another Don Juan cruising the canals and breaking hearts as easily as his boat can break the ice?

The noise that a steel hulled boat makes as it moves through unbroken thin ice is eerie. It sings. I am not sure whether it is caused by reverberation from the first shattering crack of the bow or the sound of the splintered ice rubbing along the side of the metal hull. The singing has a weird extra-terrestrial note which I fancy might sound like the so-called "music of the spheres".

To stand on the bow of the boat is fascinating. As the stem of the hull splits an unbroken sheet of ice, a crack runs forward like a living thing. It zig-zags ahead of the boat and faster, seeking out weaknesses in the ice plate caused by debris which had been floating on the surface before the water froze. As the boat carves its way forward, jagged chunks of ice slide sideways like daggers, quite capable of piercing the hull of a fibreglass boat if one should be unfortunate enough to be moored nearby.

Burst water pipes were common that winter and we were no exception. The first one made its appearance during the same brief thaw which the Bryces had mentioned. Since then Maurice had protected the vulnerable plumbing of the outside lavatory with a paraffin heater that he lit every night.

One evening in early January, the temperature fell sharply to (as we learnt the next day) a record low and he went out to light the heater at about nine o'clock. We will never know exactly what happened but we think that Brynne must have slipped out behind him, unseen in the dark. Her bed was in a dim corner of the shop near the stove and she had been asleep in her basket a short while before; he never thought to check on her when he came in as most of her time she spent sleeping. It was not until he called her to come outside with Tansy for their routine nightly exodus that he realised she was missing.

Since our move to the Wharf we had not worried too much about the dogs getting out of the garden. Neither of them were young and they had ceased to be wanderers. They were accustomed to canals and it was many years since they had fallen in the water when we were boating. In any case, with a canal frontage as long as ours, it would have been impossible to prevent a determined dog from escaping onto the towpath. The biggest danger was the A5 and until that day they had shown no inclination to stray further than the front of the pub where they scrounged crisps and peanuts.

But Brynne's behaviour on this particular day had not followed its usual pattern. She had trotted off in different directions, not once but four or five times and even along the main road. Each time we had rescued her before disaster struck. Until now.

We put on boots and anoraks and searched the garden, the orchard, the towpath and the road. By eleven o'c1ock she still had not been found.

"Go to bed, Mum," insisted Bruce, "you've got to get up at half-past five - I haven't. I'll find her, don't worry."

He did find her, within a few minutes. Bruce did what I had not had the courage to do; he shone the torch down onto the dark water at the bottom of the lock.

Much later, after Bruce had descended the slippery iron ladder into the clock while Maurice held the torch and I had shivered in my dressing gown by the door, clutching a towel in the forlorn hope that she might still be alive, we stood talking and grieving in the kitchen. I wanted to give Bruce something - a token, I suppose, of my recognition of a strength of character which I had not known he possessed.

"Would you like a beer?" I asked. He nodded.

"There isn't any." He said flatly.

"Yes, there is." I reached up to the top of the kitchen cupboard and took down a pack of Marston's Royal Lager, brewed in honour of the Royal Wedding the previous July.

The following morning, while I was busy delivering Her Majesty's Mail, Maurice and Bruce buried Brynne in a small grave beyond a ridge in the garden. They had to use a blow-lamp to thaw the ground and even after the next fall of snow and many after that, I could still see the indentations of their footsteps and the spade. It was not until the spring when the snow melted and the grass grew fresh and green over the grave that I was able to push the unhappy event to the back of my mind.

    Bruce was glad when term started and he could go back to Oxford. It was his first direct contact with the death of a loved one and it had been a shock. Once back at college with his work and his friends he knew that he would think of the episode but rarely. I knew that it had changed him. He had grown up.

-8-
Boats and Pieces

February is a depressing month, I think, and March only marginally less so. By February, the Christmas and New Year festivities are merely memories or an overdraft. Spring seems to be aeons away. If one has the cash and the inclination it is a good month to spend on the ski slopes of one of the countries which are in the happy position of having sunshine and snow at the same time. I lost the inclination when I broke my leg halfway down an Austrian mountain so I did not regret that at Buckby Wharf there were more important things on which to spend our cash.

Besides, in 1982 I felt different. February was delightful. It was bliss to be able to whizz along the roads and pavements with the mail, unhindered by ice and snow. It was exciting to notice the first shoots of spring appearing here and there in other people's gardens which were more sheltered than our own. There were snowdrops growing wild along the grass verges at the Wharf, nodding their graceful heads next to the two post boxes that I cleared every morning and on the wall of the former post-office shone a profusion of yellow winter jasmine.

No boats were moving on the canal for the Buckby flight of locks was closed for routine maintenance. Balks of timber (known as "stop planks") had been dropped into slots in the canal walls above the top lock to retain the water there. The rest was drained away down the flight until all seven locks were empty. In the lock-pounds only a trickle of water flowed between the banks of evil smelling mud that sloped up on either side. Local fishermen rescued bucketfuls of suffocating fish which they transferred to the water that was dammed above the stop planks.

I watched two British Waterways men replacing stones in the tumble-down canal wall at the very spot where "Bix" had been frozen in. The weak sunshine had inspired one of them to strip off his shirt. He'll be itching tonight, I thought, looking at the cloud of midges dancing in the sunlight around him.

Suddenly, everyone I spoke to was cheerful. It was not that the weather was specially good for February but by comparison with the previous two months, it just seemed wonderful to us all. The ground had been hidden for so long that I found myself taking particular notice of everything I saw. Clumps of willows growing along the canal bank were already showing their downy white catkins and small furled violet leaves were pushing their way through the leaf mould. As I strode home along the towpath, swinging an almost empty mailbag, I saw a thrush sitting on the bare hawthorn twigs of the farmyard hedge with pieces of straw in its beak. Close against the Watling Street bridge the catkins on a group of alders glowed red.

Pushing open the white wicket gate and walking round the shop to the back door, I glanced affectionately at our latest acquisition - sheep. To be exact, two ewes in lamb of a breed known as the Jacob.

With the smell of spring in the air, Maurice had firmly stated that something would have to be done about the grass. I absolutely agreed. We had both spent a disproportionate amount of time on a very unrewarding task. Action must be taken before the wretched stuff began to grow. We were unanimous on that.

Clearly, recycling the grass (through a stomach) would be more sensible and more interesting than investing in yet another expensive cutting machine. We debated all sorts of possibilities, poring over innumerable books from the library as we examined each idea that popped out of our heads.

Maurice fancied keeping goats but I was not keen on them. They are not hardy animals and would need warm, draught-proof winter quarters. A nanny goat would have to be milked twice daily, every day, and I knew who would end up doing that! They are also browsers rather than grazers which would probably mean that they would leave the grass and eat the hedges and trees. A goat is a genius at escaping unless it is tethered and I foresaw all my flowers and vegetables being recycled into milk as well!

Geese were a possibility and we have not entirely discounted that idea. They make good "watch dogs" as I learnt painfully when I was delivering letters to a house at the other end of the Wharf. The gander's owner excused the bird's ill temper by telling me that a fox had recently killed the goose and he was pining for his mate. The Co-op milkman, who delivered there too, said:

"Don't you believe it! He was just as mean before - I've got scars to prove it!"

On second thoughts, I think geese are out as lawn mowers! But not wanting to admit my cowardice, I put a good case against them to Maurice on the grounds that they were bound to go swimming in the canal where they might get run down by a boat or poached for someone's Christmas dinner.

"You'll have to dig them a pond," I said slyly, knowing that I had played my trump card.

In the end we decided on sheep. They would nibble the grass beautifully short and leave the fruit trees alone. Hm! One glance at the de-barked apple trees will tell you that we were wrong on one count. But we were right about the rest. As ruminants, they are particularly good at recycling grass and garden waste. Their droppings have been through so many stomachs that they do not smell unpleasant and they spread it evenly themselves, treading it in with dainty feet. We are pleased to have them.

I wanted to have Jacob's sheep for I am a bit of a romantic at heart. They are creamy coloured, distinctively spotted with dark brown, and usually have two pairs of curved horns. It is an ancient breed for whose history one has to go as far back as the Book of Genesis.

Jacob went to work as a shepherd for Laban on the understanding that after seven years he would be given Laban's beautiful younger daughter as his wife. But Laban cheated and gave him Leah, the elder daughter, promising him Rachel only after he had served him for another seven years. When Jacob had worked for fourteen years without wages, greatly increasing Laban's flock, he wanted to return home with his two wives.

"I will pass through all thy flock today, removing from thence all the speckled and spotted . . . among the sheep . . . and of such shall be my hire," he said to Laban, who instantly agreed and almost as quickly double-crossed him by giving all the mottled beasts to his own sons.

There is an old wives tale that one should take care what one's pedigree stock is looking at while they are mating. Jacob took advantage of it. Having peeled scraps of bark from branches and twigs to give a spotted effect, he stuck them in the ground around the water trough during the breeding season. Many of the offspring were mottled. For several seasons Jacob repeated the experiment, breeding only from the best. Eventually he returned home with a large flock of healthy, hardy animals - all speckled.

I was not being entirely romantic in wanting to have Jacob's sheep, for they really are hardy. Not only that, they have useful fleeces and the meat is sweet and lean. We asked around and learnt that a neighbour owned a small flock of Jacob's sheep which grazed the meadow around his boatyard at Weltonfield. Hugh agreed to sell us two ewes and suggested that we left them to run with a ram that he had rented for his other ewes. The thought of lambing made me gulp (Maurice flatly refused to make any promises to help in the mid-wifery) as there are heaps of things that can go wrong at lambing time. But Judy, Hugh's wife, jollied me along with the reassurance that our two ewes were experienced mothers with no history of trouble.

As soon as the snow had melted, Hugh had brought the two skittish goat-like creatures over to us in his horse box. They settled down quickly and looked perfectly at home in our orchard. When they arrived they were stained with raddle (a dye put on the chest of the ram) and before many weeks had passed they looked noticeably fatter. I was sure that they were in lamb.

"Don't worry," said Chris, the milkman. "Give me a ring if you have any trouble and I'll come over. You'll need a little old shed for them to lamb in, though."

We did not even have a lean-to in the orchard and we did not really want to buy a little new shed just then. So we compromised by setting two sheep folds, which are like low fence panels, across a corner of the hedge to give extra shelter from the wind. We might as well have saved ourselves the money and the effort for the ewes never went near them. I had decided on names for the sheep even before they came. We called them Rachel and Leah. Their markings and horns were so distinctive that they were easy to tell apart. I thought they added a touch of class to the garden.

With canal traffic at a standstill, trade in the shop almost ground to a halt. Customers from the road were a rarity. We blamed the District Council for that.

Some time at the tail end of the previous season I had found pasted onto our two roadside sandwich boards a couple of sheets of paper covered in typescript. We were informed that we had no right to put the signs there and if they caused an accident we would be held responsible. Furthermore, we should remove them forthwith.

We were not the only ones to have been so honoured. "Weltonfields boats" sported a similar message and so did "The New Inn". According to the regional news there was a positive epidemic of the typed sheets throughout the East Midlands!

I could not believe that our sandwich boards (which fell flat at the first breath of wind) were more likely to cause an accident than the huge hoardings dominating urban highways, but being law abiding citizens we removed our boards from the roadside. Our trade from the A5 died an immediate death.

As the weeks went by, we began to get really worried. I decided to write to the planning department and appeal to their sense of responsibility to local traders. My letter was most polite in explaining our predicament and describing the signs and their late position. All it achieved was an equally courteous reply. Or did it? I read their letter again carefully. It was their policy to resist the erection of such signs. "Resist" not "forbid". Well I reckoned that I had unscrambled enough red tape in the past to recognise a bureaucratic weakness when I saw one.

"I don't believe they have the legal powers to enforce the removal of signs," I said to Maurice, "if they had - mark my words - they would have said so!"

"Could be," he nodded, "I think I'll put them back." .

"Let me paint some roses on them first," I said mischievously, "to make them more eye-catching! "

It seemed a good opportunity, while the shop was so quiet, to think over the first year in business and do our sums. Not as good as we had hoped was what the account books told us, but not bad either. At least until Blisworth Tunnel reopened, we needed a complementary income if we were not to drain away our precious capital. I sighed. It looked as if I was stuck with the Post Office. Thank goodness I had the summer to look forward to, anyway.

The news about Blisworth Tunnel was dismal. A promising announcement by the British Waterways Board early in 1981 had not borne fruit, neither had another one made in the summer. There were pessimists among the waterways fraternity who were sceptical of the tunnel ever being reopened for navigation. For our own piece of mind we were determined not to admit to that possibility, but the thought lurked there in the shadows all the time. And what if something happened to close Braunston and Crick tunnels to the north of us as well? We would be marooned. Finished.

The February edition of the waterways magazine told us that the British Waterways Board were proceeding with investigations to assess the work necessary in Blisworth Tunnel. The probable method of repair would cost four and a quarter million pounds and take about two years. A start could be made by mid 1982. Humph! Had we not heard this refrain before?

I have a friend who maintains that if there is a problem over which he has no control he does not allow himself to worry about it. A sensible philosophy, but one that is easier to preach than follow, I suspect. Well, I had written to my Member of Parliament and we continuously supported a waterways pressure group. It was out of our hands. Our best course was to forget the tunnel and devote all our energies into increasing turnover and keeping ourselves afloat.

Boats meant customers: lack of boats meant loss of trade. So - was there any way in which we could increase the number of boats that passed the shop? One way would be to encourage people from the north to come down to Northampton and cruise the River Nene from its link there with the canal. Indeed, downstream on the river, at Peterborough, it was possible to enter the Middle Levels (the navigable drains of East Anglia) and from thence the River Great Ouse and the River Cam from which the university town gets its name.

It used to be simple to take a boat onto the River Nene. From Gayton junction, just north of Blisworth, one dropped steeply down through seventeen locks to Northampton where it was possible to obtain, for a small deposit, a key to unlock the gear on the river locks. Nothing else was needed.

Then came a massive re-organisation of water authorities and at the same time the lock-keeper who issued the river keys retired. Not only that, but a licence became a prerequisite of obtaining a key and both were only obtainable from the Anglian Water Authority in Oundle. In advance, of course.

We had listened to so many talks of woe from boaters who had painstakingly traversed the Northampton Arm and knocked at the door of the little toll-house to be met by a shake of the head. Angry and disappointed, they were unlikely to cruise our way again in a hurry.

Perhaps we could make it easier for everybody and do ourselves a good turn at the same time?

I wrote to the Anglian Water Authority and offered to sell navigational licences and provide lock keys for the River Nene on their behalf. They seemed pleased with the idea, admitting they knew of the difficulties (I should think that their telephone line must have been red-hot) and said that a Mr Fred Martin would call on us nearer the start of the season to discuss it. We nearly had second thoughts when Mr Martin told us how much red tape and form-filling there would be, but we do not as a rule give up easily (as you have probably noticed) and in view of the princely sum of fifty pence commission they promised to pay us for each transaction, we went ahead.

In anticipation of all the boats which were going to come flocking down from the north, we ordered scores of charts covering the Fenland waters. Then, because Maurice likes maps, we opened an account with Ordnance Survey so that we could stock those as well.

We hit a few snags in the arrangement at first, but Mr Martin helped us iron them out. I wrote to many of the hire boat firms and the waterways magazines telling them of our new service; gradually the word got round about it and only a few unhappy boaters knock at the toll-house door in vain nowadays. It increased our trade marginally, mainly through the sale of maps and charts, but it did a lot for our morale in helping to entrench us more firmly in the waterways scene.

What else could we do? We had received many requests for beer and wine, and considered the possibility of applying for an off-licence. The landlady of the New Inn naturally enough took a dim view of that, so in the interests of good neighbourly relations we shelved the idea for the time being, and decided to expand the gift side of the business. Unhappily we had become thoroughly disillusioned with groceries although we had no intention of discontinuing them entirely. But it was hopeless trying to compete with the supermarkets and pointless to keep ourselves stocked up during the winter with perishable items on the off-chance that one of the locals might run out of self-raising flour or cornflakes.

There was a limit to the amount of painted ware that I could produce and be a postwoman at the same time. What we needed were gifts of good quality that were unique to our shop. Fudge was the first thing I thought of because I have a passion for it myself - especially the homemade crunchy sort. Fudge in personalised packages.

"Hm!" said Maurice when I told him, "you'll get fat as a pig!"

"Nonsense! I've far too much self control. We could use the drawing I did for the postcards and the peppermint rock labels."

The pen and ink sketch of the cottage and shop with the lock in the foreground has become almost a "house logo" now, decorating notelets and writing paper — even match boxes. Surprisingly, it did not take long to track down a confectioner who made the most delicious fudge. He was pleased to pack it in small bags with header cards printed to my design that could be displayed on his handmade wooden counter stand. Secretly I was amazed at my self restraint. After sharing one of the first bags of fudge with Bruce, I have not touched another piece since!

The International Spring Fair is held in February at the National Exhibition Centre near Birmingham. This is a trade fair which concentrates on gifts. One or two of our existing suppliers had written advising us where their stands could be found at the Spring Fair, so we went along in search of new ideas. We had never been to anything quite like it before. It was vast.

There were five halls with over a hundred and fifty stands in each. Thank goodness that only two of the halls contained products which interested us. Even so, our feet were aching and our heads were spinning by the time we had walked round all the stands, pausing frequently to have a discussion with the

"Almost our 'house logo' now ..."

various representatives.

There was no shortage of ideas. The main drawback was the extent of the order demanded by many wholesalers. Two hundred pounds was not unusual for a minimum requirement, which is a lot of gifts of one sort at a few pence each. Still, I scribbled furiously in a notebook and underlined names in the catalogue energetically, and for good measure agreed to be visited by a whole galaxy of salesmen. In the event, very few of them followed it up - perhaps they had a sixth sense which whispered that we were unlikely to give them a substantial order. They could have been right but I would have thought it was worth a try. Even the ideas about which we were positively enthusiastic turned out to be hard to put into practice.

For instance, on one of the greetings card stands we spied a postcard that we wanted very much. It was both colourful and humorous without being bawdy. Delicately executed in pen and wash (captioned "Enjoying the peace of the inland waterways"), it depicted a narrow boat firmly embedded in the canal bank and surrounded by every noisy and irritating hazard which could be encountered on a boating holiday! There was a big demand for postcards, and

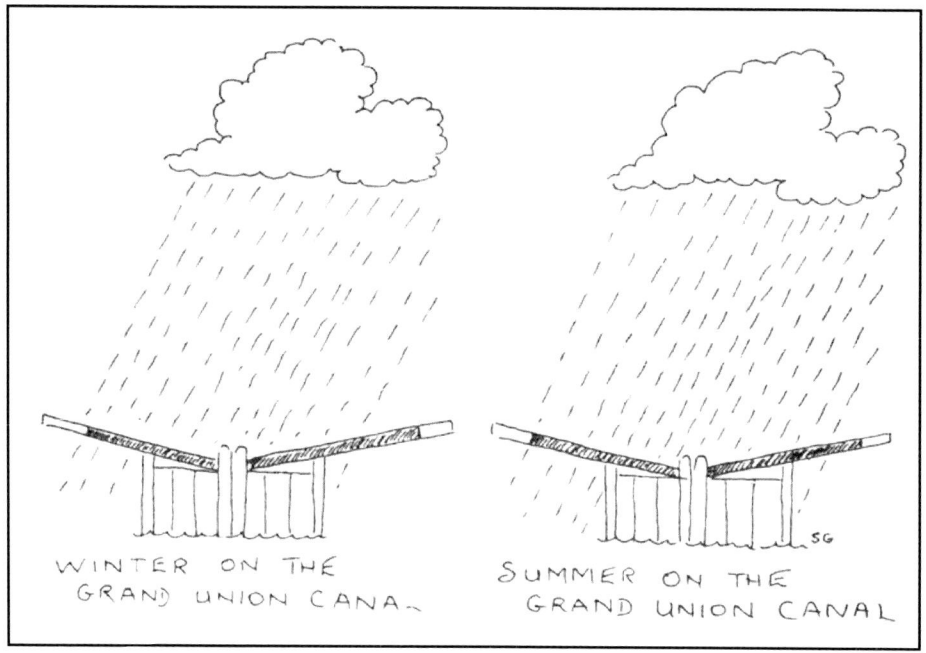

" I designed my own funny postcard ..."

as all our present ones were either conventional views or photographs of traditional working boats, this one would complement the range very nicely. The representative on the stand at the Spring Fair was most helpful in giving us all the details of the transaction and promised us a visit from the salesman within a fortnight to process the order.

It seemed incredible at a time when Britain was floundering in the depths of a recession, but in spite of our best efforts on the telephone and on paper, it was nearly a year and just before the next Spring Fair that our first delivery of those postcards arrived! The theme of this tale is not unique and in some cases we got tired of waiting and found alternatives. That postcard wholesaler not only lost a complete season's trade to us (at least a thousand cards), but he also reduced the size of our future orders. So irritated was I by the delay that I designed my own funny postcard and took it to a local printer. It was well established and selling fast by the time the others arrived, and has continued to sell in competition (with a greater profit) ever since!

The lethargy of these British businessmen showed a marked contrast with their Far Eastern counterparts with whom we came into contact at about the same time.

Wooden spoons painted with roses on a dark background are one of our most popular gifts. I cannot think why - they are utterly useless - but that is a fact. Kitchen spoons are usually waxed and do not take paint. That we had learnt by experience. Unwaxed spoons are hard to find and there were none at the Spring Fair. My nephew, who travelled widely, gave us the name of the Taiwan trade representative in London. A quick telephone call from Maurice and within a short while we were inundated with letters and brochures from Taiwan offering us the most competitive terms for every sort of wooden ware that it is possible to imagine. The letters were a delight to read. Without exception we were "much esteemed" and they were "highly honoured" to deal with us. One company informed us that we were the leading importer of wooden spoons in the United Kingdom which was a slight exaggeration!

All the correspondence was addressed to "Ginger's Channel Store, Top Rock", which foxed us until we remembered that Maurice had given the address over the telephone. I laughed when Walter said, as the sorting office overflowed with airmail envelopes,

"Where's the lighthouse, Shirley?"

We still receive the Taiwan trade journal every quarter and I have enough wooden spoons to last me a lifetime!

I cursed myself for not keeping a record of the painted ware that we sold during our first season. I had to rely on memory and mine is more fallible than most. The trouble was that I had been racing to keep up with demand. I resolved to do better in future - or is that the way to Hell?

We knew that teapots, coffee pots, enamel mugs and tobacco tins had sold well and we could check the first three against the invoices for the unpainted goods. But tobacco tins had cost us nothing. It was guesswork. Maurice had been an inveterate pipe smoker for years and never threw away a tin if he could avoid it - storing them away like a magpie. We must have sold a fair number for the supply was nearly exhausted (discounting those in which he kept nails and screws). I needed more than he could smoke.

"What about offering to swap a box of Swan matches for every tobacco tin in good condition?" I suggested.

"Good idea - pipe smokers hate throwing away their tins."

"You don't have to tell me that! And if you're anything to go by - they smoke as many matches as tobacco, so we'll be doing them a service."

He looked affronted but ignored my remark, saying,

"And if they don't want matches, we could offer them a packet of crisps or even ten pence - if we're pushed."

We were pleasantly surprised at the response. The "Object" soon filled up with cardboard boxes full of gleaming tobacco tins waiting to be decorated with roses and daisies. One school teacher had her whole class collecting in aid of the school fund, and several pipe smokers developed a habit of travelling along the A5 at regular intervals so that they could drop off a carrier bag full of tins in exchange for the next few months supply of matches.

I was constantly on the look-out for novel articles to paint, particularly if they were cheap, or better still - came free. Empty bottles painted up most attractively, especially those whose contents had originally been expensive; squat liqueur bottles in rich brown, smoky green Remy Martin bottles, tall textured cylinders aptly named Black Tower and slender graceful shapes in clear glass that had once held Galliano. All these were likely candidates for my paintbrush.

I passed the word around my affluent relatives and hard-drinking ex-army friends, even the cocktail conscious younger generation. Soon we had a plentiful supply. Bottles are fun to paint. As they cost nothing, one can let the brush have its fling and experiment with bold new designs. It always works. The flowers seem to glow against the rich glass backgrounds. I arranged the painted bottles along the top shelf of the shop window with a huge one-gallon Bell's whisky flagon as a centrepiece and the colourful display could be seen clearly from the other side of the lock.

Maurice bought the heavy one and two gallon Buckby Cans that we used from another member of his chess club. Colin was a tinsmith and took great pride in the manufacture of his cans. They were made of galvanised tin which would not rust if the cans were used for their original purpose - that of carrying drinking water on the roof of a narrow boat. It is difficult to get enough cans because they need a good deal of hand finishing by the tinsmith. Colin is one of the few who still make them and goodness knows what we will do when he retires. He threatens to - all the time!

I was surprised at the large number of Buckby Cans that we had sold during the year, for when one adds the hours of work to the cost of the specially made can, they are expensive to retail. Occasionally, people jibbed at the price. I usually shrank out of sight when that happened because Maurice would say severely,

"Would you work for less than a pound an hour? That's what my wife does - selling a Buckby Can at that price! Have you any idea how many hours of work there are there?"

They had not, of course, and sometimes looked sheepish although they never bought a can on that account. It made Maurice feel better though. Artists and craftsmen are rarely paid a fair price for their work and it annoys him as much as it does me. And yet the days are past when one was expected to work for love and starve in a garret, surely? I could paint faster than I do, I admit: if I thinned the enamel, painted bigger roses and half the number, left out all the finishing details that take so much time, and (Oh! Horrors!) painted every can exactly the same as each other - then I would be quick. What is the point? I might as well be putting nuts on bolts in front of a conveyor belt. So I am painting for love, in a way, except that nowadays it is called "job satisfaction". Times do not change for the artist.

A register of painted ware would be the best way of keeping a check on myself, with each item entered as I finished it. A quick calculation at the end of each season would demonstrate how many had been sold and roughly how many I ought to paint during the winter in preparation for the following year. If I had known what a daunting prospect that would turn out to be, I might have had second thoughts about keeping a record at all but it did make our annual stock-taking easier when it came to the end of the financial year.

That was when we had a nasty shock! Not (as you might think) because we had done so badly, but because we had done better than we thought. We had failed to notice that our turnover had risen above the minimum required by law to register for Value Added Tax.

"Oh, Lord," groaned Maurice, "we should have registered in October!"

"Never mind, I don't suppose they'll send us to prison - we ought to be pleased that we've done well enough - do you remember that chap in Brum who fancied himself as a tycoon? He told me before we moved here that if we didn't have to register for V.A.T. in our first year we'd got problems."

"He was probably right and we may actually gain to begin with as we can claim V.A.T. back on purchases. It'll mean a lot of extra work, though."

"It's a closed book to me. I don't know what you're talking about," I said gloomily. "Do you suppose they'll show me how to do it?"

"I can show you," said Maurice.

"That's what I'm afraid of - I've never forgotten your attempts to teach me to drive. You seem to think that the louder you shout the more easily I'll understand. I was nearly deaf by the time I took my test!"

The inspector from Customs and Excise, when she arrived at our request, was quite understanding about our oversight. Her main problem seemed to be in fitting us into one of the special schemes for retailers. None of them were tailor-made for our set of circumstances. To use modern jargon - we were deviants. In fact, I think that it was the visit from the V.A.T. Inspector and her wide-eyed amazement at our set-up that inspired me to think about writing a book. I had never before considered that we might be oddities! She spent the greater part of a morning with us. Once or twice she thought that she had got it sorted, then we mentioned something that we made or grew or embellished and she sighed and began again. Eventually she allocated us to a scheme that involved me in hours and hours of extra book-keeping which I resent. Not that I blamed her - I just wish the government would undertake its own work in collecting my taxes.

We still had the Inland Revenue to contend with, so Maurice went into Daventry to search for the financial wizard who had been recommended to us by the coal merchant. The accountant's eyes sparkled at the thought of a battle with the tax office on our behalf and he turned out to be every bit as good as we had been told, winning tax repayments for us on grounds which we never knew existed. I began to see the attraction of a profession which I had always thought of as rather dry and fusty.

Stock-taking takes place on the anniversary of our start in business and always comes at an awkward time - slap in the middle of the school Easter holidays. We realised even before the time came to do it that we could not afford to shut the shop, even for half a day. If one's trade depends on tourists, every penny has to be squeezed out of the holiday seasons. It had not taken more than one winter to teach us that! Maurice hit on the notion of counting everything a few days before the schools broke up and amending the list every time he made a sale. It was tricky but he did it. I was not much help as British Telecom chose that precise time to issue the new edition of Yellow Pages. I think I had about two hundred and forty to deliver on my "walk". They were heavy and I could only manage to carry ten at a time on the front of the bicycle with safety. That was without any parcels. By the time I reached home, counting wooden spoons was definitely not at the top of my list of priorities.

Easter Saturday marked the beginning of a whole week's holiday from the Post Office. I lay in bed feeling wonderfully lazy until eight o'clock. I had woken at dawn, of course, out of habit. One minute perhaps, or two, and I was snoring again (according to Maurice) until the clang of windlasses on the metal lock beam beneath the window sang out the beginning of the boating day.

"Gardening leave" was the name it used to be given in the army, when one did not go away but pottered about at home. For me, that is exactly what it was. I intended to sow in the vegetable plot all the crops which were not already germinating in trays on every windowsill. We had other plans for the garden, too. Nothing to do with self-sufficiency and absolutely uneconomic, we wanted to develop a small part of it as a habitat for wildlife. Not at all pretentious, just a few patches uncultivated and unmanicured so that (with a bit of encouragement) our natural flora and even fauna could survive and multiply.

There was a dearth in our immediate vicinity, of copses in which small mammals could take refuge and wild birds feed on the myriad creepy-crawlies that are an essential part of their diet. A bird table, however well spread with goodies, is not enough. There are few old pastures untouched by plough and harrow, unsprayed by pesticides, fungicides, herbicides, in which wild flowers, grasses and fungi can grow and set their seeds or fling their spores.

I admit that I was not anxious to encourage wild creatures to use my vegetable plot as their dinner table, or my poultry house as their larder. I get impatient with some naturalists who try to persuade us to turn our gardens into nature reserves, never spraying or dusting or weeding. Do they eschew fruit and vegetables as part of their own diet, I wonder, or do they buy top quality produce from the greengrocer and thus let someone else do their dirty work? Maybe we were over-ambitious in trying to achieve two apparently opposite goals. We shall see.

You may think that creating a wild garden is easy. All one has to do is - nothing. That might be true if the garden already has the makings of a natural jungle growing in it. Except for potatoes, nothing much had ever been planted in ours. I thought that I might learn a few lessons about native woodland if I explored Cornerhill Spinney, a little wood not far away on the other side of the main line of the Grand Union Canal. The spinney tumbles own the western side of an embankment which carries the Leicester line of the canal round a sharp right hand bend from Norton junction. It was well named Cornerhill.

The wood is triangular in shape; the base runs along the side of the canal, sweeping the water with the willows and alders at its edge; scrubby hawthorns clung to the apex which jutted into the field below. In between the two, the steep slope supported tall, round-headed sycamore trees interspersed with huge dead elms, pale against the grey sky. Several of the elm trees had fallen and long white branches pointed across the canal like skeletal fingers. The prostrate trunks were thickly matted with glossy green ivy, whose tentacles were already seeking out young saplings of sycamore and ash to carry them towards the sky again. Even in early spring, the decaying undergrowth and mouldering wood was alive with colonies of woodlice and beetles. The bare branches and twigs trembled and rustled with the passage of birds seeking food. A robin perched on the bleached parasol of a wild parsnip seedhead, its beady eyes watching me while it shrewdly waited to forage among the dead leaves scuffled by my boots.

In the outward corners of the triangle there were smaller trees growing, mostly hawthorn, hazel and young oaks. Beneath them, long brambles lay like snares hidden by ghostly nets of silvery goosegrass. One dome of briars was enveloped in a goosegrass snood and round about it the soft earth showed the tracks of rabbit feet. Was Brer Fox nearby too, I wondered, keeping watch on the rabbit's den? We could do without him paying us a visit!

On the rim of the spinney and at the edge of the field grew clumps of thistles over which a group of goldfinches were busy working to extract the last few remaining seeds that had not been blown away by the wind on their parachutes of fluffy silk. As I walked past, the birds twittered off in a cloud of colour and settled on another patch of thistles to continue feeding while I carried on across the field to the canal bridge.

Well, what had I learnt? A wood is made up of tiers of growth. On the ground lay fallen leaves and rotting timber threaded with the filaments of fungi and seething with insect life. Out of the soil grew annual plants which flowered and set their seed in the same year, and some perennials that spread by root and sucker as well as seed. The middle tier was made up of young saplings and shrubby growth with autumn berries and nuts. At the highest level there were tall trees, a haven for all sorts of birds, and more nuts for squirrels.

For my wild garden, the major problem was going to be the top tier, for apart from the orchard (which was not part of our conservation plan) we had very few mature trees of any height. Trees were part of my planting programme but it would be years before they would signify. The crab apples and the rowan, which had seemed enormous when I bought them and stuck yards out of the rear window of the car, looked as if they had shrunk once they were planted.

However, we did have a sixty year old thorn hedge surrounding almost the whole of our property. Excluding the orchard, there were fifty yards of hedgerow between ourselves and the neighbouring field. On our side there was a ten yard wide strip of turf which had probably not been disturbed for sixty years either. (We could see where the edge of the potato patch had been, for the turf must have been stacked in a long ridge which was still there.)

Having discounted the length of hedge alongside the drive, which was too close to the pub car-park and the road to be much use as a wild garden, we made our plans. Twenty-five by ten yards of ancient hedge and turf were to be the base from which we worked.

Judicious pruning of the hedge, sufficient only to prevent it becoming top-heavy, left one young alder tree growing above it. So we had four trees altogether - all of them youthful and spindly. Hardly a dense forest! Five sparrows looking for a perch and there would be an argument!

I remembered a tip about woodland gardens in Philip and Marjorie Blamey's beautiful book "Flowers of the Countryside". They suggested that for quick results, three Silver Birch trees should be planted eighteen inches apart to form a triangle. A mini-spinney in fact. I was not quite bold enough to plant the trees as close together as that, but I managed to put them two feet apart without a qualm. Then I copied Cornerhill's layers of growth by planting Hazel bushes around the birches and a Guelder Rose, with several Dogwoods in between. Lastly, to the floor of my spinney, I transplanted from other parts of the garden, flowers which would flourish in the half shade - violets, primroses and celandines. Many more would arrive unbidden, I was quite sure. A few dead branches sneaked from Maurice's wood pile completed my efforts. Nothing more needed to be done until late September when the seeds would have set. Then the grass should be cut and cleared to let in light and air.

"You can come and admire the spinney now," l called to Maurice when I had finished."

Any stranger glancing over the hedge just then, might have looked askance at the odd couple who were standing, arm in arm in the cold drizzling rain, smiling at a scattering of bare twigs sticking out of circles of brown earth and surrounded by straggling unmown grass. A casual spectator could not have known that we were visualising a meadow full of wild flowers and a little spinney busy with birds feeding on insects and other invertebrates and with small mammals scratching about on the woodland floor. Such is the power of the gardener's imagination!

-9-
Spring Greens

I was busy serving in the shop and Maurice had gone up to the orchard to collect the eggs and give the ewes their evening meal of concentrated feed. It had been a good day; a fine and sunny Bank Holiday with plenty of gongoozlers. My watch said five o'clock. The shop was still crammed with customers and I knew that my smile had become fixed and was probably more like a grimace. A woman (who appeared to own hoards of children) was coming to the end of a long grocery order. At the same time the kids clamoured for ice-cream and sweets, leaning far over the counter and kicking the front of it with what sounded like hobnail boots. She managed to turn a deaf ear which was more than I could do. Lucifer was forcefully weaving back and forth against my legs to remind me that it was his teatime and Tansy was dancing about on her hind legs trying to attract the attention of a small boy who was eating a Kit-Kat. I lost count of which of the two animals I tripped over most often! Fraught was the only way to describe my frame of mind.

Maurice came in and said something to me very quietly. Not unnaturally, I could not hear him above the din. He raised his voice to parade-ground level.

"Would you like to go and see Rachel's lambs?"

"Gosh! Not really? Are they alright? Is she alright?"

Without waiting for an answer to any of my questions, I turned back to the customer, anxious to end the transaction so that I could hot-foot it up to the orchard to see Rachel. I must have been genuinely smiling all over my face, because the woman stopped arguing about the price of orange squash and smiled back suddenly.

"We've just had lambs!" I said. "This very minute. Isn't that wonderful?"

"Hear that children? This lady has just had lambs. Now hurry up and choose your ice-cream so that she can go and look after them."

Within minutes I was quietly closing the orchard gate after myself and walking unhurriedly towards Rachel. Not unexpectedly she was nowhere near the sheep folds but in the opposite corner beneath the oak tree. Looking calm and complacent (as well she might), she was industriously licking a moist-looking speckled lamb that stood, swaying slightly on splayed legs, against her flank. Close by, her first lamb lay on the grass with its legs tucked underneath it and its little head alert as it watched its mother. She snorted softly as I approached and it struggled to its feet and tottered towards her.

I did not go any nearer, but stood for a few minutes looking at the little family and checking (with my limited knowledge) that all was well. They looked fine. What a relief! Leah was grazing contentedly on the other side of the orchard, no doubt replete after consuming Rachel's helping of concentrate as well as her own. It was Rachel's absence at the feed trough that had alerted Maurice to her condition. Normally both ewes would have been standing by the gate, bleating like fog-horns for at least ten minutes before their suppertime!

Leah did not show any signs of imminent birth (neither had Rachel the last time we looked), but she could lamb in the night without us knowing. I frowned. Being responsible for pregnant animals worried me. I had been frantic when Brynne had puppies, convinced that she was dying of gross calcium deficiency. In fact, she was just a very anxious, inexperienced mother. I think the vet only gave her an injection of calcium to keep me quiet!

I wished now that I was not so ignorant. It was all very well to learn by experience, but not at the expense of one's livestock. I had asked Chris how long a ewe normally took to lamb from the onset of labour to the birth. He had said that it was usually a couple of hours.

"What if it's longer?" I had asked.

"You lamb 'em," was his short answer.

"How?"

He looked puzzled and thought carefully.

"Well . . . just lamb 'em." He could not - or would not - elaborate although I rephrased my question ever so many times. The book to which I turned in exasperation was of little help either. It told me that if a ewe had been labouring for a long time she needed assistance but a beginner should get a vet to do it. Well, it might come to that. I cursed the stupid author who had not seen fit to tell me how to do something that shepherds did all the time. However, the book did say that perhaps five in every hundred ewes might have difficulty in lambing and so I fervently hoped that Leah, like Rachel, would be one of the other ninety-five!

Nothing had happened by the next morning except that Leah had become excessively interested in Rachel's lambs. She kept running round and round them, with Rachel butting her whenever she came too close. Poor Leah! She thought that she had already lambed and that they were hers. It was several hours before she accepted that her time was still to come.

Meanwhile, I knew that there was one unpleasant task which had to be done fairly soon. Both lambs would need tailing to avoid blow-fly attacks in the summer, and as one was a male, he would have to be castrated as well.

This is done by using high tensile rubber rings and I would need a shepherd to show me how to do it. I asked Joe, who looked after a thousand ewes at a neighbouring farm, if he would mind giving me a lesson. Ringing the tails was easy but I was not at all sure about my ability to deal with a ram lamb!

Joe showed me how to tell whether the lambs were suckling by the simple expedient of feeling their stomachs. Obvious really.

"Watch them when they've been lying down," he advised. "A healthy lamb stretches when it stands up - see - like that?"

I did not like to take up any more of his time by going into the question of lambing problems; I doubted that it was a subject that could be dealt with briefly. But I was learning.

I am less diffident about asking for advice now. All the farmers I have met have been pleased to share their experience and sometimes their time. On one occasion I was touched by the concern shown by Joe's family for one sick lamb of mine when I knew that they had successfully lambed their own large flock.

Leah's lambs did not arrive for a fortnight; perhaps she could run faster than Rachel! The first one was more black than white so we called it "Sooty". It was a chilly Sunday morning, so I dried Sooty on a towel while we waited for the second lamb. Leah was much too pre-occupied to bother. Sooty's twin seemed in no hurry and by the time she emerged it was to an audience of fascinated week-end guests watching through binoculars.

I heaved a sigh of relief. Two ewe lambs meant two tails only to be dealt with! It was all over for another year.

Stephanie was thrilled to have been present when Leah lambed. It made her last weekend with us more special. She had resigned from the BBC and accepted a job with United Press International in Athens. As parents are wont to do, we "ummed" and "ahed" about the folly of such a decision. Working for "Auntie Beeb" had seemed such a nice, secure thing to do. Stephanie retorted that we were fine ones to preach about safe jobs! Of course, she knew that what we really hated was the thought of her living umpteen thousand miles away in a foreign country. We were accustomed to her frequent visits and welcomed her bright ideas and hard work. Inheriting her father's sense of humour (sadly unappreciated by his commanding officers in the past), she had become popular with many of our regular customers. I overheard her saying to a dear old man who called every Saturday for a vanilla wafer.

"You want to be careful about standing still round here - Mum paints roses on anything that doesn't move!"

Three of the boating regulars were Harry, Harvey and Henry. The only characteristic common to all three was an affinity with canal boats and a disposition to stop and have a long natter with us about this or that on the waterways. We were always more than willing to oblige so we were invariably pleased to see them.

Harry was a professional steerer employed by Northampton Education Authority. It was not easy to tell his age. Not young, I should think, for his bald head was as brown as a nut and when he smiled, which he did often, one could see that he had not a tooth in his head. He always called Maurice, "Ginger love" and me, plain "love". Like many people he probably thought that Maurice had acquired Ginger as a nick-name and may have wondered why he did not have red hair. When we first married, my new surname embarrassed me and I used to get annoyed at the wisecracks. It does not bother me at all now although I have heard all the jokes before. I once met a man called "Dr Livingstone" which must be much worse as it invites but a single comment.

"Neysa Rose" (which stood for Northampton Education Youth Services Association) was an ugly tub of a boat, painted bright green with a distinctive acid yellow guard rail in front. The letters of the name looked as if they had been cut out of coloured paper by a child and stuck on the cabin side. Perhaps they had! The boat was always loaded with youngsters from tots to teenagers. Brilliant in their orange life jackets, they spilled off the deck and the cabin roof to run around in all directions like an army of exotic ants.

Harry always gave his human cargo plenty of time to buy all that they wanted in the shop, which was a kindness to us all. He bought cigarette tobacco and papers for himself. We could tell how long each trip was going to be by the amount he bought - sometimes he took all we had. Then he would lean against the counter and carefully roll himself a fag and gossip while each of the children came in and out a dozen times to dribble away their pocket money. If "Neysa Rose" was only out for a day's trip, Harry left the boat at the bottom of Buckby flight and cycled up the steep towpath to the shop. No-one could move the boat until he got back, so if we were not too busy we made him a cup of tea to refuel him for the return ride.

The passengers on "Neysa Rose" fed Harry - sometimes like a king but occasionally not so well. If he bought food from us we knew that things were really bad! But he liked our gifts. His bright blue eyes would scan the shelves and when he saw something that took his fancy he asked us to put it on one side until the end of the season. On the last day of October he collected the large box which we had labelled "Harry", said "Cheerio till next year" and went home to Huddersfield.

A few days after we had moved in to the Canal Stores, we saw a working narrow boat called "Tadworth" loaded with coal which was partly sheeted over with green canvas. Surprised that there were any boats still carrying cargo in the Midlands, I went out to have a chat with the steerer. Harvey was a young man in his early twenties. His face was pale beneath the coal dust and he was very thin with a slight limp and a stoop that belied his years. His mother had owned a well known hire-boat fleet and the canals were in his blood. He lived aboard "Tadworth" in the tiny boatman's cabin and carried coal on a regular basis to some of the canal-side dwellings between Rugby and Gayton. It cannot have been a very profitable business because Harvey did other work in Daventry or Long Buckby or anywhere on his route. Perhaps he was not a very good salesman, because I had to ask him to call on us next time he was passing. He would not have done so otherwise.

We always supported waterways enterprises when we could, but I think that Harvey's was a lost cause. He rarely seemed to move his boat, sometimes tying up at the top of Buckby for weeks at a time. I would have thought that to compete with a land-based coal merchant, one would have to travel non-stop and knock on the door of every canal-side house that boasted a chimney.

Poor Harvey. I was sure that he did not eat properly. He often called in the shop after his day's work shifting paving slabs in Long Buckby (he must have been stronger than he looked) for a cup of tea before he lit the stove on "Tadworth" to cook his supper. Unless he found time to shop elsewhere, he must have lived on baked beans, sweet biscuits, Mars bars and (curiously) Dairy Milk chocolates in expensive boxes.

One day he showed us a coin that he had found. It was a token - the currency in which the canal companies used to pay the "navvies" and "cutters" who were employed in digging the canals and designed to prevent them spending their pay in shops other than those owned by the canal companies themselves. It was a mean practice which was abolished by the Truck Act. Harvey had his coin valued on our advice, but alas, it was so worn that it was worth very little - not even a square meal!

There must be many historical gems luring in the murky depths of canals or among their neglected environs. Bruce used to join the working party of the Birmingham Canal Navigations Society regularly on Sundays. Their aim is to improve the filthy, rubbish strewn waterways of the industrial Midlands. He would arrive home at dusk on a Sunday evening, black with oil and streaked with mud, triumphantly bearing his latest find. Once, it was a lethal Napoleonic bayonet whose scabbard disintegrated in his hands, another time he found the brass nameplate from the front of a nineteenth-century safe, thrown into the canal no doubt by the thief who rifled its contents. Unfortunately, Bruce was not fussy about the quality and condition of his trophies. Worthlessness I could put up with - stink, never!

I first made Henry's acquaintance one Monday evening at about a quarter past five. He called in the shop to buy a pint of milk and I noticed him particularly because he was wearing a smart camel-hair overcoat and I caught sight of a collar and tie; an unusual phenomenon in most of our customers. I had glimpsed him the previous evening, comfortably dressed in a scruffy grey pullover and a baggy track suit, filling the water tank of a handsome narrow boat at the stand-pipe opposite. The boat, "Leo", was still here and tied up beyond our own. I mused (nosily) about his circumstances but restrained myself from prying on so short an acquaintance!

He brought two children into the shop with him - a pretty, elfin-faced girl, slightly built, whom he addressed as Tamsin and a younger boy of about ten called Giles. Both of them wore school uniform which was also unusual on boating youngsters. I told Henry that we had often run out of milk by five o'clock so he asked me to save him a bottle daily which he would collect after school. By that remark I jumped to the conclusion that he was a schoolmaster. I would never have guessed his true occupation - that of a V.A.T. Inspector! Mind you, it took a long time to drag that information out of him, and only after we had got to know him quite well. It must be off-putting if one has a guilty conscience!

Actually, he was a great help in giving me tips about claiming V.A.T. Back from the government. It is a strange thing, but I have a comprehensive leaflet explaining to me how I should work out what I must pay the tax-man, but scarcely a written word on how I can work out what the tax-man owes me! Such information depends on one's friendly neighbourhood V.A.T. person; happily

I now have one; Henry even offered to help me fill in my return (I was not in his area so it was quite legal) but I felt that would have been too much of an imposition on my part.

Although "Leo" looked like a converted working boat, it had only been built eight or nine years before for cruising, and was home for the three of them. They did not travel far in term time, for the children were at school in Coventry, but stayed at least five days in one place. Every morning Henry drove the children to school in a little red van before doing the rounds of the accounts to be inspected. I could almost set my watch by the time that they returned and gossip with Henry made a pleasant finish to the afternoon.

On Friday evening, out would come the mooring spikes and off they would chug aboard "Leo" to another spot a few hours cruising away leaving the red van to be collected at some convenient time during the weekend. I think that they went a bit further afield in the holidays. He even went as far as Nottingham in the summer though I could not resist suggesting that he should take a survival kit for such a long voyage! I was quite relieved to see them return safely to Buckby Top lock in the autumn.

When they did, Henry paid me the compliment of asking me to repaint his old Buckby Can. It had come with the boat and been left out when "Leo" was given smart new livery and "Henry May & Co." in elegant sign-writing on the cabin side. I took a sketch-book and pencil and walked along to his boat to copy the name so that the style of lettering on the can would match and also make a note of the colours. It is important that a Buckby Can looks part of the boat to which it belongs.

Henry had scraped the old paint off the can and primed the outside with red lead. And the inside. How funny? He won't be able to use it for drinking water, I thought. I realised why when I came to paint the underneath — it was riddled with holes. One day, I anticipated, Henry will be in the market for one of my brand new cans. And he was! He was pleased, though, with his old can which still sits proudly on the roof of "Leo" and the next time he came to Buckby Wharf, Henry gave me a polyanthus to plant in the garden. It is always the first of its kind to bloom in the spring and flowers alongside the snowdrops. When we see the pale yellow faces smiling against the cold earth, we cannot help thinking of Henry May & Co.

May Day brought a welcome change in the weather that was to last the whole of the month. The large field behind us which sloped up to the brow of the hill had been planted with oil-seed rape that instantaneously burst into bloom. The brilliance was almost blinding. It was as if the sun was constantly shining; the vivid yellow blossoms reflected on the walls and ceilings of the cottage.

Yvonne kept eight hives of honey bees near the farmhouse on the other side of the big field. They exploited the pollen. She called in the shop one morning, leaving her three collies obediently sitting outside the gate, to tell us of the glut of rape honey that she was extracting from the hives. I bought several jars from her to sell in the shop and one for ourselves. It was the most delicious honey that I had ever tasted and most unusual in texture and colour. Pure milk white and very thick, it could stand up by itself and be spread smoothly. Three hundred pounds of it, she had! I glimpsed a gleam in Maurice's eye. Oh dear! We were a step nearer to keeping bees.

The apple trees followed the example set by the rape and unfurled tight pink buds into a froth of whiteness that decked the entire orchard. From the top of the hill, it looked as if a lacy shawl had been dropped on a yellow-green carpet. I walked beneath the trees with a sense of unreality. The pale pink canopy overhead almost blotted out the sky as the unpruned branches of one tree mingled with another. The heady scent of the blossom pervaded the air that I breathed and my ears were full of the constant humming of innumerable insects. A pair of carrion crows had nested halfway up the tall pear tree. Their raucous clamour woke us abruptly at first light, cutting short my precious hours of slumber. Crows have been known to peck out the eyes of young lambs, and the pullets too, ran from them in fear so Bruce climbed up and poked away the heap of twigs with a garden cane. The nest was empty.

One which was not, judging by the squawking and fluttering emanating from it, had been impudently built in the cypress tree overlooking the kitchen garden by a couple of wood pigeons. But whenever I saw the parent birds emerging with a great commotion and flapping of wings, they swooped across the garden and over the hedge into the field to forage. So long as they left my cabbages alone, I would overlook their cheek. Not Lucifer! He scrambled up the bole of the tree with claws like crampons embedded in the soft bark and tried without success to force his way through the dense green growth at the top. One day, I thought, he'll make it but I hope by then the fledglings will have flown away. I know that pigeons are the farmer's pest but I cannot help but take pleasure in their beauty — the soft-grey wings, the pale grey rump and rosy breast with a flash of iridescent green at the nape of the neck.

No sooner had one brood of young pigeons grown up and left the nest than the adult birds were preparing to hatch another clutch of eggs. The conveyor-belt production went on all summer and well into the autumn by which time Lucifer was extremely slim and athletic but still unsatisfied. I have read books by people whose cats have been trained never to catch birds and I do wish that I knew how it is done. I remonstrate with Lucifer whenever I find a sad little heap of grey feathers on the lawn, but I cannot bring myself to punish him for following his instinct. His feelings would be dreadfully hurt. And how can I tell him "Yes" to rats and "No" to birds? Occasionally I catch him looking speculatively at the bantams, in which case I growl "No" very fiercely. It may be that he has learnt to recognise them as part of the same establishment as himself or that they are a wee bit too big!

Another instinct of Lucifer's with which I was displeased was his habit of scratching up my seed bed. In that respect it was merely a question of catching him in action before I made him fly!

I was pleased with the way the vegetable garden was progressing in spite of the set-back of the severe winter. I had lost all the purple-sprouting broccoli but the lambs' lettuce was growing faster than we picked it and the autumn sown broad beans were well ahead. There were two long rows of Primo cabbages in the fruit cage between the young bushes and safe from the pigeons - more than enough for us to eat but we could sell the surplus. In the past, I had always had far too many vegetable seedlings because I sowed all the seeds in the packet in the belief that seeds did not keep well. Then I crammed my garden with plants set much too close together and forced the remainder on reluctant friends.

With Walter and Jim as mentors, I changed my ways. Jim made a packet of seeds last years, he said, though some varieties kept better than others. He reckoned that one seed meant one plant and would have been disappointed to find it otherwise. Not only that, he saved seed from most of his crops choosing the biggest and the best. It was twenty years since he had bought his original packet of runner beans, he said, and he could not remember rightly what they were! I was not surprised.

Jim sowed a few seeds of each of half a dozen different varieties of cabbage which would mature in succession. He prided himself that, be it Lent or Michaelmas, if his wife required a cabbage in the kitchen then she should have one. It was a good example to follow as we all enjoyed eating cabbage. One sort that I certainly meant to try was Holland Late Winter, which Jim said grew so tightly balled that the caterpillars could not get into it. Maurice had the idea of growing a row of Jerusalem artichokes parallel with the towpath hedge to give extra shelter from the north wind to the other vegetables. Walter and Jim had no advice to offer.

"To my mind, they taste like dirty pond water," said Jim.

"I've never grown them either," said Walter, "and I think I agree about the taste."

I know what they meant, although I have not made a habit of drinking dirty pond water! The nearest I have come to it was when I fell off the boat into the canal at Dudley in the Black Country. "Warwickshire Lad" was brand new and we proudly attended a boat rally to celebrate the re-opening to navigation of the famous tunnel which runs beneath Dudley Zoo. The heavens opened and turned the rally site into a sea of mud, a lot of which found its way onto our hitherto pristine deck. Anxious to look our best, I grabbed the mop and stepped onto some loose canvas. Splash! The water was deep and absolutely filthy. My one thought as it closed over my head was that I must keep my mouth shut and I concentrated on doing just that. I was so long in surfacing that Maurice was just about to jump in after me! My clothes were so disgusting afterwards that I had to throw them away.

Actually, we came to like Jerusalem artichokes. The earthy flavour is an acquired taste. They are pleasant boiled or steamed like new potatoes but at their best when made into soup or a thick vegetable sauce. We have probably got them forever now, as no matter how conscientiously Maurice digs them up, there are always a few tubers left to carry on the following year.

Salad vegetables always sold well to boaters and I had reared dozens of perfect Ailsa Craig tomato plants on the kitchen window sill to cope with the demand. The bathroom sill acted as nursery to the outdoor variety called Pixie which was to cater for our own fondness for green tomato chutney.

Alas, as the plants burgeoned I got bored with cooking and bathing in botanical gardens and put Ailsa Craig and Pixie out in the cold greenhouse too hastily. To be fair to myself, we provided a little warmth from the small paraffin heater that had protected the water pipes during the winter. It was not enough. One unexpected night of frost on May the fourth and the thermometer in the greenhouse dropped to thirty degrees Fahrenheit. Only seven hardy little Pixies survived among the blackened corpses of the others.

I had never known such a catastrophe happen in our sheltered garden in Birmingham. But it was situated on the side of a hill. The frosts rolled past us most of the time. I had forgotten that our greenhouse now stood at the bottom of a hill. A sitting duck for the ammunition of Jack Frost! But there was just time to start again with a fresh sowing of seeds - yes, on the bathroom window sill.

Seed catalogues make fascinating reading if one can avoid being carried away by the glorious pictures of perfect produce and keep a grip on the reality of one's own imperfections and that of one's gardens. This is difficult. I had been sitting in the sunshine perusing one catalogue in particular, when Maurice came outside to join me, carrying two tankards of beer.

"Shall we grow some exciting vegetables for a change?" I suggested, "things that are expensive to buy, like Mangetout peas, for instance. You eat them pod and all. I loathe shelling peas."

He looked over my shoulder at the catalogue and turned a page.

"What about French beans as well, then? They don't need stringing. And those globe artichokes look nice - you eat them like this!" He made a pantomime of tearing imaginary leaves off with his teeth.

"Celeriac's awfully useful in the winter, but you'll have to build me a cold frame for it."

"There's the shop bell!" He disappeared inside. I knew he would, even before I heard the bell. I had been trying to get a cold frame out of him for weeks. It is no good trying to be subtle with Maurice. He sees through it straight away.

Determined not to be beaten, I improvised a frame myself out of a barrow-load of half bricks and an old window. With the celeriac coming along nicely, I decided to postpone my gloating until Maurice was eating and enjoying it in December!

Another useful winter vegetable is kale which some people dismiss as rabbit food. Certainly it can be tough and lacking in flavour, but the young shoots are tasty and quite tender and we had to remember that there were other, less pernickety mouths to be fed during the lean months of the year.

The ewes were lying in the deep shade of the overgrown thorn hedge, their chins on the turf, watching me with bright brown eyes. They were breathing quickly. It was very hot, unusually so for late May, and for the past week we had been expecting a visit from the mobile shepherd to shear them. I had discovered his name with some relief when I visited the Central Wool Growers to buy some electric fencing to divide the orchard in half. The theory was, that if you rested the ground for about four weeks, most of the parasites to which sheep are prone died off and the land was sweet again. This avoided what seemed to us the rather unpleasant business of drenching the sheep, which entailed shooting a liquid dose of sheep wormer down their throats periodically.

I walked back into the shop by way of the small room we euphemistically called the stock room. It had once been the wash-room of the old cottage and now housed, in addition to a washing machine and an ancient camping gas cooker we used for preserving, shelves and shelves of reserve groceries, sweets, maps, charts, boxes of fudge and canal rock. Lucifer slept on a cushion on top of the washing machine at night (when he wasn't prowling outside or creating havoc among my shop window display).

"We'll have to ring Mr Hayton and chivvy him, Rachel and Leah look really miserable, they're glaring at me," I said to the only portion of Maurice that was visible, the rest of him having disappeared into the depths of the ice-cream freezer, no doubt to satisfy the desires of the two urchins on the other side of the counter who would not be palmed off with any other sort of ice-lolly but the one he could not find.

"Mm," he straightened up, having finally found half a box of the missing Starships and dealt with his young customers.

"I'll give him a ring now but I don't suppose he'll come today - it's Sunday."

"Right you are," I heard him say, "lunchtime today. Great. See you later."

"Funny time to come, don't you think? Sunday lunchtime," I asked, having failed to appreciate that, bearing in mind we lived next door to a Free House, it was the obvious time to come!

Just then we heard the "Ker-plunk" of a narrow boat diesel engine and we could see the familiar sight of "Water Ouzel" chugging gently astern to tie up at the gnarled oak bollard above the lock. "Ouzel" was a trip boat operated by

" the familiar sight of "Water Ouzel" ..."

Willow Wren Canal Transport Services from the nearby village of Braunston. George Walker gave us a wave as he strode briskly past the window towards the pub. He too, was careful to time his arrival at Buckby Wharf, anxious to miss not a minute of Sunday licensed drinking time. He was closely followed, more slowly but with equal determination by his passengers.

It looked like a Darby and Joan outing this time. We glanced at each other and sighed. Not that we had anything against senior citizens, far from it, but we knew the form. After they had partaken of a moderate amount of liquid refreshment next door, they would surge into the shop in waves, all sixty of them and demand one sort of ice-cream only - vanilla - between wafers and known to the more mature as a "sandwich". It would clear our stocks of that particular line for a week. In vain we had explained to the Wall's representative at length that at Bank Holiday weekends it was useless to telephone for our order on the Friday for delivery on Tuesday. So much depended on the weather. We might sell everything or scarcely any.

It was too much to expect, however, that small fry like ourselves could alter a delivery pattern worked out by a computer any more than we could plead successfully to have our order arrive early in the morning while the ice-cream was still firm rather than at four o'clock when it was oozing out of the cartons. Surprisingly, the vans are not refrigerated, only insulated, and as ours was the last drop, they were full of warm air instead of cold ice-cream. I could put in a claim to the computer for spoilt goods but that did not boost our sales much. Clearly, this Bank Holiday we had got it wrong again. It would be "Sorry, no vanilla" from now on.

With the reassuring sound of "Water Ouzel's" engine becoming fainter, we sank into armchairs in the dining room, each with a pasty and a mug of cool beer. I pulled up another chair on which to rest my throbbing feet.

"I would never have believed a shop assistant's job could be such hard work. The miles we must walk! We must rearrange things so that the ice-cream and the sweets are nearer the till."

"Not now," implored Maurice, "some time when we're quiet."

Almost as he spoke, we heard another sound. The crunch of lorry wheels on the pebbles of the drive.

When we had first moved to Buckby Wharf, it had seemed a matter of some urgency that we should have something done about the drive. It was in a terrible condition: full of pot-holes and craters, it had a high ridge of old tarmac on the bend and a sunken trough halfway along that flooded when it rained. We asked for a couple of estimates, looked at them and decided that perhaps it was not as urgent as we had at first thought! In the meantime, I had discovered that there was a market for canal roses painted on pebbles of a certain size. Armed with a paper bag containing half a dozen of the right sort of pebbles, I toured the local builder's merchants until I found a supplier. One and a half inches was the size I required to paint, but some of the load would be smaller. Hence, one and a half inches down. We had nine tons delivered in all, which we spread ourselves, sorting out the best pebbles to paint as we did so. The drive may not be perfect, but it is a great deal better than it was, and it does give us advance warning of any arrivals at the back. I went to the door. It was Bob Hayton, the shepherd.

"Thank goodness he's brought a dog."

We knew the ewes would be difficult to catch. They were very wild. Some people said that it was too much inbreeding. For some years the Jacob has been listed as a rare breed; now there are quite a number of flocks about all over the country. It could be that the breed expanded too fast. I think with our two, the problem was lack of handling. They could also run like smoke and were far from stupid when it came to anticipating our movements.

Maurice had made a small sheep pen in a corner of the orchard out of baker's trays and surrounded this with a larger pen in which we always fed them. The strategy was to lure them into the big pen with food then drive them into the small pen for capture. Baker's trays, incidentally, are incredibly useful items. We were fortunate in that the large bakery which supplied bread for the shop was changing from metal trays to plastic ones, and Ken, who delivered our bread, suggested that we kept the trays as they arrived. We eventually fenced two thirds of the orchard with them before they were phased out.

I nipped up to the orchard with a shovel of sheep nuts to put in the trough in the large pen, and stood at a discreet distance from the entrance and waited. The ewes were too clever. They knew that they were normally fed morning and evening. This was lunchtime. Something was up! They were curious but they were not going to come nearer than halfway down the orchard to investigate. I returned to where Bob was just finishing assembling his gear on the grass between the drive and the orchard fence.

"It's no good. I thought I could catch them, but they're too smart. You'll have to use your dog."

He grinned, and whistled a black and white collie, still sitting with ears pricked and tongue lolling in the back of the lorry. It seemed to me that Bob and his dog had those ewes, together with their lambs, penned in a matter of minutes.

I was so envious.

"I wish I had a dog," I said.

"Thought you had," grinning again and looking at Tansy asleep in the sun.

"Humph! That's a matter of opinion!"

Bob grabbed Rachel first, maybe because she had a less belligerent look in her eye than Leah, although she bucked and kicked as he frog-marched her from the orchard around the spring cabbage towards his mechanised shears. Flinging her over in one movement, he sat her on her rump so that she was leaning against his knees. Suddenly she stopped struggling, and seemingly docile, sat quietly

" He sat on her rump ..."

while he sheared her using a precise pattern of strokes as he controlled her with his legs. The fleece rippled to the ground like a fur coat being shed tantalisingly by a strip-tease.

"I'll trim her feet," he said, "they need doing." He was still holding her steady against his knees.

I handed him the powerful clippers and leant closer to watch. The hoofs of lowland sheep are not worn down naturally by stones like those of the mountains and require frequent paring if the animals are not to go lame. Obviously, I had not been ruthless enough at my first attempt. Her feet trimmed, Bob changed her position so that he could shear her back and then he had finished. The fleece lay in one complete piece on the grass. The whole operation had taken about five minutes.

"I'll show you how to roll it up," he said, after he and Rachel had danced their way back past the vegetables to rejoin the little flock. She looked laundered and rather naked beside the others. Spreading out the fleece, with the clean inside facing outside, he turned in the legs and rolled it up, twisting the neck into a rope and using it to fasten the bundle. To my tidy mind, this seemed illogical. I would have kept the inside of the fleece clean by doing the opposite and said so.

"You want to sell it, don't you? Well, this way the customer sees the best Part - the inside shoulders - without undoing it, see?"

Yes, I do see and of course I want to sell the fleeces, I thought. Jacob wool was supposed to be ideal for hand spinning because of the long fibres and dual colours. A card in the shop window would sell the two fleeces in a trice, I was quite sure. The money would help us pay for their winter keep.

Ideally, wool should be spun within a year of shearing, and before the natural grease dried out. I could smell the lanolin as I carried Rachel's fleece to the storeroom. It was a strong smell and almost masked the scent of animal and outdoors. I liked it. I knew that before those two ewes were sheared again I would have learnt how to spin and somehow found myself a spinning wheel. Knitting was another matter!

-10-
Summer Scene

Many gardeners enjoy seeing in their own homes the flowers they have grown. Very occasionally I feel the same. We have a large oak mule chest whose gleaming surface sometimes cries out to reflect a mass of the colourful blooms that are nodding outside the window. It may have seemed as if I am only interested in growing plants that are useful. This is not true. As an artist I cannot do without form and colour in the garden, not just to look at but also to paint. I rarely pick the subjects of my watercolours but sit on a low stool and paint them as they grow. My small flower pictures are usually sold as fast as I can paint them which is lovely for me as I enjoy doing them so much. More, I confess, than painting roses and castles on Buckby Cans! At first I concentrated on wild flowers but when I could not always find appropriate subjects without going far afield, I tried garden flowers and these were just as popular. The only criterion seemed to be that the customer could recognise the flower easily.

So I grow well-known cottage garden flowers in drifts all over the place, even following the old-fashioned way of sowing annuals as a catch crop between the long-stay vegetables. But I rarely think of picking them to bring indoors. I am not sure why.

As spring matured into summer, the garden flaunted such a vivid display that I was spurred into action. I would arrange some flowers for the house for once. I cut the partially opened buds in the early morning. The woody stems I bashed with a hammer, others I plunged first into boiling water and then ice cold. The whole lot was then "conditioned"; steeped up to their necks in a bucket of water for several hours. In the afternoon I rolled up my sleeves and pushed and pulled and bent and tweaked those recalcitrant stalks until the conglomeration adopted an "artistic" shape. Finally, I picked up my arrangement and placed it carefully on the mule chest. Then came the moment to stand back and admire it. With a gentle sigh, the focal point keeled over, taking everything else with it and collapsed in a welter of water and crumbling Oasis, leaves and petals, onto the polished oak.

That was the moment when the chicken wire, the pin-holder, the container and all were flung into the farthest corner of the stock-room. I found a large brown earthenware jug and filled it to the brim with fresh sparkling water. In went the flowers that were not too battered or broken. Loosely bunched and more or less upright. A non arrangement. No! More than that - an anti arrangement. A glorious jugful of colour that would last for a week without wilting.

I know a demonstrator in the art of flower arranging, and of course that happened to be the day she chose to call.

"The garden is looking lovely," she said, averting her gaze from my jugful of glory on the mule chest and pointedly staring out of the window. I could read her mind. She was remembering her own house, where tables smirked beneath containers of Hogarth curves and every arrangement alike except for the colour of the flowers. Pink for the drawing room - so welcoming. Blue for the dining room to match the curtains. Green for the hall, so cool . . . Each display of flowers would be as self-conscious as the velvet drapes, the porcelain cherubs, the artificial birds which had been added to give meaning to the arrangement.

If I went to classes like hers, she has told me, I could learn the tricks of the trade, the formula for successful arrangements of floral art. Art? Is that how Cézanne learnt to paint oranges tumbled onto a table or Van Gogh the riot of apple blossom in the asylum garden. To a formula?

I think not. When the floral art movement began nearly four decades ago (perhaps as a reaction to the austerities of the War), it acted like a shot in the arm on horticulture. People became not only interested but often enthusiastic about unusual flowers and foliage, fruits and seed heads. Plants which hitherto had been virtually unknown to the average householder became a familiar sight in private gardens throughout the land.

Now, old favourites are scorned. The fashion is for the outré. No longer do Bachelor's Buttons and Aubretia trim the borders, but Alchemilla Mollis is favoured instead - and a more boring, invasive plant I have yet to find! For some reason its lime green flowers are a flower arranger's dream. The same goes for the citrus green form of the cottage garden annual Nicotiana or Tobacco flower which is sought in preference to the glowing carmine or the white, although it smells nowhere near as sweet. Roses, too stubborn to be popular with the flower arranger, are given away to friends; lilies and carnations, spiky dahlias and pom-pom chrysanthemums are grown instead.

I realise, of course, that this is my problem when I come to adorn the mule chest. I grow the wrong flowers! I should not grow those I like but those that arrange well. It is no good going out into my garden and picking an armful of roses and marigolds, delphiniums and hollyhocks, expecting them to fall into an arrangement even if I knew the formula. But I do not want to grow the flowers of the funeral parlour and the marriage ceremony. Let the professional florists have that prerogative. I have reached an impasse.

In my view the Floral Art Movement has become stale. Collectively, it has lost the freshness of its youth. There are few sparks of individuality and rarely an original idea in flower arrangements today. They are predictable. They are contrived. They conform. I believe that it is time for the movement to give itself a shake and a dust and then take a good hard look at itself. It is time to throw away its edicts, its rules and its formulae. And if its followers cannot recapture some of that genuine simplicity with which the movement began, perhaps it is time to leave the flowers where they belong - in the garden.

The house in which we had lived in Birmingham backed on to the nursery garden of a large park although it faced a busy thoroughfare for traffic and pedestrians. We had pleasant gardens both front and back and a broad, open driveway.

I cannot remember, in all the twelve years that we lived there, strangers sitting on the rockery to eat their sandwiches, spreading a rug on the lawn for a picnic, or going round to the back door to look for a lavatory. The very idea is ludicrous!

And yet - take townies out to the country for the day, take them to Buckby Wharf - and then see what happens.

One sunny morning in June, I was sitting at my table by the window in that part of the shop which had once been a miniscule office and which I had adopted as my studio. A shadow fell across my work. Looking up, I saw a woman turn away from watching me and walk out of the gate. The idle thought crossed my mind that I had not seen her when she first came in through the gate from the towpath. I must have been too deeply engrossed in transforming empty Nescafé tins into waste paper bins.

Oh no! Another woman passed out of the gate, then another, then another…Mesmerised, I sat there while a seemingly endless procession of middle-aged ladies walked past my window and out onto the towpath like rabbits coming out of a conjurer's hat.

" As self-conscious as the velvet drapes ..."

I jerked myself into life and ran out of the back door to see the tail end of the crocodile disappearing round the corner of the garage. I managed to catch up with the last of the stragglers.

"Excuse me!" I panted, "but would you mind telling me what you're all doing in my garden?"

"Not at all, dear. We're all going on a canal-boat trip. Sixty of us there are, from Bradford. Is this your garden? Very nice it is I'm sure. Goodbye dear. I must hurry or they'll go without me."

Helplessly, I stood and watched the two coaches pull away from the gate. Why the passengers had traipsed through our garden instead of down the wide concrete steps from the bridge onto the public footpath I shall never know. I stood at the gate and tried to view the mistake dispassionately. But I could not see it. There was no clue from the back that it was possible to get through to the canal. No hint of a shop, even. There was a house and a garage, a greenhouse and a line of washing, a flower garden, trees, shrubs, lawn, vegetables, and an orchard with sheep and chickens. It looked every inch what it was - private property.

But this incident was only the beginning. I became obsessive about an Englishman's home being his castle. We tried keeping the gate closed which was a nuisance for our delivery drivers but it did not make a lot of difference. I painted a board for the gate which said "Private Drive" but that was ignored as often as the one which asked drivers to leave the entrance clear.

Even Maurice, who is more phlegmatic by nature than me, found his gall rising when a couple drove in and parked their car by the greenhouse. They had spread a groundsheet on the grass in front of the dining room window and were just unpacking their luncheon hamper when he went out and asked them to take their picnic elsewhere!

A frequent occurrence is for patrons of the New Inn to bring their dogs into our garden before the animals are shut in the car while their owners imbibe at the pub. The dogs are released to romp and relieve themselves, chase sheep and chickens if they will while the owners stroll round admiring what is left of the flowers. It has not been unknown for the patrons to relieve themselves in our garden either. But more often it is our outside lavatory they are after. I often stumble across people wandering around in the region of the back door searching for the "Public Convenience" although why they think there should be one there is beyond me.

One man got more than he bargained for when he invaded my privacy. We had closed for lunch on a gloriously sunny day and I had been tempted to snatch a post-prandial nap on the sun bed. The little terrace beneath the dining room window was secluded so I whipped off my shirt to get full benefit from the sunshine. I lay back and shut my eyes. Bliss. Menacingly, Tansy growled. I opened an eye. An elderly man was approaching about a yard away. He held a River Nene lock key in his hand.

"*Do* you mind?" I was caustic because of my state of undress, "we're closed and this is my lunch break."

"Yes, I know the shop's closed but I knew you'd be round here." No word of apology.

"Did you now." I said aloud, and silently - bloody cheek!

It was probably our fundamental desire to draw some sort of demarcation between conviviality in the shop and seclusion in the home that decided us not to repeat the exercise with the tea-room for a second season. It had been such a relief finally to restore it to a dining room after we had redecorated it in the autumn. I was tired. The early start to the day and the physical strain of the postal delivery on top of everything else I was doing began to make itself felt. A six day week at the post-office left only one day to refresh me and the seventh was often our busiest day in the shop. Sundays meant merely and irreverently two more hours in bed!

One Saturday night I was particularly weary. Maurice was tired too, for the harder I worked for the post-office the more work he tried to take on himself at home. As darkness fell I said:

"Why not leave the hens unlocked tonight so that they can get themselves out and about early tomorrow and we can have a decent lie in?"

Oh! How I wished later that he had not agreed with me!

It must have been in the small hours that I was awoken by a noise outside. I held my breath. There it was again - a sort of muffled cough. I nudged Maurice.

"Listen! Could that be a fox?"

He listened obediently or perhaps just gave the impression of doing so. I doubt that it mattered much for the damage had already been done by the time he muttered,

"Don't think so," and turned over with his back to me to indicate that the dialogue was at an end.

The next morning I was cooking breakfast when Maurice came in from attending to the livestock. I could see by his face that something was horribly wrong.

"You were right." His voice was flat and unemotional. I could tell he was upset.

"A fox?"

"Yes. It's dreadful. Feathers . . . everywhere!"

"How many?" I could not trust my voice to say very much.

"I don't know. I haven't really looked - it was such a shock. I saw Gandalf, he seemed to be alright, and the bantams, I think. That's all I noticed."

We went up to the orchard together to undertake the grisly task of searching for feathered corpses, for foxes have a murderous habit of killing for amusement. There were two of the brown hens left alive, two of the bantams, and Gandalf (Aragorn's successor) who looked very subdued. The only two bodies that we found were those of our lovely home-reared cream pullets. They had been such big, heavy birds that the fox had been unable to take them away. The fact that all the others had disappeared indicated that the culprit had been a vixen feeding well-grown cubs. Perhaps that should have made us feel less angry. But just then I hated foxes from the depths of my soul. And we only had ourselves to blame.

We looked at the two brown hens not really expecting that one could be our clever broody. No, she had been taken with the others. And that was the only hybrid hen we have ever owned which has gone broody. As for the bantams! They have turned out to be useless for anything but decoration. So much for their reputation. What we needed were some proper hens - good old-fashioned Rhode Island Reds or Light Sussex or Leghorns. We are still looking!

I cleaned up the mess in the hen-house and in the evening we drove over to see Mr Penny at Canon's Ashby. We decided not to mention our catastrophe as I thought he would be displeased with us for being so careless with his hens, but we looked so woebegone that he guessed straight away. He was full of sympathy for he had a sorrier tale to tell.

Several nights before, two foxes had got inside one of the sheds which houses several hundred of his point-of-lay pullets. The beasts had dug their way beneath the foundations of the building and created havoc within. They had bitten the heads off two hundred and forty birds!

"Carnage," said Mr Penny with tears in his eyes, "it isn't just the financial loss - it's the suffering. I can't bear to think of it."

"You're insured, of course?" asked Maurice.

He shook his head.

"You know how it is. I kept meaning to get round to it like I kept meaning to sink metal sheets at the bottom of the walls to stop the foxes digging."

What could we say? We bought some more of his hybrids because they were all he had and although not quite ready to lay, they might cheer up Gandalf and share the marital duties of his remaining wives. We had learnt a hard lesson that would not readily be forgotten. Particularly as I can guarantee that not a single year passes without some dear friend sending us a Christmas card with a picture of a fox on it!

Nearly all my life I have pursued landscape painting as a hobby. Often, using charcoal and watercolour, I made a sketch outdoors and then developed it into a large oil-painting when I got home. When Maurice was stationed in Somerset, I made a half-hearted attempt to sell some of my canvases to an art dealer in Minehead, thinking that in a tourist town there might be some demand for pictures of local scenes. I recalled his advice and the germ of an idea formed in my mind.

"Watercolour views are what people want, nicely framed and small enough to fit into a suitcase."

We chose narrow, inexpensive beech frames of the appropriate size and bought ourselves a mitre cutter with which to cut cardboard mounts of a dark soft brown colour. With an ingenious easel converted from a camera tripod and a block of course-grained paper I was ready to put my idea into practice. It was several weeks, though, before I got round to it. There always seemed to be more urgent painting to do.

Pushing back my chair from where I had been sitting in my comer of the shop, I announced somewhat rebelliously,

"It's a lovely day and I'm stifling in here. If I paint one more beastly rose today I shall scream! I'm going for a walk."

"Why don't you?" Maurice sounded so unbearably reasonable about it that I waited for the catch. It came.

"Take your sketching things," he said.

He knew full well that in spite of my pained expression I found the thought quite attractive. I gathered my gear together in a canvas bag and put a folding stool under my arm.

"Come on, Tansy!" and airily, "expect me when you see me!"

We walked along the towpath which, as we got nearer to Norton Junction, deteriorated markedly. At its best slippery and uneven, the dry hot weather of late after the fierce winter frosts had created yawning chasms that waited to catch and twist an unsuspecting ankle. Some of the huge coping stones, each one the size of a small cabin trunk, had broken away and lay a foot or more out in the channel while the path, left without its retaining wall, had sunk in places several inches below the invading water.

I negotiated the pitfalls while Tansy paddled in the shallow water and, as dogs will, had a good long drink from the muddiest puddle that she could find. We passed beneath the rosy bricks of the junction bridge and the cool deep purple of the archway flickered with the dancing, dappled sunlight reflected off the water. The blazing sun dazzled as I came out from under the bridge on the far side and it was several seconds before my eyes adjusted themselves to the glare. Ahead of me the canal curved in a broad right-handed sweep, its bed terraced out of the smooth green hillside which fell away to the stream below. On the left, great oaks and sycamores dominated the line of the canal until it disappeared where the parapet of the next bridge was just visible.

After the first few yards beyond the bridge the towpath ceased to exist - it had been completely washed away. The water's edge was shallow and stony like a beach, with little inlets where tree roots made hiding places for shoals of minnows. Underneath the trees the undergrowth was dense and impenetrable, smothering the steep bank until it met the field above nearly at the level of the tree tops.

The air was quite still. The heat was intense - almost tropical. There was no bird song. It was so quiet that a dragonfly whirring past my shoulder with a flash of turquoise made me jump.

I stopped where the towpath gave up and turned round to face the way that I had come. The sun shone full on the bridge. The mellow brickwork seemed to radiate a whole spectrum of colour in the shimmering light, from pale ochre through a fantasy of reds to dark grey-purple. Placing my hands together, fingers crooked, I squinted through the tube I had made at the view. Yes - it would make a picture.

The contrast of light and shade was dramatic; the colours were vivid and subtle at the same time. The arch of the bridge framed a softly coloured stone cottage in marbled shade and on the left, the deep shadow of the path in front of the Toll House accentuated the brilliance of a clump of blood-red peonies. The broken water on the other side of the bridge was still beneath it where it lay cool and darkly green. In the foreground, creamy meadowsweet drifted down the bank to contrast with the rich blue-green of elder bushes bending low over the yellow-brown water that was stirred only occasionally by the passage of a boat.

" The arch of the bridge framed a softly coloured stone cottage ..."

I could hear one now. A red narrow boat approaching from the north, the steerer coming upon the junction unexpectedly turned sharp right and hit the side of the bridge with a resounding "crunch". I flinched. The peace being shattered, I set to work laying out the tools of my trade. There was a tremendous barking on the other side of the bridge as Bobby, the big Airedale from the Toll House, took exception to the antics of the crew who were trying to extricate the boat from the confusion caused by the inattentive steerer. The boat was broadside across the cut. Its bow was stuck in the reeds and mud and its rudder was firmly wedged against the coping stones on which Bobby stood, teeth bared. Very sensibly, the crew did not attempt to disembark to push the boat round but after much dangerous windmilling with a long shaft, one of them managed to wedge the boat-hook against a stone toadstool on which a painted gnome sat, and eased the stern out into the middle.

By that time, Mr Fielding had come outside to see what the commotion was about. He glanced at the boat but did not say anything, just checked that his gnomes and miniature farm carts and gypsy caravans were intact. I expect he had seen it all before. Somebody did take one of his gnomes once. Underneath the stone on which the gnome had been seated, he found a pound note with a telephone number written on it.

"Why would anyone want it?" he said next day when he showed me the note, "it was only a plastic gnome — must have cost me one and sixpence when I bought it."

The Fielding's tiny cottage had been built in 1914 by the Grand Junction Canal Company as a gauging and toll house, and with no more thought for convenience than was necessary for the two clerks who collected the tolls.

But Mr and Mrs Fielding were used to a hard life; before they retired they had lived and worked on the boats. Both of them were retired Salvation Army Brigadiers whose mission had been to the families of the working boat people. With a well equipped school on board one of their pair of boats, "Aster" and "Salvo" , they travelled the waterways where they are remembered with affection. When they celebrated their Golden Wedding recently, they received over two hundred cards!

There is no mains water connected to the cottage; the supply comes through a rubber hose over the wooden foot-bridge from a stand-pipe which often freezes up in winter. Mr Fielding lights a fire beneath the tap to thaw it which does the trick unless the frost is as severe as it had been the previous winter. Even when he thawed the tap, the hose was still frozen and he had to carry the water up the steep steps to the bridge and down the other side. It cannot be easy but I have never heard him grumble.

At one time there had been a cast-iron swing bridge there which was level with the path, and would have been less trouble for him (provided boaters swung it back when they had passed through). Swing bridges pivot on a central point above one bank and are counter balanced to make them easier to move. They can be stiff and awkward to shift though, if dirt and grit get in the mechanism. One day in 1973 a heavy boat collided with it, destroying it utterly, and the cheap replacement is the white painted footbridge we see today.

Boating on canals is not always the idyllic pastime which many people expect. It is easy to forget, now that there is a thriving leisure industry on the inland waterways, that the canals were not built for pleasure. They were constructed as a means of transport when the standard of living for most people was low and when human life (in particular that of the labouring classes) was held cheap. The existence of a working boatman was not expected to be easy by his employers and least of all by himself.

Thus there are many hazards on the canals which the holiday-maker needs to treat with respect or else court disaster. I suspect that there are a few hire boat firms whose managers are not too conscientious about warning their clients of the dangers. After all, who wants to tell a potential customer that he could kill himself or one of his children if he is not careful! But this is so.

Between the four of us we have had our fair share of narrow squeaks which could have ended in tragedy.

The one I recall most vividly was the occasion when eleven year old Bruce rode a bicycle into a full lock! He said he had swerved to avoid Tansy. I only heard the splash. He could swim like a fish and bobbed up quickly, but it took hours to retrieve the bicycle after emptying the lock, for it was a deep one. I cannot bear to think of the outcome if his foot had been trapped in the pedal. Five years later one of Bruce's best friends was killed on a boating holiday. He slipped between the steel hull and a stone bridge and was crushed.

I think that locks and bridges are the biggest hazards. Over the years we have developed our own canal vocabulary which is invariably connected with some incident or other. "Doing a Bindweed" means hitting your head on a bridge as the boat passes underneath. We were travelling behind a cruiser of that name and several youngsters were up on the cabin roof, larking about. We could tell they were paying no attention to the bridge which was looming ahead. No amount of shouting and hooting on our part could prevent the awful inevitability of the sickening thud which one poor lad sustained on the back of his head. He was knocked right out.

"Jump Stephanie" is a synonym for immediate action. At the start of our very first canal holiday I gave both children a lecture on the importance of obeying instructions straight away and without their habitual arguments. We were on the Oxford Canal and between two locks when we spied a horse-drawn trip boat which Maurice went off to photograph, leaving me in charge - I hesitate to say "in command". Oh horrors! The wind caught the boat and slewed it round. I had already told Stephanie to be ready with the mooring rope and shouted,

"Jump Stephanie," not realising that the boat was drifting away from the bank instead of towards it.

Remembering my lecture, Stephanie immediately jumped smack into the middle of the canal. Brynne thought this meant that it was time for a swim so jumped in as well. Bruce got in a panic thinking Brynne would drown and in trying to fish her out, fell in too! By the time Maurice returned to chastise us for hanging about instead of entering the lock that he had set for us after taking his photograph, we were all in tears. Except Brynne, who was dripping all over her puppies.

At Buckby Top Lock we were not the actors but the audience. During the summer the action was pretty well non-stop - mostly amusing but occasionally frightening for the participants. The New Inn was not one of those pubs that forbids coaches so it was not unusual to see a charabanc draw up on the verge at the side of the road on a Saturday evening and pour its occupants into the inn.

We were sitting at the dining room table eating supper. I had half an eye on the activities which were going on beyond our low box hedge. Self interest not curiosity on my part - it is amazing what people will do when they have had a few drinks! We were fast learning the drawbacks of living next door to a public house.

Four people were sitting on the lock beam having a drink. Their glasses would probably be left behind them when they had finished. There was nearly always broken glass around the lock on a Sunday morning waiting to cut bare feet and paws. Sure enough, the two men and one of the girls put their tumblers on the concrete beneath the beam and sauntered off towards the junction. The other girl stepped up onto the beam and, in her four inch high heels which were attached to her feet by narrow thongs, teetered across the lock. She stopped in the centre and stood with one foot on each of the lock gates, one hand on the rail and the other holding her glass which was half full. She bent over and stared at the water.

"Honestly! Some people have no sense!" I said impatiently as I cleared the plates and took them out to the kitchen.

"Hmm." Maurice looked out of the window at the girl and yawned.

When I returned with the fruit and cheese there was no-one outside and Maurice was sitting at the table with his eyes half shut, nearly asleep.

"Brown bread or cheese biscuits?" I asked as there was a sudden flurry of activity outside.

"Good heavens!" he announced, sitting up very straight and staring out of the window.

The two men had arrived by the lock gate at a run, one of them leant over the side while the other held his legs. Together, they hauled the girl out of the water and hoisted her onto the path. She was ashen white but alive, vomiting and choking with inhaled canal water.

We have never seen a boat sink in Buckby Top Lock - yet. But there have been one or two near misses. One week there were two separate incidents involving experienced boaters and they were caused by a moment's inattention on both occasions.

I had been watching an immaculate fifty foot long narrow boat entering the top gates and silently admiring the excellence of its paintwork and the cabin decoration. The castle panels were exceptionally well executed, a bit Eastern in flavour with dark red onion domes capping the towers. The boat's crew of two looked very competent. The man closed the top gates and then briskly wound up the lower paddles before going up on to the bridge to cross the road (there being no towpath under the bridge) and see whether a boat was coming the other way. The woman steered the boat right up to the far end of the lock until the front fender was touching, left the engine in forward gear to hold the boat there, then went below into the cabin.

As the water level fell and the embellishments dropped out of sight, I lost interest and turned away. The next thing I knew, there were screams echoing from inside the lock chamber. I rushed out and arrived at the lock-side at the same time as the man, who had dashed (dodging lorries) back across the road. He dropped the paddles without a second's thought but it took both of us a few more to appreciate what had happened.

The front fender (the "button") had become wedged between the top beam of the gate and the lock-gate itself. As the lock emptied, the stern of the boat dropped with the water, leaving the bow stuck in the air. The boat was at an angle and any minute the water would start flooding in through the fuel and gas vents which were just tilting below the water-line. The man did the only thing possible; he ran to the top paddles and wound them up as fast as he could (praying aloud that it was not too late) to refill the lock and raise the back end. I think Madam had little faith - she was clinging to the iron ladder on the lock wall and yelling her head off as she clambered up it!

All was well. The boat levelled off as the lock filled and the button slipped off the beam. The fellow leapt on board and starting pumping the bilges like a madman - more as a therapeutic exercise than anything else, I think.

The other incident was not dissimilar, but instead it was the stern that was left high and dry by the rudder being trapped in the mitred top gates. This was not so critical as far as sinking was concerned because the bow stands higher out of the water anyway and has no vents in it. But if the rudder snapped and the boat fell, it would almost certainly break its back on the exposed stone sill beneath. Once again, someone was saved by the bell - the shop bell actually, as I ran outside gesticulating wildly at the lad who was dreamily gazing across at the shop window.

We witnessed the passage of one sorry looking boat, "Knapweed", being towed back to its hire base after being sunk in the River Soar. It is a river which is inclined to flood quickly after heavy rain and I believe that was what happened although we heard conflicting reports of the events which led to the sinking. I understood that the people on board were safe although they lost most of their belongings and must have been very scared. The boat had been built by Chris Barney and was the twin of "Warwickshire Lad" in basic design and length although painted in different colours. Not that much was visible when we saw it! Smeared with thick, grey river mud and encrusted with weed, there were large patches of orange rust on the hull where the paint had been scraped off. I could not see a single pane of glass left in the windows. Amazingly, it looked as good as new by the following season but it must have made a mess of the boatyard's bookings for the rest of that one.

I heard of another Barney boat being sunk - in the Warwickshire Avon, another river which is notorious for flooding. Perhaps there is a jinx on Chris's boats! I do hope not. We are not very fond of rivers actually, even the ones that rarely flood, except as a useful link between canals. All of us agree that it is nice to get back onto a canal from a river and feel comfortable and cosy again.

Many people who own narrow boats believe they are superior to those who possess fibre glass cruisers, and the epithet "Noddy Boat" is not infrequently heard from the more patronising boat owners. It is sad to relate that the typically British class system is quite noticeable on the canals today.

The boats which are generally considered to be the aristocracy (by their owners) are the genuine old working boats which have not been converted for modern use in any way. They should, of course, have their original engine or one of the same vintage, and each component part of it will have been polished until the owner can see his grimy face in it (authenticity depending on looking like a real boatman and not a holiday-maker - even if he is).

Lower down the social scale are the working boats that have been converted. Then come full-length boats like "Leo" - and "Leo" climbs the ladder a rung because Henry lives on board. "Leo" steps up even higher now that Henry tows a butty boat called "Hereford". He is well on the way to his earldom!

New, traditional style narrow boats are the middle classes of the boat world and the longer the boat and the more graceful its lines the further it moves to the upwards side of middle. "Warwickshire Lad" is just about plumb in the middle of middle. There will not be many narrow boats much shorter than our thirty-five feet, so if one looks down the social ladder one will see boats less well built with inferior materials and poorly designed, but nevertheless narrow boats.

Which brings me back to where I started, the fibreglass cruiser. To my mind, they have two disadvantages and those are their vulnerability in locks and the tendency of their engines (or maybe their owners) to go a bit too fast in between. But they do have one enviable advantage in that they draw less water than a narrow boat and can be moored comfortably close to the bank in places where a narrow boat would be stuck in the mud with gangplank precariously balanced between towpath and deck.

I was distinctly grateful one day to have been given a lift in the merest whisp of plastic when Brynne and Tansy had, unnoticed by the rest of us, run out of towpath. They had been trotting alongside "Warwickshire Lad" when their way was barred by a tremendous tangle of briars. Being a determined sort of dog, Brynne swam round them and Tansy followed. Unfortunately the towpath did not reappear for some distance and by the time my friend, with barely six inches of water beneath his hull, dropped me off to rescue them, they had swum and paddled for nearly a mile.

One of the splendid bonuses of living at the Wharf was the indulgence of standing and staring without feeling guilty. I stood gazing idly at a pretty little cruiser being led like a dog on a lead into the lock. Its motor was switched off and the small boat was obviously the pride and joy of the couple who carefully tied its fore and aft ropes to a bollard on the lock-side. The man wound up the bottom paddles and sat dozing on the comfortable oak beam in the sunshine - a special delight of canal cruising - while the woman stood by the bollard with her mind heaven knows where. The lock emptied. The little boat swung gaily in mid-air. I waited. Nothing happened for ages. Suddenly - action! The chap woke up and hissed at his wife who turned scarlet with embarrassment. I retired into the shadows at the back of the shop while they partially refilled the lock and let the blue and white craft drop with a gentle "plop" onto the water.

The grand finale of the summer was undoubtedly the scene that stopped the traffic. Not on the Grand Union - that was moving pretty sluggishly anyway as the weekend build up of boats queued at the top lock. I mean the A5. And so efficient was the towpath telegraph that cars from Long Buckby were screeching to a halt on the Wharf bridge two locks down, occupants frantic not to miss the show!

Only a few startled farm hands and lorry drivers had stumbled out of the New Inn, eyes popping out of their sockets, at the start of the performance but by the time it was played at Whilton Marina alongside the bottom lock of the flight, vehicles were parked nose to tail on the bridge with others converging from both directions. All five bars of the capacious "Bannaventa" public house had been deserted. A buzz went round the audience. She had arrived. The beautiful blonde riding "topless" on the roof of a narrow boat!

Maurice's birthday falls in July and the temptation to be reckless and have a really good splurge overwhelmed me. Bruce was a willing accomplice and Maurice was easily persuaded when I rashly offered to foot the bill out of my post office wages. It swallowed a whole week's plus overtime but it was worth it.

Whether it was chance or whether someone "up there" decided to give us a break, I cannot decide. But after a miserable week of rain and wind, the birthday weather was perfect for the plans which Bruce and I had laid.

I booked a table at "The Stag's Head", a restaurant with a delightful garden overlooking the canal just short of Watford locks. Bruce had accumulated the ingredients of something called a "Harvey Wallbanger" and stowed them together with a cocktail shaker, a Thermos of ice and various appetizers like nuts and olives, aboard "Warwickshire Lad". It would be about a forty minute cruise each way with no locks and provided at least one of us was not so intoxicated as to be incapable of having proper control of the vessel, no worries about drinking and driving!

The trip there seemed all too short. The warm evening sun after the rain drew out the fragrance of flowers and grasses. Clouds of swallows darted in front of us, skimming the water in their search for insects. We tied up the boat at the wooden jetty, using the posts thoughtfully provided, and walked up the colourful terraces, savouring the heady scent of roses and jasmine. Jack, justifiably proud of his lovely garden, asked if we would like our drinks outside while we studied the menu. The meal was delicious and we economised on nothing! After liqueurs and coffee we wended our way (slowly) down the steps through the garden to the jetty where the boat lay waiting with Tansy on board ready to wag her tail in ecstasy at our return. The air was heavy with dew and the smell of honeysuckle.

Our journey back was mystical; the countryside was quiet and still once we had left the rumble of the Watford Gap Service Station behind. Tall sentinels of reed-mace were picked out crisp and clear by the rising moon. In one field, a whole flock of sheep were lying down motionless. A moorhen softly squawked, "cock . . . cock". They never seem to sleep at night.

Bruce throttled down as we reached the junction and turned left, the headlight sweeping the undergrowth ahead. One or two curtains were pulled back and faces peered out as we slowly chugged past the boats that were moored above Buckby Top Lock.

    Home! After, Maurice said, one of the best birthday treats he has ever had.

-11-
The Wheel Spins

Imperceptibly it was autumn. The summer had slipped away more quickly than any that I can remember since my childhood. Around noon it was warm but a penetrating chill crept into the air when the sun sank (a little earlier each day) behind the oak tree. On September the first I worked my last day at the post-office. It would be untrue to say I was sad to leave but I had not given up easily.

"Look at this!" I had attacked Maurice with a copy of The Guardian about a month earlier. "That's the last straw - I have absolutely and finally had enough!"

"Steady on," he said, calm as always. He was used to me being melodramatic but this time I meant it.

I spread out the newspaper and stabbed with my forefinger at a half page advertisement. Maurice obligingly looked at the charcoal drawing of a postman who was staggering under a tower of a couple of dozen parcels and smiling. Grinning his silly head off - poor fool! Of course the postman had just driven up in a van because it was sketched in behind him. The caption was what enraged me. It said that if "You" were in the habit of sending more than twenty-five parcels per week, the post-office would generously deliver the first twenty-five free. It then went on to say what a simply super service they were offering all over Britain by (presumably) the lovely cheery chap illustrated. Then came the crunch. The maximum permitted dimensions of the parcels were given. I had already fetched a tape measure.

"One and a half metres long and one and a half metres in circumference - good heavens - and what's twenty-two kilos?"

"About half a hundredweight," said Maurice beginning to look sympathetic.

I cut out the advertisement and pinned it on the wall of the sorting office, having first crossed out the van and drawn in a bicycle. The post-master did not find it very amusing, I think that he sensed what was coming. Not that it was his fault. He said that he quite understood my reasons for leaving and by the time my due leave had been subtracted from the period of notice I had the whole autumn of freedom in front of me.

My successor is a six foot rugby player with shoulders like an American footballer so half a hundredweight to him will be like peanuts. He has a cross-bar too, on his bicycle to which he can strap packages that are one and a half metres long. That is, until Long Buckby enters the twentieth century and gets itself a post-office van!

The first of September was important to us in one other respect, for I see from my sheep diary that the ewes were taken by Bob Hayton for dipping on that day. Perhaps I ought to explain that one does not keep a sheep diary in order to reminisce or to write a book. It is primarily a record of the movement of sheep between agricultural holdings or to market. This information would be important should there be an outbreak of foot-and-mouth disease or scab. It makes it possible to trace contacts and control the spread of the disease.

Dipping against scab is required by law which is absolutely specific about how and when it should be done. That year, it was permitted in the autumn. Bob took Rachel and Leah and all four lambs, for although the young ram was destined for the butcher, poor chap, it would not be until after the specified dipping period had ended.

Barely an hour later, they returned. I could smell them coming as they came in through the gate! A fresh, strong carbolic sort of smell it was to me, but I doubt that the sheep liked it much. Bob backed the lorry up to the orchard and lowered the tail-gate. They bounced out, the lambs giving a vertical twist and jump on the ramp, seemingly pleased to be home. Their fleeces were damp and curly. I was glad that it was a warm, fine afternoon so they would not get chilled before they were dry.

"I've got some good tups if you're thinking of it later on," offered Bob as he fastened the back of the lorry.

Fortunately my back-yard sheep book had a glossary so I knew that he meant a ram to mate with the ewes. It is said that ewes tupped on Guy Fawkes day will lamb on April Fool's day which seemed early enough for us - not having a "little old shed" in which to house them.

"Thanks," said Maurice, "we haven't really thought about it. To tell the truth, we only got them to cut the grass and now they're beginning to take over the place!"

Bob adopted his usual grin when dealing with us. We must have been a supreme pair of ignoramuses when it came to sheep.

"I've got Down rams - Suffolks - give you fatter lambs than those. They'll be black, of course."

I wondered why they would be black as I thought Suffolk Downs were white. However, they have black faces so I supposed that added to the spots on the Jacob, the black genes would predominate.

"Are we going to have them tupped?" I asked Maurice when Bob had gone.

"Seems silly not to - we could be self sufficient in meat, lamb anyway, and we didn't have any trouble."

"We may not always be so lucky," I said thoughtfully, "but if we do, oughtn't we to stick to Jacob's?"

"I don't see why. We've got our five Jacob's ewes, that's more than enough to feed through the winter and maybe even too many for the orchard. Any more lambs will have to be for the chop so they might as well be fatter."

"Yes, you're probably right. I'll have five Jacob's fleeces next year too. I must learn to spin, the lambs have lovely wool."

"The ram has the best fleece," said Maurice, adding heartlessly, "you'll have to make a rug out of him! "

I believe much more strongly in opportunities than I do in luck or coincidence. An opportunity which presents itself at just the right moment when one is in a position to grab it with both hands may be fortuitous but not coincidental. What the chain of events really hinges on is one's recognition of the opportunity in the first place. How many opportunities are lost because of one's dullness in appreciating that they are there waiting to be grasped?

So it was with the question of spinning. I had gone along to a Festival of Wool in the village of Ravensthorpe in June, to see what I could find out about spinning. Every cottage and farm in the village had some sort of stall or display connected with wool. The highlight of the event was the production of a tweed jacket from sheep to finished garment in (it was hoped) record time.

Brian, one of my milkman acquaintances (there is a great camaraderie between milkmen and postmen), started the sequence of work by shearing a bunch of Jacob's sheep from the superb flock owned by Earl Spencer. The fleeces were then sorted into black and white wool and spun by a team of spinners, one of whom was a man. My ears were glued to a heated argument between him and two of the women on the respective merits of spinning "in the grease" (unwashed wool) and of spinning washed wool to which a lubricant had been added. He got so angry that I thought he was going to walk out of the barn in a paddy and leave them one spinner short. He calmed down after the work began in earnest though.

As fast as the wool was spun, it was given to the weavers who had set up their looms in another barn. One of the looms seemed to be giving a bit of trouble and the tailors who were waiting for the cloth began to get edgy and stood around giving the poor weaver advice which he obviously did not want. Then the black wool ran short and Brian had to be fetched back to shear two more sheep. It was very exciting. Tension mounted as time began to run out for them to beat the record; they just made it, I believe, by a few seconds.

Interesting though the Festival of Wool had been, it had not advanced me towards my goal of learning how to spin. I had been offered an expensive course of instruction which took place a considerable distance away and I had picked up various leaflets on spinning and spinning wheels - the latter also beyond my pocket.

On action-packed September the first, the question answered itself. I was hastening along the steep, unmade road which clung to the ridge flanking Long Buckby's southern aspect. It was the last street in the village for me on my last day as a post-woman so for once I was bounding up and down the steps to each of the little terrace houses that lined both sides.

Do builders ever consider, I wonder, how much harder they make the task for a delivery person when they put six steps up (and therefore six steps down) to the front door? Trivialities, you might think, but it is surprising how they add up. Every porch door and garden gate that has to be opened and closed contributes minutes to the day's work. Each letter box with a powerful spring on it means time and effort - if it leaves the skin on your knuckles. Every wheelbarrow, scooter, line of washing, banana skin that impedes your progress makes you slower and sometimes leaves you bruised.

As for dogs! I have always liked dogs, but being a postman can be guaranteed to give you a jaundiced view of the canine species. The jolly little yap-yap of your own household darling strikes quite another note to a postman, many of whom have scars to show for it. My heart used to thud in the most unpleasant fashion as soon as I turned into the lane where an Alsatian called Star lived. The owner worked shifts and if he was at home in the mornings the dog was allowed to run loose. I had to walk round the house to the door which had the letter box in it and not until I turned the corner could I see whether the dog was about. If it was - whoosh - out it came, snapping and snarling. The only time that I was actually bitten was by a dachshund, scarcely bigger than a large rat and easily as ferocious as one which had been cornered.

Opening the porch door of one of the houses in this particular street of steps, I saw on the mat a yellow leaflet that had been dropped there by someone before me. My eye was caught by the word "spinning". Feeling rather guilty, after a quick look about to make sure that I was not being observed, I picked up the slip of paper.

I saw a list of Further Education courses to be held at Long Buckby Junior School. Spinning classes would be under the instruction of one Bob Donnelly on Monday evenings at a cost of two pounds and fifty pence. That was more like it! I jotted down the date and time of the enrolment on the only paper I had with me (a handkerchief) and put the yellow leaflet back where I found it.

But it was not all smooth sailing after that. The minimum number of students to make the class worthwhile from the point of view of Northampton Education Authority was eight. We were six. Just my luck, I thought, beginning to doubt the value of opportunity versus the rest. But determination won after all. When Bob saw how disappointed his six students were at the prospect of the class being cancelled and how keen they were (especially me) to learn how to spin, he persuaded his friend Jack, a first rate spinner, to come along to swell the numbers. Then we all talked the organiser into relenting and she let us go ahead with a class of seven.

Actually, I think I learnt as much from Jack as from Bob, so we ended up with an excellent pupil to teacher ratio for our money!

Both Bob and Jack were advocates of the "spinning in the grease" method, I was interested to discover why. Bob said:

"Why wash the grease out just to put it back again - it's silly."

I told him about the argument at the Festival of Wool and he laughed, "I bet I know who that was! He and his wife are nutty about cleanliness, they say they won't have unwashed fleeces in the house. Don't pay any attention to him!"

I find the smell of an unwashed fleece quite pleasant as I spin it, but without a doubt there is a lot of muck in it, particularly round the tail end! I wear a long carpenter's apron to protect my clothes now. The apron was soon stiff with strong smelling grease. The dirt washes out of the wool surprisingly easily after it has been spun and plied because the sheep's body secretion, which is present in the fleece, contains its own cleansing agent.

Bob taught us to spin using a hand-spindle to begin with, so that we would understand and practise all the processes involved. It seemed a simple enough device, consisting of a flat disc with a stick shaped like a crochet hook stuck

" I practised on the spinning wheel ..."

through the middle, but it was remarkably tricky to manipulate properly. I was glad to progress to a wheel.

There is a knack to spinning and I had not got it! I practised and practised on the spinning wheel which Yvonne lent me and became more and more cross with my own ineptitude. I had always been secretly proud of my nimble fingers. Eureka! One evening I did get it! Then I never looked back and could scarcely control my impatience to own a spinning wheel.

The opportunity (there was no other word for it) arose to buy a wheel through Bob who was offered a discount for his students. I did not hesitate for a second but ordered a beautiful new wheel made of Silver Beech, carders to tease the fleece and a "lazy Kate" to store spare bobbins. Maurice made me a gadget called a "niddy-noddy" on which to wind the spun wool into a skein and I was ready to begin. Except for one vital thing. I had sold both our fleeces. How I cursed myself!

But I am rushing ahead too fast. All I had done was enrol on Bob's course by the time Maurice and I went "up the cut" for our second canal holiday since moving to the Wharf. The season was still in full swing but as Bruce had volunteered to take over from us while we were away, we had to fit in our holiday before his term in Oxford started. We were not absolutely sure who kept him company or even how many of them there were! We knew that Becky, his girl friend would be there some of the time and her friend Polly who was an agricultural student and bound to be useful with the livestock.

Then there was Rick and Jacky . . . oh and Kurt. I lost track about there. I think people came and went.

I wrote a check list for the shop and another one for the animals and, stifling any misgivings but promising to telephone often in case he had any problems, we disappeared with Tansy. Telephoning is not simple when one is on the canal. There never seems to be a 'phone handy at the precise time one wishes to use it but over the years we had accumulated mental lists of useful items near canals and telephone boxes fell into that category. Sometimes we found that the one on which we were depending was out of order or had been vandalised. This happened once when we were desperate.

A convenient place to moor for the night but not one to be recommended on account of local hooligans (we were set adrift at night once), is just above the two Cape locks in Warwick. Early in the morning while I was cooking breakfast and Maurice was tinkering with the engine, Bruce was playing around outside. Unexpectedly, without the customary thump and rocking of the boat, he appeared at the top of the cabin steps. His face was grey.

"I've hurt my leg," was all he said before he swayed into my arms.

I put a sterile field dressing on his left shin which was slit to the bone from knee to ankle. (He had been pretending to be Tarzan, he told me later, and swinging from tree to tree when he slipped onto a pointed dead branch.)

Meanwhile Maurice had run to the nearest public telephone to find it smashed, so he charged into a small factory by the locks and asked the night watchman to let him use his 'phone.

We had only just moved the boat close to the road bridge when the ambulance arrived with impressive promptitude. The men did not seem at all put out that their patient had to be lifted off a boat and up the steep canal bank. Bruce gritted his teeth manfully (he had looked better the moment the wound was out of sight) and said afterwards that the most annoying part of the whole episode was lying the next day with his foot on a cushion while we sweated up Hatton's famous twenty-one wide locks.

Hatton is often described as the twenty-one golden steps to Heaven. I do not know how the saying originated and I disagree! It would be more logical if Heaven was traditionally down instead of up; descending the flight, the spire of the church of Saint Mary in Warwick is clearly visible. Climbing up, the only building which could be considered of the slightest importance is The New Inn at the top of the hill. It is one of the few pubs which once to my knowledge, actually had no beer!

The New Inn does not have direct canal access, so having fought my way through brambles and nettles and puffed and panted up a steep field to the door, I was pretty thirsty by the time I got there. A notice on the door told me that Davenport's brewery was on strike. Marvellous! I almost threw the half-gallon container I was carrying into the blackberry bushes in my rage and seriously considered what my life was going to be worth when I returned to the boat and its parched crew empty handed!

We had made a conscious decision to climb Hatton Twenty-one again without Bruce when we set out on this holiday, for we hoped to complete a circuit which had come to be known as "The Warwickshire Ring". In the event, we swept up the locks in the company of another boat carrying a splendid crew of hefty young Germans. They did nine-tenths of the work in exchange for picking our brains exhaustively about English canals. I had not entirely forgiven Davenports for their debacle of a few years before so we waved goodbye to our helpers as they sprinted up to The New Inn and we cruised on to Shrewley Tunnel and The Durham Ox.

It was a pleasant pub with a large garden. The wide lawn was dotted with families that spanned several generations, from crawling baby to Great Grandpa. There was a happy holiday atmosphere entirely suited to our mood. The smooth pint of Brew XI made the short steep walk up from the tunnel entrance worth while.

You may have observed that beer has featured rather predominantly on the preceding pages. It all began on one Easter cruise when Bruce had reached the height of passing for the age when he was legally allowed to drink alcohol. The weather was even more appalling than it usually was for our spring holiday, but I had brought with me a publication which is sadly now out of print (and out of date). It was "Nicholson's Real Ale Guide to the Waterways" and it opened our eyes to a delight of canal cruising which we had hitherto neglected. It may have been instrumental in persuading Bruce to continue holidaying with his parents long after the age when he might otherwise have found us dreary and tedious. No doubt it has some bearing on the fact that he and his pals, now in their early twenties, find canal holidays so entertaining! Certainly he never leaves our home mooring without making sure that he has an up to date copy of "The Good Beer Guide" on board which comes back carefully annotated.

We became fairly discerning about the various beers and critical about the way they were kept by the individual landlords. I think that the three of us are unanimous in asserting that the best pint we have ever drunk was a Border Ale at The Cross Foxes in Llangollen. Of course, once one develops a taste for real beer there are few lengths to which one will not go to achieve a good pint. We walked miles down back alleyways in Nantwich, seeking out The Bowling Green because The Real Ale Guide sang its praises so loudly and justifiably. The landlord responded to our enthusiasm and showed Bruce round his cellars to sample his selection of Great Northern Ales.

Feeling content and drowsy, we strolled back to the boat from the Durham Ox, waving cheerfully from the road above to our German friends as they approached the southern portal of Shrewley Tunnel. We met them again at Kingswood Junction where our routes diverged. As they had a whole fortnight to complete the same circuit as ourselves, we suggested that they might prefer to take a detour up the Northern section of the Stratford Canal which would bring them in to Birmingham from the south west, a more attractive route altogether. At King's Norton they would pass through the unusual but obsolete stop lock with its pair of guillotine gates permanently (one devoutly hopes) raised before travelling through the middle of Bournville Garden Factory. The canal wharves where cocoa and chocolate crumb were off-loaded had no more useful purpose any more than as home mooring to boats owned by employees of Cadbury Schweppes. I expect that even that tenuous link with canal transport will disappear when the plans to develop the area for residential use are put into effect. My heart sinks; in our experience, housing estates and vandalism go hand in hand (Cape Locks in Warwick for example).

After skirting the grounds of Birmingham University and the Queen Elizabeth Hospital, the canal enters a secluded, wooded cutting where kingfishers dart between the overhanging trees and golden rod drifts down the railway embankment alongside. We anticipated our foreign visitors being struck with surprise as we had been, when they erupted from the short tunnel at the end of the quiet woodland setting into the hurly-burly of Gas Street Basin in

Birmingham's City Centre.

Our way lay more directly past our old mooring due south of the city at Copt Heath Wharf. The M42 bridge had been the scene of a terrible massacre of countryside there when it was built in the mid seventies. It seemed to have settled a little more comfortably into its surroundings since we last saw it. Trees and bushes had sprung forth suckers from their macheted stumps, and bracken and rosebay willowherb had spread over the raw embankment. Hoards of rabbits had recolonised the field on which thousands of tons of motorway spoil had been spread - a profitable crop from what I heard! It must be nearly ten years since all this took place and the M42 still grinds to a halt a few miles from the scene, petering out in a grassy slip road that leads nowhere.

North of Copt Heath the pleasant rural aspect was brief. The water became thick with oil and cluttered with rubbish until we dropped down the six narrow locks to Bordesley Junction and the link with he Birmingham Canal Navigations. These locks were never widened when the Grand Union Canal improvement took place in the thirties and used to create an infuriating bottleneck in the old days. Neither were the following five Garrison Locks on the last leg of the Grand Union rebuilt between Bordesley Junction and Salford Stop Lock which marked its terminus.

Narrow locks are usually light work even for a crew of two and our progress down the two flights would have been quite snappy had it not been for the rubbish. Garrison Locks were the worst. There was a complete three-piece suite in one lock, jamming the gates so that they could not be opened fully. In another floated a large Butane gas cylinder - on fire. When Maurice opened the gate it drifted out and the wind took it towards the bank which was set alight to our dismay as there was a used car lot on the other side of the wire. There was not much we could do about it though, except shout to the mechanic to warn him. We fished a door out of the bottom lock, a pair of trousers (after they had been caught round the propeller), a roll of wire netting, a doll's pram, a crutch . . .

Disenchanted with mankind, tired and filthy, we passed through the perpetually open gates of Salford Stop Lock. With a deafening report an aerosol can exploded in the heart of a bonfire which was smouldering next to the lock cottage. I just had time to register the fact that it was the twin of the cottage that stood opposite our own, before I joined Tansy who had hurtled down the cabin steps in terror at the bang.

We slid into the shadows of Spaghetti junction. The rhythmic thud of wheels overhead on the bearers which carried the Gravelly Hill interchange was soothing balm to my shattered nerves. It is a view of that notorious conglomeration of concrete that few people see and less appreciate. There is a majesty and elegance inherent in the massive pillars that stand like great trees of the forest supporting huge boughs which interweave in a gigantic canopy aloft. Some of the columns actually stand in the water of the canal like mangroves in a swamp, reducing the width of the channel to little more than that of the boat. Here and there are clearings where small ornamental trees have been planted and flourish, unmolested. It was a surprise to see a man exercising his labrador in the concrete jungle - but why not? In spite of the continuous traffic overhead it was strangely quiet. The sound of the boat's engine, thin and echoing, seemed to be obtrusive. It ought not to have been so, for the canal was opened nearly two centuries before the motorway interchange was even begun.

The Birmingham and Fazeley Canal was authorised in 1784 as a useful junction canal. It remains an important link and is much more pleasant than its name implies, escaping the tentacles of industry with unexpected speed. As we journeyed north-east the water got progressively clearer; in the three locks at

" Like great trees of the forest ..."

Minworth it was seething with tiny fish. Between the bottom lock and the short Curdworth tunnel the canal banks were so verdant that it was easy to make-believe we were in the country and far from the industrial conurbation. This feeling was enhanced by an enormous fallen tree that bridged the canal. As we ducked our heads to dodge the sprays of leaves, a wood pigeon flew out with a great flapping of wings and headed off towards a small coppice on the right.

"That fallen tree would make a picture," I said wistfully as I looked back, "although the light's not very good."

"We'll stop if you like," said Maurice, "it's quiet here. Maybe the light will be better in the morning."

Landscape painting always looks better when there is sunlight and shadows (or storm clouds and lightning), so it was disappointing to wake up to an unimpressive day with a sky of opaque white cloud. Still, I managed to make a fair sketch which pleased someone enough to buy it almost as soon as it was framed and hung up in the shop. I was glad to have painted a picture when I did because things went wrong shortly after that and the weather turned nasty as well.

We had just left Warwickshire and crossed into Staffordshire when a clattering in the engine compartment heralded a red warning light on the control panel. The drive belt had snapped. Buying a spare belt had been one of those chores that had been shelved along with a lot of other maintenance the boat should have had over the past year. Maurice was not too worried as a motor-car fan belt of the right size would do and we knew there was a garage in Fazeley (on the corner of our own A5).

The first fat drops of rain started to fall as Maurice struggled with the extraordinarily heavy and awkward swing bridge at Drayton Manor Park. The appearance of the bridge is eccentric. On either side of the canal there is a castellated turret which supports a white wooden footbridge. Pedestrians have to climb up inside the tower to cross the bridge above the heads of the boatmen and descend within the tower on the opposite side. The adjacent vehicle bridge is the one which has to be swivelled. It is very difficult to start the bridge moving and inevitably, each time Maurice thought that he had got it going, a car appeared with the driver sounding the horn to indicate that he wanted to cross first. Considering that the track seemed to lead into an empty field, the number of cars which disappeared down it was incredible!

We were almost halfway round our planned circuit with time in hand when we stopped in Fazeley to do our shopping. We called at the British Waterways

Yard to top up with drinking water and dispose of our refuse and sewage before going in search of a fan belt. There was not one to be had anywhere. Dodging the muddy spray being thrown at us by lorries as they thundered through the town, we darted from one garage to another without finding a belt of the right size. At the last garage, the mechanic suggested that we ought to try using a pair of ladies' tights!

"It's well known in the motor trade," he said, "I once knew a chap who did five thousand miles between services on his girl friend's tights!"

"Not mine!" I said firmly to Maurice, "you buy your own. I only brought one pair — for when you take me out to dinner!"

"What shade would you like?" I asked mischievously as we sorted through the packets in the newsagent's.

"I'm not fussy - you choose and then you can have them afterwards," he said generously.

The tights were not only useless as a drive belt (five thousand miles - my foot!) because they kept slipping but they stretched to eight feet long in no time at all. So Maurice gave in and telephoned a boatyard in Braunston to ask someone to come out with the right size drive belt. He knew that I would have been impossibly grumpy with no cabin lights or shower pump for the rest of the holiday. The thought of swinging the engine to start it every morning probably did not appeal to him either.

I would like to say that we learnt by experience. Alas no! The same thing exactly has happened to us since. Worse actually, for the bulb in the red light blew at the same time so the battery was dead flat before we knew what had happened.

Nothing untoward happened during the rest of that week, however, and the weather picked up after its hiccup and turned warm enough for a crowd of girls on one boat to plunge into bikinis. Personally, I thought it was carrying stoicism a bit too far! They all had goose pimples.

Hawkesbury Junction was basking in sunshine when we arrived there on Friday, the eve of a boat rally being organised by the local branch of the Inland Waterways Association. These rallies are held from time to time throughout the boating season at various places all over the waterways. Usually, they are designed to draw attention to a particular area that needs renovation or a canal that is underused. Occasionally, they are held just for the fun of a local get-together, which was probably the reason for this one at the end of the season. A number of boats had already arrived for the rally, including a pair of well maintained ex working boats with fine decoration and Buckby Cans.

We were not too late for a pint of M&B at The Greyhound, one of the few canal-side pubs in which one sniffs the atmosphere it must have had when canal transport was at its peak. I popped into the small shop nearby to have a chat (and compare their goods and prices with our own) and then we were through the shallow stop lock and off down the Oxford Canal on the last segment of our circular journey.

There was one more holiday task that was yet to be completed, that of loading the roof of the boat with wood for the stove. We had selected a fair bit from the debris at Garrison Locks but not enough to make any appreciable difference to our winter warmth. Towards evening I spied a fallen elm tree at the edge of a field beyond the towpath. Limbs had been torn off as it fell and were strewn about the field; nettles and brambles were growing through the twigs and branches which were overgrown with long grass. It was obvious to me that the owner of the field must be disinterested in potential firewood.

Leaving Maurice to make the boat fast (he always rearranged the knots if I did it, anyway), Tansy and I went to explore the possibilities. Most of the bigger pieces of timber were out of the question - it was a far larger tree than it had seemed at first glance - but there were three or four good sized branches of the diameter preferred by our finicky stove. I hoisted one of them out of the grass. What was this? Gosh! In triumph, I ran back to the boat carrying the largest mushroom I had ever seen. It was at least the size of a tea plate and heavy, too. At least, I thought it was a mushroom and so did Maurice. We both looked at it, smelt it, looked at it some more and then at each other. Was it - or wasn't it?

"Fungi are so difficult," I said, "and yet there are lots of edible ones. We ought to be able to recognise them. I mean - it's stupid to live in the country and not be able to tell a mushroom from a toadstool."

"Oh, I'm not sure it's stupid," said Maurice, "remember Ali, our servant in Ghana? He reckoned that all snakes were poisonous - killed them on sight just in case - I never could persuade him that some were harmless. He used to say 'all shnek be bad Sir' and that was that. No use to argue."

"What are you getting at? Are you trying to tell me that we should assume that all fungi should be treated as if they were a Death Cap?"

"Not at all. There are more that are harmless than poisonous and I think the poisonous ones are few and far between."

"You don't need more than a few," I said drily, "one if it's a Death Cap."

"I'm sure this one isn't a Death Cap - Amanita Phalloides. We'll give it a try for breakfast."

"The fact that you can show off with its Latin name does not convince me that you know what you are talking about. I think that only one of us should have it for breakfast, then at least the other one can explain to the doctor what happened. "

"Okay," said Maurice, adding generously, "you can have it as you found it."

"No thanks. You have a bigger appetite - you have it."

He did, too. It smelt delicious while it was frying and Maurice said it tasted "fine". I think that he would have enjoyed it more if he had been absolutely certain what it was. I forbore to enquire about his health until lunch-time, when we both agreed that he was probably not going to double up in agony after all.

We have bought a field guide to fungi now but it is still a tricky business. I think that we could identify a Horse Mushroom again, for that is what it was, but we have nearly been caught out with Yellow Stainers once or twice. And not having the field guide at the time, we missed out on a meadow at Hawkesbury Junction full of Shaggy Parasols which are said to have a very fine

" Then - it was winter ..."

flavour. It must have been a good year for mushrooms because on our return we found that dozens of fairy rings had sprung up all over the orchard and the garden. Having always considered mushrooms to be a luxury, I suddenly found that I had punnets full of them. We had mushrooms for breakfast every day, we ate them with fish and with chicken. I slung handfuls in every casserole and finally we made soup. That was the pièce de résistance and we froze it in pint containers against the day that the mushroom harvest was over. Then - it was winter.

-11-
Roll in The Barrel

The bitter winds with which we were becoming familiar swept across the canal from East Anglia. But as the thermometer fell, the warmth of optimism in the future of Blisworth Tunnel began to rise among the waterways fraternity. We heard that the main contract to repair the tunnel had at long last been awarded to a construction company. Work had begun!

At a meeting of the Northampton branch of the Inland Waterways Association, a British Waterways Board engineer gave a talk illustrated by slides on the rebuilding of the tunnel. The hall was packed. He did a grand job of improving public relations with the Board - so often the Big Bad Bogeymen of the canals. All of us who were there began to understand the magnitude of the problem and even the rationale behind the Board's insistence that the money was forthcoming before the giant task was undertaken. We had no sympathy for a sluggish Treasury!

The official opening date was given as Spring 1985. Two more years at least. (It was opened six months early in fact!) So - back to our sums. Clearly the full potential of the business would not be realised until we had through traffic on the Grand Union between London and Birmingham. Meantime, one of us ought to prop up the enterprise with other work.

Maurice reckoned that it was his turn so he accepted a job with a Friendly Society selling Life Insurance. He was suited to it about as little as I had been to the task of post-woman but it got us through that winter and beyond. We would take each one as it came.

The time had come at last to apply for an off-licence. We had shelved it as long as we could in order not to create ill-feeling between ourselves and the New Inn but our survival depended on an increase in turnover. It was the obvious way. The demand was there and judging by the number of customers who signed a petition on our behalf, we would be filling a need. Not everyone who has a holiday on a boat wishes to drink in a public house although they may not be teetotallers - a lot of boaters dislike having to stop cruising at all in the hours of daylight! Then it can be difficult to go out in the evening if they have small children; boats are not safe places for toddlers to be left alone even if they are supposed to be asleep. We would be catering for a different market from the New Inn.

I tried hard not to be too hopeful. We had read so many horror stories in the magazine for independent retailers about small grocers who had been refused off-licences time and again without ever knowing the reason why. But the same periodical also published a helpful leaflet which told us how to set about it and the pitfalls to avoid. We followed the advice to the letter.

After a considerable search Maurice found a solicitor who was prepared to quote us a set fee for the work involved in applying for a licence. His clerk came to see our stores and tell us what we had to do. Quite a lot, in fact.

I had to draw a scale map of the district and mark on it every single off-licensed premises within a radius of five miles. Being canal rather than road oriented, I made a point of marking on the map the distance and cruising time in all three directions to the nearest off-licence. As the latter was in every case at least three hours plus a fifteen minute walk, I think that it may have tipped the balance in our favour.

A scale plan of the shop was needed too, with the proposed whereabouts of the alcohol marked on it. The clerk warned us that we were unlikely to be granted a full licence at first, so we applied for a licence to sell beer, wine and cider only. In any case, not as many people had asked us for spirits as the other three. This was to be one occasion when the fact that we were not a self-service store was a positive advantage. The clerk did not think we would have stood a chance if our shop had been open-plan.

The next hurdle was a visit from fire officers and the police and (most frightening of all) the magistrates themselves! They were charming people but I was unable to tell from their manner what the decision was likely to be. The solicitor collected a stack of supportive letters from customers living as far away as York and Cornwall. Our lock-keeper at Buckby wrote too, and so did Chris Barney in his capacity as the owner of a hire boat firm. The aim of all this and of the petition was to prove the need for an off-licence.

We had decided that the licence was to be in my name, so putting on a smart coat and (good heavens) a hat - off I went to the Brewsters Sessions in Daventry on my own to learn the worst. The solicitor put my case. Feeling nervous, I went to the stand when I was called, to answer a few questions and describe the alcoholic state of the canal. Then ;

"Licence granted," said the chairman of the bench. Yippee!

Naturally, the first thing that had to be done before I even took off my hat when I got home, was to organise some "real ale" to sell in my newly designated off-licence. There was a small brewery in Daventry that brewed a smooth pint known as Northamptonshire Bitter. Bruce and I had tried it, so I knew that it was good. In no time at all it was arranged. We would kick off the season with a barrel (or more correctly - a firkin) of good beer.

If one is selling draught beer in an off-licence, the brew has to go into something to be carried away. The law says that it must be in a covered container and quite often the customer does not have one of his own. Bruce produced a sample flask that he had bought somewhere else which was perfect for the job. It was made of stone-coloured plastic with an air-tight stopper and held four pints. Unfortunately, the maker insisted that we placed a bulk order for three hundred and sixty of them. They arrived in ten boxes, each of which measured a cubic yard! The "Object" nearly burst at the seams.

Then we found that we could not fill the flasks from the firkin without burping ale all over the floor. A special funnel was needed. Maurice rang up a real ale off-licence where he and Bruce had been regular visitors in Birmingham.

"Hello boys," Syl used to say, "Sunday wouldn't be Sunday without you!"

She was as helpful as ever and gave him the name of a brewer's supplier who sent us an elegant copper funnel which had an air vent and a long slender stem. Tansy was not too pleased, though, as she had developed a taste for Litchborough beer when it dripped on the floor and she still lingers by the barrel occasionally, sniffing and licking her lips hopefully.

Another idea that we had, was to attend weekend craft fairs throughout the winter. Craft fairs are big business for the organisers, less so for the exhibitors. But there are plenty of people who produce work at home, small cottage industries even, for whom a craft fair is the only outlet. Some of them do quite nicely out of it. For others, it is an adjunct to their main point of sale. A potter rented the stand next to ours at Bedford Craft Fair. Most of his pottery was sold at the twice weekly market in the small town where he lived, but his wife went to all the craft fairs in the county as well "just to keep the stuff ticking over".

Some craft fairs, especially the large ones in densely populated districts, are fussy about the wares you sell. The organiser will probably send you a fiercely worded letter, stipulating that the goods must be "true crafts" with nothing "bought in for resale". You may be required to fill in a form stating exactly what you propose to have on your stand and promising to abide by it. They often try to dragoon you into working on your craft at the fair to "add interest". I only tried this once. The light was dim and people manning stands behind me kept bumping into the back of my chair just as I was making a delicate brush stroke. Finally, the dust which floated about as soon as everyone started packing up, stuck to the enamel and ruined the finish so that I had to rub it down and begin again.

At the first large fair that we attended, we were meticulous about the "true craft" ruling. I stayed up half the night before, painting, in order to comply with my agreement that everything would be hand-painted. We agonised and eventually left behind, notelets and postcards which had been commercially printed to my own design in case they broke the rules.

A likeable extrovert at a nearby stand was selling glove puppets. The most successful of these was a large monkey with a long tail that the man hitched in his belt. The monkey's hands were tied round his owner's neck as if it were clasping him lovingly. The salesman waited until a child of any age was within earshot, not bothering whether or not the infant was looking in his direction. Often they were not, for the mothers were more interested in the jewellery stand opposite. No matter, it was all the same to our man.

"No!" he would say crossly to the monkey, "be quiet! That pretty little girl doesn't want to talk to a rude monkey like you. Do behave or I'll leave you at home next time!"

Of course, the little girl would turn round to see what all the racket was about, and before a minute or two had elapsed, that monkey would be clasped round her neck and our friend had five pounds in his pocket!

We talked to the monkey man quite a bit during the slack period before lunch. He had designed his glove puppets many years before - there were three or four different ones but the monkey was easily the best seller. He bought the fur fabric in bulk and cut it out with a stamping press. Out-workers (people who worked at home) sewed the pieces into the finished puppets using domestic sewing machines. After a round trip all over the Midlands collecting the puppets he sold them through all sorts of outlets, often employing sales-people on a casual basis. He told us that his sales were always higher when he did the selling himself and I believed him. He was a natural mimic. But his product was certainly not a "true craft" by any stretch of the imagination and I felt sorry for the hand-beaten silver jewellery lady who scarcely made a sale all afternoon.

A scented stall of fragrant cosmetics, herb sachets and pomanders caught Maurice's attention or maybe it was the lovely young woman behind it! (Being a pipe-smoker, Maurice is not renowned for his keen sense of smell.) Maggie made the face creams herself, he said, cooking beeswax and other wholesome ingredients on the kitchen stove. Her pot-pourri mixture was "going like a bomb", sold by the ounce from large paper sacks. He was sure that I could make this at least - I already grew everything that was needed in the garden.

"I'll give it a try," I said, resolving to buy a large pot of Maggie's moisture cream when I had the chance. I think his interest in her waned rather when she told him that she only ate nuts and yoghurt and could not bear the idea of keeping sheep as they would dirty the grass on which she held her yoga class.

Across the hall someone was warbling old familiar melodies; mellower than a flute, softer than a recorder. I found myself humming in unison as the unseen musician played The Ashgrove then Greensleeves. Shades of my schooldays I thought as I heard the opening bars of The Minstrel Boy.

"I must go and find out what instrument is making that lovely sound," I told Maurice, "will you mind the stand while I have a walk round?"

It was some time before I located the source of the music. There were so many distractions. I kept getting side-tracked. A large Pyrography stand could not be ignored as I had just bought myself a Pyrography machine and I was still a beginner at the craft. The name is derived from two Greek words meaning fire-writing and is an up-market term for the old-fashioned poker-work. My modern tool was electrically heated and there were several different working points of various shapes and sizes. So far, I had not been too ambitious. I had begun by decorating wooden spoons because we had so many that it would not matter if I spoilt a few. They looked pretty good so my next step was to burn castle scenes on chopping boards which would be more difficult.

I stopped to watch the woman working on personalised key-rings and brooches to order. I did not learn anything of her technique though, as she was only writing names and I had mastered that much. I moved on.

A girl was making pastel portraits taken from photographs of famous personalities. She worked quickly and they were good likenesses. The real test, I knew, would be when she had a commission and had to work like lightning from a live model. Portraits are not my forte. I once painted a portrait in oils of a friend of mine - it was a terrible picture but just recognisable as Beverley. Her husband insisted on buying it because he said: "That's what Bev will look like in twenty years!"

Fifteen years later and she still does not look remotely like the portrait which I sincerely hope has now been thrown away!

I tried to slide past the home-made cakes without a side-long glance but weakened and bought two wedges of shortbread to have with our coffee. The adjacent stand was quite tiny, about three feet square, and a small girl was sitting by herself in front of an array of little ceramic pots. I smiled at her and she smiled back and lifted one of the vessels to her lips. Incredulously, I listened to the pure notes of The Lass with the Delicate Air as the child played the ocarina!

Craft fairs are ideal places in which to do one's Christmas shopping. There are so many unusual gifts and prices are low by comparison with those in the shops. This is because the overheads of the traders are low. We knew that our ware seemed over-priced and yet we had no margin to reduce it. I am not sure that we had a suitable product either. Canal ware was out of context. A few members of the public recognised it for what it was and they tended to be our only customers. Others found it eye-catching, paused, and moved on. They were probably the sort of people who drive across hump-backed bridges without ever wondering why they are there or what passes underneath. The world is full of them!

At about that time I was offered the chance to enlighten some of those persons whose eyes had not been opened to the delights of the canals and the traditional art of the boat people. An acquaintance in Birmingham invited me to talk to a ladies' circle about the history of canal painting. Oddly enough (and I rebuke myself for the oversight), I had scarcely bothered about the background of the decoration at which I was trying to make a living. It had been enough for me to discover that I had the skill to execute my own designs within the constraints of the original techniques used on the working boats. To learn this I had looked at scores of old photographs of painted boats and the utensils owned by the boat people, but my interest had always been "how?" and not "why?" Having been given this brief, I needed to do some research. The more I found out, the more curious I became.

Unfortunately, there are fewer hard facts about the early days of canal boating and the people who worked the boats, than there are about the construction and the politics involved in the early waterways. There were hardly any contemporary records that I could find and a lot of the other information was guesswork. I felt that the history and expansion of the canal system itself must have played an important part in the introduction and development of boat painting, so I examined that first.

In the 1800s there were some four thousand miles of navigable waterway in England with an interconnecting system stretching from as far north as Ripon to Portsmouth in the south. At the heart of the system lay the Birmingham Canal Navigations. This in itself is an extensive complex which was formed originally by the merging of several canal companies. In its heyday (the mid nineteenth century), there were a hundred and sixty miles of waterway and even today it is reputed to have more miles of canal than Venice.

Of the hundred and sixty miles of canal, only six in the south-east corner of the Birmingham Canal Navigations were actually in the city, the rest was spread over the Black Country in a rough square with Wolverhampton in the opposite corner. The B.C.N. (as it is commonly called) was the only canal network to benefit from the coming of the railways; it had numerous private branches and wharves with as many as twenty-six railway interchanges. It declined recently (in canal terms) - only after the Second World War.

It is generally accepted that the Duke of Bridgewater's canal which opened in 1762 was the first viable canal in England. The early boats were called "Starvationers" and went deep into the Duke's mines at Worsley Delph, and being double-ended vessels, reversed out and carried coal to Manchester. The nick-name should tell you that they were spartan craft with no provision for the comfort of the all male crew.

After connections were made with other waterways, make-shift cabins were erected on "day boats", but journeys were still short so no other refinements were deemed to be necessary. It was not until half a century later, when competition with the railways caused the proprietors of the canal companies to cut their prices, that living accommodation on the boats was provided for families. The exploitation of women and children during the industrial revolution is well known and the canal companies were no exception when it came to taking advantage of cheap labour.

I am inclined to believe, on negative evidence, that it was the feminine influence on board the boats that gave rise to the decoration. In other words, I could not find any written or pictorial records which suggested that there was a tradition of narrow boat painting in the days when the boats were crewed by men and boys. The earliest ornamentation (if one can call it that) was illustrated in a set of engravings dated 1827 by Thomas Shepherd. Narrow boats owned by Pickfords had the boat's name painted on the top plank of the hull and the company name on the cabin side next to a large diamond which may have been the company logo. Hardly a work of art exactly!

And yet only thirty years later, narrow boat painting as we know it today, had become established. There was clear proof of that. A series of articles entitled "On the Canal" was written by John Hollingshead and published in the periodical "Household Words". Vivid descriptions of flamboyant roses and castles were likened by Hollingshead to "the great teaboard school of art".

He was referring to a style of painting which began as "Pontypool Ware" in Wales in the late seventeenth century. Japanned sheet metal was used in a variety of useful and decorative objects, oriental-looking to begin with, but by the 1830s a high standard of landscapes and rustic scenes had evolved. Tea trays and caddies were a speciality from which the name of the style was derived.

Nearly everyone will have heard of the rather damning epithet "Brummagem made", so it will come as no surprise to learn that numerous factories sprang up in the Black Country churning out cheap copies of the highly regarded Pontypool Ware under the direction of an ex-Pontypool workman called (would you believe it?) Jones. By 1850, block-printing and stencilling speeded the process of embellishing tea-trays with floral motifs similar to the stylised roses and daisies characteristic of canal painting. As for the castles - they were nearly always fairy-tale mediaeval turrets with conical roofs - rarely seen in the vicinity of the canal system but not uncommon in the Welsh Marches near Pontypool.

At this point in my investigations I began to get excited. I was certain that the proliferation of inexpensive teaboard ware in the very heart of the canal system at a time when narrow boats became floating homes for whole families was the key to the puzzle.

But picturesque landscapes and wreaths of flowers are only half the story. Less romantic but more striking at first glance is the bold juxtaposition of pattern and colour using abstract designs and geometric devices. Try as I would, I could not track down the source of all of them.

Playing card symbols were often used, perhaps because like most travelling people, boat families were highly superstitious. The diamond, first recorded on the Pickfords boats, occurs over and over again. A vertical band of diamonds was commonly painted in the centre of the cratch (a flat triangle at the front of the boat), up the stands and masts or in a row on either side of the bow. But why diamonds? I entered the realms of supposition.

One evening when we were slowly cruising down the middle of a straight stretch of canal, the banks of which had been reinforced, Maurice chanced to look back. He noticed that as the bow cut through the water it was pushed sideways to create ripples which fanned out towards the bank in a band of

"But why diamonds ...?"

perfect diamonds. Shimmering in the late sunlight, the pattern was deflected off the canal wall to form a second, fainter band of diamonds and so on until a bend in the canal disrupted the process. We have seen the phenomenon several times under similar conditions. Was it the source of inspiration to the boat painters of old?

Hearts and clubs were popular too. Like diamonds, they always followed the rule of contrast - dark against light. A red heart, for example, on a scalloped white ground against a dark green backdrop. There was a wealth of geometric motifs - crescents, circles, compass roses - perhaps because they were less difficult to achieve than freehand designs. At about the time the Prince of Wales reached the height of his popularity, the fleur-de-lys was first used on the handles of dippers and water cans.

I was specially anxious to find out what I could about the latter as the Buckby Can was our "stock in trade". Maurice was very fond of telling customers that our shop was "the home of the Buckby Can". But I could not trace the Water can further back than 1858 when Hollingshead's description was published in "Household Words". Both that and an engraving in the "Art Journal" of 1873 showed that the construction and decoration of water cans became a tradition soon after their innovation and changed very little in subsequent years.

The joints and seams made by the tinsmith were exploited by the painter who picked them out in garish yellow. The panels thus divided were adorned with clusters of roses and maybe a few daisies and a sunflower or two. Sometimes the widest panel boasted a castle scene while the strengthening centre band carried the name of the boat or its owner or occasionally a motto. The proportions of the can varied slightly according to its origin but came to be known by the district rather than the tinsmith. An Aylesbury or a Buckby Can, for instance. Sometimes the style of painting was similarly accredited. Hence, a Braunston rose, although I expect that every boatman could have told you who painted his can if he had a mind to!

Not being an experienced speaker, I thought it would be easier and more fun if I illustrated my talk with colour slides. Maurice and I had a great time running our collection of photographs through the projector one evening. We had dozens of pictures of painted boats, buckets, cans and dippers all smothered in roses, mops with handles striped like a barber's pole and cabin doors illustrated with castles fit for Sleeping Beauty.

"We might as well do the job properly," said Maurice as we sorted the boat pictures into piles, one for each section of the boat working from bow to stern, "I have a feeling these talks of yours might catch on, word gets around you know."

"Oh! Look! We must use these 'photos of "Iona", I'd forgotten that fantastic castle on the fold-down table in the boatman's cabin."

"Iona"! How long ago that seemed now. It was almost at the start of our long love affair with the canals. So much had changed since then. We were different people.

Maurice asks all our customers how much they are enjoying themselves. It is not merely salesman's patter - he genuinely wants to know. If it is their first canal holiday and they are having a marvellous time, he says gravely, "Canalling is a very dangerous thing to do — look what it has done to us!"

" A liberal dose of fresh herbs ..."

Postscript

I have talked a lot about food production as a means of partial self-sufficiency not just for the sake of economy, but because home grown stuff tastes better. It has not travelled for a start, or been handled by umpteen different people. Naturally, the preparation of our harvest for the table is of equal importance although I try to reduce the time spent on it to the absolute minimum. This is mainly because I prefer gardening to cooking, but I do believe that if the produce is absolutely fresh (which it ought to be if you have grown it yourself), you are halfway to cooking a good meal.

We are not obsessive about "organic gardening". I would not dream of asserting that a lettuce grown with compost and horse muck tastes any better than one which has utilised artificial fertilisers or that it contains more vitamins or whatever. But there are facets of the "old fashioned" methods which appeal to me strongly. I do worry that mankind today is taking more out of this planet than it is putting back into it and I know that I am as big a culprit as anyone. It also seems more sensible to me to walk round the orchard with a bucket and shovel for half an hour and spread the resulting sheep droppings around the blackcurrant bushes, topping it off with a panful of wood ash from the stove, rather than buy an expensive bag of fertiliser and potash from the garden centre.

Maurice uses garden sprays occasionally but not regularly and then only as a last resort in dire cases such as gooseberry sawfly attacks. One winter wash of the trees in the orchard in four years has improved the quality of the fruit no end without any of the recommended spraying at pink bud and petal drop and all the rest.

I prefer to let the wild birds and the chickens have first refusal of most of the creepy-crawlies that would damage our crops and I have at last found a useful occupation for the two remaining bantam hens. They have unfettered freedom of the vegetable garden away from the persecution of the bigger hens and the unwelcome advances of Gandalf . Being small and light, they do no damage to perennial plants and from November to April they work away at the soil consuming everything that moves except worms which they dislike!

In the summer, when we are selling our garden produce, it is sometimes difficult to laugh away the fact that caterpillars have left the cabbages looking more like the leaves of a Swiss Cheese plant but we do our best. I am currently trying a method known as "companion gardening" which means using one plant to discourage pests from attacking its neighbour - garlic between carrots and parsley between onions for example. I doubt if I will ever be certain that it works, though.

I think it is easier to grow vegetables which can be harvested in the winter than to bother with the storage of earlier crops which would lack the important quality of freshness. We tend to use the freezer whenever we have a glut and of course that is where the lamb goes when it is has been jointed by the butcher. Some root vegetables will remain quite happily in the ground until they are required provided that one is reconciled to doing without them when the earth is frozen. But then there will always be something else which will do instead, like sprouts or curly kale. We always reckon on eating our own tomatoes until New Year's Day - green ones that have been ripening in dribs and drabs since October. Apples are a problem. Some varieties do not keep at all. Of the ones we have that do, any specimens which are less than perfect go bad. We need somewhere really cold and yet frost-free in which to store the good apples. I am working on that! Meanwhile, apple slices can be dried or frozen and apple pulp is a useful standby to have in the freezer.

I have gathered together for those readers who might be interested, the recipes that I have mentioned in earlier pages and added a few more of our favourites. The main ingredient without exception is home grown and the cost is low of any that have to be bought. For instance, I always use Maurice's homemade yoghurt as a substitute for cream. Those who, like me, cannot bear the taste of raw yoghurt need have no qualms. It is undetectable when used in cooking. Butter is my one extravagance. For that there is no real substitute that does not ruin the flavour. I need a cow!

When it comes to quantities, I admit I am rather haphazard, tending towards "handfuls" rather than "ounces". But I will be specific, I promise, where it matters. I often remember the customer who asked Maurice to pick her "enough spinach for two greedy people". A woman after his own heart. He knew exactly how much spinach to pick and it was much quicker than using the scales!

Incidentally, as those scales are nearly thirty years old and perfectly accurate, I have resisted any attempts to metricate me in the kitchen. New-fangled readers will have to make their own conversions.

The collection of brief notes which follow is not intended to be a cookery book in miniature. My aim has been two-fold; one is to offer a rationale for behaviour which may have seemed to many people as being imbued with an over-abundance of enthusiasm for growing things merely for the sake of growing them; the other is to infect others with a little of that same enthusiasm and what better way than through their stomachs!

STEAMED VEGETABLES

One inexpensive cooking utensil that I can recommend is a steamer which fits inside any size of saucepan. Vegetables that are steamed are supposed to retain more of their nutrients. They keep their colour better and we prefer their texture. Steamed brussels sprouts for instance, are brilliant emerald and firm and crunchy instead of looking (and smelling) like soggy yellow compost.

Put an inch of boiling water in the bottom of the saucepan which is going to hold the steamer. Remember that greens shrink so you will need twice as much uncooked by volume as you think you will need when they are cooked. I never add salt to the steamer - individuals add their own at the table - but I often put herbs and spices in with the vegetables when I steam them.

The following vegetables steam well:
Perpetual spinach with a few young sorrel leaves and grated nutmeg.
Runner or French beans with parsley and savory.
Carrots (young) with parsley and fennel.
Peas (young) with apple mint.
New potatoes with any sort of mint. Experiment; try dill or green coriander.
Cabbage. All varieties steam well with dill, fennel or chives.
Kale. Very young leaves only, with grated nutmeg.

Place the steamer on top of the water in the pan and fill it with as many vegetables as you require. Put a well fitting lid on the pan and place on sufficient heat to maintain steam without the lid lifting to allow steam to escape. The vegetables will cook in slightly less time than you would ordinarily allow. Do not overcook.

Most green herbs can be used to make herb butters. Try leaving the herbs out of the cooking sometimes and dressing the vegetables with a dollop of herb butter before serving.

BAKED VEGETABLES

Baked Jacket Potatoes with curd cheese and chives
1 x 7oz potato per head
¼ pint curd cheese fills 4 potatoes
Bunch freshly cut chives
Scrub and dry the potatoes and prick the skins with a fork.
Bake for 1-1½ hours, testing by piercing with a skewer.
Slit skin like a cross, lift corners and make a dent in the middle then fill the depression with a mixture of curd cheese, chopped chives and seasoning. Alternative flavours can be added to the cheese by using different herbs.

Beetroot
Medium sized beetroot should be scrubbed and cooked in a baking tray in a slow oven. They take about 2½ hours, less if wrapped in foil.

Onions
Large or medium sized onions, wrapped in foil can be cooked the same way. They should not be peeled, and take less time than baked potatoes. It is advisable to inspect them now and again as the cooking time can vary according to the variety of onion.

Vegetables wrapped in foil can be baked in a barbeque.

BUTTERED VEGETABLES

Celeriac stewed in butter
Wash and peel a celeriac root and cut it into thin strips. Fry in butter for about ten minutes, tossing frequently. When it is nearly cooked add salt, pepper, a tea spoon of French mustard and a teaspoon of chopped parsley. Do not overcook - the celeriac should be crunchy.

Courgettes or Marrows sweated in butter
Peel a marrow, remove the seeds and cut into one inch cubes.
Melt a nob of butter in a fairly heavy saucepan with a well fitting lid. Put a layer of marrow pieces, crushed garlic, a pinch of salt and a good twist of black pepper. Continue in layers until all the marrow is used, then top with another nob of butter. If there are many layers do not salt them all. Put the lid on the pan and place on a low heat. Shake the pan now and then, but resist the temptation to look for at least 15 minutes. Cooking time depends on the age of the marrow but avoid huge old ones which will be dry.

Courgettes can be cooked in exactly the same way, but do not need peeling or seeding, just washing and slicing into pieces about ¾ inch thick. They need less cooking time, of course, about 10 minutes.

Buttered leeks
Trim and wash the leeks and cut into slices ¾ inch thick. Wash well in a colander under running water and drain. Melt a nob of butter in a heavy saucepan with a well fitting lid and add the leeks, stirring them around in the butter to coat them all. Add a pinch of salt and a good twist of black pepper and a crushed clove of garlic. Put lid on pan and place on a low heat for about 10 minutes or until tender, shaking pan frequently.

Mangetout or Sugar peas
Pick these very young - before the peas have developed fully. Top and tail the pods. Melt a nob of butter in a frying pan and stir in enough mangetout to coat the bottom of the pan thickly. If you wish to cook more than that, you will have to have another go. Sprinkle with sea salt and toss the peas about for a couple of minutes. The results will be bright green and very crunchy.

Roots as salad vegetables

Grated celeriac, carrot and beetroot are all delicious when mixed with chopped fresh herbs and used in salads. Wash and grate the root raw. They add flavour and colour to a green salad.

SOUPS

Artichoke and Carrot Soup *serves 6*
1½ lb Jerusalem artichokes
1 lb carrots
1 large onion
Bunch fresh or dried celeriac leaves or 1 small peeled, sliced root.
3 oz butter
2½ pints chicken stock
Peel artichokes (be ruthless about discarding nobs) and slice them into a bowl of cold water to prevent discolouration.
Scrub carrots (young home-growns will not need scraping) and slice. Peel and chop onion. Melt butter in a saucepan, soften onion in it for a few minutes then add drained artichokes and carrots (celeriac root if used) and seasoning. Allow vegetables to sweat with the lid on for ten minutes on a very low heat. Add celeriac leaves, chopped and pour in the stock stirring well. Simmer until all the vegetables are soft. Liquidise or pass through a sieve. Check seasoning.

Mushroom Soup *serves 4*
About 1 lb mushrooms
2 oz butter
1 thick slice crustless white bread
2 pints chicken stock
Garlic, parsley and seasoning
Wipe mushrooms and cut into small pieces. Melt butter in a heavy pan and soften mushrooms until the moisture runs. Add 1 clove of garlic, 1 tablespoon of chopped parsley, a pinch of salt and black pepper. Stew for a few minutes. Meanwhile soak bread in some of the chicken stock, squeeze out surplus and add to mushrooms. Stir well. Add the rest of the stock and simmer for 15 minutes. Either mash and put through a sieve or into liquidiser. The result should not be a smooth cream but have obvious mushroom particles. Return mixture to pan to reheat and swirl in some top of the milk and sprinkle with finely chopped parsley before serving.

MAIN COURSES

Artichoke and Tomato Sauce
Cooked in sufficient quantity this dish could be served on its own or as a vegetable, but it is very rich so we prefer it as an accompaniment.
For each pound of Jerusalem artichokes (peeled) add 2 skinned and chopped tomatoes.
1 clove of garlic crushed.
A sprinkle of sweet basil and marjoram.
Simmer the artichokes whole in salted water until they are almost cooked and then strain and cut in half. Heat a little olive oil in a heavy pan and add the tomatoes and the artichokes with the herbs, salt and black pepper. By the time the tomatoes have run the artichokes should be soft and the whole dish ready to serve.
This freezes well to serve at Christmas with goose or pork.

Potato and Onion Pie
A complete supper dish or an accompaniment for roast lamb.
Twice as much potato as onion according to the number of servings required. (For 4, 20 oz - 10 oz)
2 oz Cheddar or Edam cheese
4 fluid oz natural yoghurt
½ oz margarine
¼ pint milk
Preheat oven to 300°F or gas mark 1 — 2
Peel and slice onions and potatoes very thinly and place in alternate layers in a greased casserole, starting and finishing with a layer of potato. Each layer should be sprinkled with salt and black pepper and smeared with yoghurt and dotted with margarine. Pour milk over and top with grated cheese. Bake for 1½ hours removing lid for last ¼ hour to brown cheese.

Spicy Stuffed Marrow
Peel a large marrow, cut an oblong 'window' in one side and remove seeds.
Preheat oven to 350°F or gas mark 4
1 lb minced beef or lamb
2 cloves of garlic crushed

2 onions peeled and chopped
4 tomatoes, peeled (red or green)
1 green pepper deseeded and chopped
1 teaspoon chilli powder (we like it hot) or two chopped chillis
½ teaspoon marjoram
Fry the meat and onions in a pan in sufficient oil to prevent it sticking until the meat is brown. Then add all the other ingredients and stock or water to moisten. Simmer on a low heat for about 20 minutes or until meat is cooked, stirring occasionally and adding a little more stock if necessary to prevent sticking. When it is cooked, stir in 1 dessertspoon of soya flour or 1 teaspoon plain flour to absorb surplus liquid and cook for a few minutes, stirring continuously. Test seasoning. Pack into cavity of marrow and replace 'window'. Wrap in foil or put in a roasting bag on a baking tin. Bake for ¾ - 1 hour depending on size and age of marrow - it should be soft when pressed.
Serve with a baked potato that can be done at the same time.

Spinach Flan *serves 6*
¾ lb spinach
8 oz cottage or curd cheese
3 eggs
2 oz grated Cheddar cheese
2 tomatoes
9 inch pastry flan baked blind
Milk
Preheat oven to 375°F gas mark 6
Steam spinach with pinch of grated nutmeg and pinch of salt. It only requires about 5 minutes. Drain well and press out water with a saucer. (Even steamed, this is necessary). Sieve cottage cheese or curd cheese. Lightly whisk eggs and stir into the sieved cheese. Fold in the spinach, Cheddar cheese and another pinch of nutmeg and salt if desired and 2 tablespoons of top-of-the-milk. Mix well but gently. Turn into flan and bake for 30 minutes until set and golden. Garnish with sliced tomatoes and serve hot or cold.

Lemon Chicken
1 Oven ready chicken
2 cloves of garlic
1 large lemon
Bunch of lemon balm
6 sprigs of rosemary
Preheat oven to 400°F or gas mark 6 - 7
Wipe and dry chicken. If you have the giblets you will only need the liver. Skin and roughly chop the garlic. Wash lemon and cut in quarters. Stuff the chicken with alternate pieces of lemon, garlic, rosemary, lemon balm in any order or ratio of one to another that you like but finish off with the liver. Put the chicken in a roasting bag, a meat tin covered with foil or a chicken brick. (I use a roasting bag - don't forget to pierce the bag). Dribble a little vegetable or olive oil onto the chicken before you close the bag. Roast for 20 minutes per pound turning the oven down to 375°F when you put it in. You can thicken the juices with arrowroot after skimming off the fat before you serve it if you like, but I don't bother. I use the juices as they are. The carcase is so deliciously impregnated with the stuffings that you must not forget to make stock from it.

STUFFING FOR POULTRY

Mushroom and Bacon Stuffing *(ideal for turkey)*
½ lb mushrooms, chopped
4 oz streaky bacon cut in strips
1 small grated onion
4 oz brown breadcrumbs
1 dessertspoon chopped parsley
A pinch each of winter savory (or thyme) sage, marjoram
Seasoning
Giblet stock
Fry or grill bacon until crisp. Fry mushrooms and onion in a little oil for Ten minutes, tossing them. Put all the ingredients in a bowl and bind stiffly with stock. Pack in the neck of the turkey.

Lemon and Parsley Stuffing *(for any type of poultry)*
4 oz butter
4 oz white breadcrumbs
Grated rind of 1 lemon
4 Tablespoons chopped parsley
1 teaspoon each of chopped marjoram and lemon balm.
Put all the ingredients in a bowl and stir in the melted butter with a fork to a moist crumbly consistency. The result should be light and very green. If you are short of time and the bird is not being prepared for a special occasion, try filling the cavity with mixed bunches of herbs picked straight from the garden. Vary the combination according to your fancy and what happens to be growing well.

YOGHURTS

Yoghurt
1 pint sterilised milk or U.H.T.
2 dessertspoons plain natural yoghurt
(For a firm yogurt add 3 tablespoons powdered milk)
Put the yoghurt in the bottom of a large wide-mouthed Thermos flask. Bring the milk to a temperature of 115°F or 46°C and check with a thermometer.
Pour the milk into the flask and stir well. Screw lid onto Thermos and leave undisturbed overnight. Decant the contents after at least 8 hours into a bowl, cover with cling film and refrigerate.
N.B. Always use plastic spoons when dealing with yoghurt as metal has a detrimental effect on the fermentation and make sure you leave 2 dessertspoonfuls to start off you next batch. It should make up to 16 or so before it starts to get thin when you will need to buy a new 'starter'.

Yoghurt Curd Cheese
1 pint natural yoghurt
1 teaspoon salt
Stand a bowl of yoghurt in a basin of hot water. When the outside water has cooled stir in the salt. Tip the yoghurt into a muslin bag suspended over another bowl and leave to drip for 24 hours. Discard the whey (the water) and pot the curd with a weighted saucer on top and refrigerate until firm.
N.B. The whey can be used for baking or feeding to dog, cat, poultry.

FRUIT

Hedgerow Jelly
This jelly varies from year to year and entirely depends on what fruits I manage to find in the hedges beside the towpath. To ensure that it sets well at least half the fruits should have a good pectin content, such as crab-apples and sloes. The colours of the jellies can be excitingly different; a predominance of elder berries gives a rich garnet red, sloes dark purple, rose hips a lighter red , blackberries a blue purple. If you are lucky enough to find some wild quinces you will have no problem with the jelly not setting - you may even have to cut it with a knife. One word of warning - do make sure you can identify the fruits that you use - if in doubt leave them out. There are fruits of the hedgerow which look edible but are poisonous.
Wash all the fruit, cutting large ones like crab-apples in half and put them all together in a preserving pan or a large saucepan with barely enough water to cover the fruit. Simmer until even the hardest fruits are soft and mushy. Pour into a jelly bag which is suspended over a bowl and allow to drip through overnight. Do not squeeze the bag or the jelly will be cloudy. Measure the juice and add 1 lb sugar over a low heat then immediately bring to the boil and boil rapidly without stirring for about ten minutes or until setting point is reached. Pour into clean warm jars, cover with jam-pot covers and label.

Dried apples
Core but do not peel good sweet apples and thread them on long strings which should be hung horizontally across a warm, dry, airy room. When they are dry the string may be tied to form a loop and the apples hung in any convenient dry place. Check them occasionally to make sure that the odd damp one has not gone mouldy to infect the others.

Apple pulp
This can use up windfalls. Peel, core and remove bruised or grub-eaten parts. Simmer with just enough water to prevent burning until mushy. Pour boiling pulp into hot dry preserving jars and seal with rubber rings and lids that have been sterilised in boiling water for 15 mins. Loosen lids slightly and immerse jars in hot water, standing them on a folded cloth, then bring water to the boil and boil for 5 mins. Tighten lids.

Alternatively allow apple pulp to cool then pack in polythene bags or boxes, seal, label and freeze. Much quicker!

Fruit Compote
This can be made with fresh or frozen fruit from the garden or the hedgerow, is very little more trouble than plain stewed fruit and much nicer. My favourite is redcurrant. For every 2 lb of fruit dissolve 6 oz sugar in ½ pint of water in a saucepan. Add the fruit and simmer gently until soft but whole and not mushy. If you are mixing different sorts of fruits (I never do) cook ones like blackcurrants first before adding soft fruit like raspberries. When the fruit is tender transfer it gently with a slotted spoon into a serving dish. Thicken the syrup remaining in the pan with cornflour in the proportions of l level teaspoon to ½ pint liquid. Stir in the cornflour blended with a little cold water and bring to the boil stirring all the time. When it is glazed and clear pour syrup over the fruit and leave until it is quite cold.

Spiced Pears *makes 4 lb*
4 lbs pears peeled, cored and quartered into a bowl of cold water
1 lb granulated sugar
1 pint malt vinegar
2 teaspoons whole cloves
2 teaspoons whole allspice
3 pieces stick cinnamon, each 1 inch long
1 piece dry root ginger
2 - 3 pieces pared lemon rind
Measure the sugar and vinegar into a large saucepan. Lightly crush the cloves and allspice and tie in a muslin bag with the cinnamon and bruised ginger (attach the bag with a string to the pan handle). Add the lemon rind and stir the lot over a low heat until the sugar is dissolved. Bring to the boil and add the strained pears, simmering gently until they are tender and translucent. Lift the fruit from the pan with a slotted spoon, remove spice bag and lemon peel and replace pan on heat. Boil rapidly until the syrup has reduced to a honey-like consistency. Meanwhile pack the pears into clean warm jars and pour the syrup over when it is ready. Cover and label. Remember, vinegar rots jam-pot covers and reacts with metal, but we have found empty coffee jars with plastic lids that screw on perfectly satisfactory for chutneys.

Green Tomato Chutney *makes 5 lb*

5 lb green tomatoes peeled (with a potato peeler) and sliced
1 lb onions peeled and chopped
2 teaspoons salt
2 oz mixed pickling spice in a muslin bag
1 pint malt vinegar
1 lb sugar

Boil the onions in a little water until they are soft then drain them. In a preserving pan or a large saucepan put the tomatoes, onions, salt and spices. Bring to the boil then reduce the heat and simmer for about an hour, adding a little of the vinegar when the mixture thickens. Stir in the sugar and the remaining vinegar and continue to stir while the chutney is cooking until it is thick. Remove spice bag and pack chutney into clean warm jars, cover and label.

WINES

Nettle wine
½ bucketful of young nettle tops washed and drained.
2 lbs sugar
2 lemons
Piece of root ginger
2 oz dried bakers yeast
1 gallon water
Simmer the nettle tops in some of the water with the lemon peel and the bruised ginger for ¾ hour. Meanwhile dissolve the sugar in some more of the water over a low heat. Add the syrup to the strained nettle liquor and make up to a gallon with water. Add the juice of the 2 lemons. Cool to 70°F and add the yeast, sprinkling it on the top and stirring it in. Keep the crock or wine bucket closely covered with a clean tea-towel in a warm place, stirring daily. Transfer the liquid in 4 days discarding the solids to a fermentation vessel with an air-lock and leave until it begins to clear. Syphon into a similar vessel without disturbing the sediment which will have settled on the bottom. Fit an air-lock and leave until absolutely clear when the wine can be syphoned into bottles and corked. If you can leave it to mature for three months, so much the better.

Orange Mint Wine
1½ pints orange mint leaves lightly bruised
½ pint strong tea
3 lbs sugar
2 lemons
2 oz dried bakers yeast
1 gallon water
Dissolve the sugar in some of the water over a low heat then bring to the boil. Pour this with the rest of the water which should also be boiling, over the mint in a wine bucket. Add the strong tea, the lemon peel and lemon juice. Stir well and cool to 70°F then add the yeast, sprinkling it on the top and stirring it in. Cover bucket with a clean cloth and keep in a warm place for 10 days stirring daily. Transfer the liquid discarding the solids to a fermentation vessel with an air-lock and leave until it begins to clear when it should be syphoned carefully into another fermentation vessel without

disturbing the solids which will have settled. Fit an air-lock and leave until it is clear when it can be syphoned into sterilised bottles and corked.

POT-POURRI

Literally translated from the French, the word means 'rotten-pot' which really refers to a moist pot-pourri, a method not often used today. Dry pot-pourris have a wider variety of uses, are prettier and luckily are easier to Make.

Any aromatic flowers, leaves and herbs which you have in your garden can be used provided they are not succulent or they will not dry out properly. There are several drying methods; the modem miss may use a microwave oven; the simplest, cheapest way (not for the houseproud) is to spread the blooms and leaves on sheets of newspaper underneath the bed. The ingredients must be rustlingly, cracklingly dry before they are used or dreaded mildew will ruin the pot and then it really will be rotten!

Crush whole cloves, cinnamon and if you have it, some orris root which is the root of Iris Florentina, in the proportion of ½ cup of powdered spices to 8 cups (pressed down) of flowers and leaves. Mix together in a crock bowl with a wooden spoon. Drop by drop add 2 or 3 drops of citrus oil and 6 drops of a flower oil, lavender perhaps. These are not essential but do enhance the fragrance just as the spices help to 'fix' it and make it last longer.

Leave the mixture for two or three weeks to settle and blend, turning it over frequently with your hands or a wooden spoon. Then it will be ready to use in open bowls, sachets or pomanders.

I included the recipe for the old but still popular pot-pourri mixture because one of the main attractions of my garden is the fragrance on a summer evening. This makes use of many cottage garden favourites as well as the aromatic plants in the herb garden.

The culinary notes are not intended to be hard and fast rules - indeed I doubt whether I ever cook home produce in exactly the same way twice running. One of the beauties of the 'grow your own' syndrome is that everything seems to be free. It is easy to forget when you are in the kitchen the hard work that went before in the garden. One is more inclined (if you are like me) to be adventurous if one has not paid out hard cash for an ingredient. After all, I often say to myself, if this doesn't work I can always pick some more. But it nearly always does.

I think that if we had to leave here and move to a place with a lot less land, the one project among the many we have tried that I could not do without now, is a herb garden. No place is too small for that - a windowsill would do. There is no doubt in my mind that a liberal dose of fresh herbs can transform the most prosaic of meals into a banquet.

" The hard work that went before in the garden …"

Glossary

Cill	or sill. Large block which supports the lock gates, bigger at the top end of a lock than the bottom.
Compass rose	Wheel-shaped decoration drawn with a pair of compasses
Flight	A group of locks close together
Lock	A box with doors at each end separating two different levels of water and a mechanism which allows the box to be filled and emptied.
Paddle	Shutter over the hole through which water enters or leaves the lock.
Pawl	A catch which prevents the inadvertent release of the paddle gear.
Pound	level part of canal between two locks
Shaft	A long pole used to push boats off the bank (or the bottom).
Sluice	A regulated outlet or inlet for water
Stem	Vertical steel post (used to be iron) at the 'sharp end' of the boat.
Tiller	An arm fixed to the rudder and used to steer the boat
Windlass	or lock-key. A handle, usually portable, which permits the raising and lowering of paddles.

THE AUTHOR

Shirley Ginger was born into an artistic family in Darlington, County Durham. She married an officer in the Royal Warwickshire Regiment when she was barely twenty and spent the first twelve years of married life globe-trotting from one army posting to another.

When her husband finally left the service for civilian life they settled in the heart of Birmingham where she had previously studied art. While their two children were growing up she ran her own small business there and achieved an Open University B.A.

In addition to the day-to-day running of Ginger's Canal Stores, painting, gardening, breeding and raising livestock, spinning, sewing, knitting and boating, Shirley managed to write this book 'in her spare time'.